The Myth of Political Correctness

The Myth

of

Political

Correctness

John K. Wilson

THE

➤

CONSERVATIVE

➤

ATTACK

➤

ON

➤

HIGHER

➤

EDUCATION

DUKE UNIVERSITY PRESS   Durham and London 1995

© 1995 Duke University Press
All rights reserved
Printed in the United States of America on acid-free paper ∞
Typeset in Minion by Tseng Information Systems, Inc.
Library of Congress Cataloging-in-Publication Data appear
on the last printed page of this book.

To all my teachers

➤ Contents

➤ Acknowledgments

This book is the product of several years of writing and thinking about issues related to political correctness while I was an undergraduate and then a graduate student; many people have helped me along the way.

My editor at Duke University Press, Rachel Toor, ruthlessly pushed me to finish and revise the manuscript and offered many suggestions with the assistance of her faithful animal companion, Hannah.

Kim Phillips, Gerald Graff, Beth Johnson, and Thomas Wilson read earlier drafts of the manuscript and offered helpful comments, as did the two anonymous readers for Duke University Press. Mindy Conner did an excellent job copyediting the manuscript.

My thoughts on some of these issues first appeared in the *Daily Illini,* the *Grey City Journal,* and the *Prism* (*Chicago Maroon*), which gave me a valuable outlet for my writings. Teachers for a Democratic Culture also allowed me to express my views on the culture wars as editor of their newletter, *Democratic Culture.*

I've also been privileged to have more than a hundred teachers, too numerous to name, who helped sharpen my thinking, improve my writing, and expand my knowledge.

Finally, I thank the following conservative foundations: the John M. Olin Foundation, the Lynde and Harry Bradley Foundation, the Carthage Foundation, and the Smith Richardson Foundation. None of them gave me any grants (I received no money from anyone to write this book), but millions of dollars from these foundations subsidized dozens of conservative organizations, books, and magazines that were indispensable in providing the errors, distortions, and outright lies I analyze in these chapters. Without their successful efforts to create the myth of political correctness, I could not expose it in this book.

I hope that *The Myth of Political Correctness* will provoke further arguments and discussions about these issues. I encourage readers with questions or comments to contact me on email (jkw3@midway.uchicago.edu) or at Teachers for a Democratic Culture (P.O. Box 6405, Evanston, IL 60204).

➤ Preface: PC and Me

When I began to hear about political correctness as a senior at the University of Illinois in 1990, I wondered what I was missing. Where were the radical students intimidating other students and teachers? Where were the tenured radicals indoctrinating me with leftist propaganda? Where *was* political correctness?

I had encountered leftist professors and students, of course, but I had never thought of them as the "thought police" that *Newsweek* told me were invading college campuses. Most of the leftists I met seemed like nice people, polite and tolerant of other people's views. And the conservative students and professors I'd encountered didn't seem like victims of a new McCarthyism. They had their own monthly newspaper funded by conservative foundations, their own organizations, and their own campus lectures. I don't recall hearing anyone called "racist" or "sexist" or "homophobic," and I certainly never heard anyone (except perhaps the conservatives) use the phrase *politically correct*. I didn't hear many students challenging the "liberal orthodoxy," but then not many of us challenged any orthodoxies. We sat in class and listened to the teachers and read the assignments and wrote the papers and took the tests.

I went to college as the culture wars erupted in 1987, back when "PC" referred only to computers. But in my first week at the University of Illinois, my philosophy professor assigned America's hottest best-seller, Allan Bloom's *The Closing of the American Mind,* which begins: "There is one thing a professor can be absolutely certain of: almost every student entering the university believes, or says he believes, that truth is relative."[1] This assertion surprised me because I'd never heard anyone say that *all* truth is relative. After all, one of the complaints about politically correct people would be that they believed they knew the truth and intimidated those who disagreed with them. In my classes and my discussions with friends, I constantly heard arguments about what was true and what was false. Perhaps what Bloom mistook for relativism was the politeness and tolerance of these arguments. Unlike the 1960s, the campuses of the 1990s are not fiercely divided by passionate debates about war and justice, and students are less likely to hold extreme views, or to occupy campus buildings to express them. But this wasn't relativism; often it was just uncertainty and a healthy skepticism about any dogma. While Bloom's outrageous statements intrigued me, I found it difficult to believe that he really knew what was going on at most colleges.

Unlike most of the people attacking political correctness and higher education, I am a firsthand witness to what has been happening on college campuses for the past eight years. As a student I've taken more than 150 classes from dozens of departments, ranging from economics to philosophy to women's studies, including the first courses on gay and lesbian history ever offered at my institutions. I had both leftist and conservative professors, and I read a broad range of books from the trendy to the traditional. If anyone could judge whether there was such a thing as political correctness, surely I could. I also read a lot of books on my own, especially books about the danger of "tenured radicals" on college campuses. But there were disturbing discrepancies between what I was reading about PC and the reality in front of my eyes.

I read that everything was being "deconstructed" and that the Great Books were being discarded in favor of books by foreigners with strange names like Derrida, Lacan, Barthes, and Foucault. I read that under the guise of multiculturalism, leftist propaganda was dominating the curriculum. But the book I was assigned most often in college was Plato's *Republic*. I read it in five classes as an undergraduate at the University of Illinois and an equal number of times as a graduate student at the University of Chicago. While I took some unusual classes with progressive teachers and read some things that will never appear on a list of great books, it was almost entirely through my own efforts to find something different. If I did what thousands of other students had done and took only the standard required classes, I would have encountered very little of the multiculturalism that is supposedly taking over higher education.

Shortly after I graduated, the conservative newspaper on campus printed a front-page article claiming that leftist English professors were trying to ban Shakespeare (along with Columbus, John Locke, Adam Smith, John Calvin, and Clarence Thomas). Ban Shakespeare? I wondered. That sounded like the PC thought police.

"Who's trying to ban Shakespeare?" asked an English professor at the booth promoting the newspaper.

"Lots of English professors," answered the woman there.

"Who?"

"Professor Cary Nelson. He hasn't had a lot of nice things to say about Shakespeare."[2]

The conservative newspaper had reported that Nelson's mission "is to forever annihilate the traditional literary canon."[3] In response, Nelson wrote in the campus paper: "I have worked to open up the curriculum to more women and minorities, but I have also published on Shakespeare, and like all my colleagues, I support the department's requirement that all English majors take a Shakespeare course. I have never met an English professor anywhere on the planet who wanted to remove Shakespeare from the curriculum."[4]

When I looked at the English Department's reading lists, I found a dozen classes devoted solely to Shakespeare, and many more that read his plays. No Derrida, no Lacan, no Barthes, no Foucault showed up in the courses. The PC thought police who won't say "a lot of nice things" about Shakespeare suddenly didn't seem quite so ominous.

"Are you politically correct?" asked the cover of *New York* magazine. Readers were told to test themselves: "Do I say 'Indian' instead of 'Native American'? 'Pet' instead of 'Animal Companion'?"[5] I had to confess that sometimes I said "Native American," mostly to avoid confusion with the Indians in south Asia. I didn't know that saying a word could make me a fellow traveler with the thought police. But the "Animal Companion" part puzzled me. By this definition, I wasn't politically correct; in fact, by this definition I'd never met anyone who was politically correct. Do people really say "animal companion" instead of "pet"? Does anyone accuse those who use the word *pet* of being a "speciesist"? Would anyone take them seriously if they did? I began to suspect that the "political correctness" movement was no more than the product of someone's paranoid imagination. Being asked "Are you politically correct?" is like being asked "Are you in favor of the international conspiracy of Jewish bankers who control the world?" Of course I'm opposed to an international conspiracy of Jewish bankers controlling the world, but I also know that no such conspiracy exists.

One of the charges I often came across in my reading was that affirmative action denies fair treatment to white males. A professor in my undergraduate political science department (whose faculty is mostly white males) wrote that white male Ph.D.s "probably never will get an academic job interview, let alone a job offer."[6] As a future white male Ph.D., this obviously concerned me. Even though I supported affirmative action, I was a little leery about accomplishing the goal of diversity by making myself unemployed.

But when I thought about my own experiences, I wondered who was really receiving these preferences. After receiving a top-notch education in high school, I went to one of the best public universities in the country, with two scholarships to pay my way and the privilege of being admitted to an excellent honors program. Then I was accepted by one of the best graduate schools in the country, offered a prestigious fellowship, and given a federal government fellowship that will pay me $40,000 over four years to get a free education. How many minorities ever get privileges like that?

I certainly don't see lots of minorities being given these special benefits. It's hard to see many minorities at all. At the University of Chicago (where I'm a graduate student), less than 2 percent of the faculty are black and white males are regularly hired. Only 3 percent of the graduate students and 4 percent of the undergraduates are black. Hispanics are less than 2 percent of the faculty, 4 percent of the graduate students, and 4 percent of the undergraduates. Is this the "victim's revolution" that is going to ruin my future career as a professor?

But "racial preferences" weren't the only threat to white males mentioned in these conservative critiques. I often read about the evils of feminism. I heard that women's studies classes had been taken over by radical feminists who were silencing dissenters, attacking men, and indoctrinating their students. But my own experience belies these charges of intimidation.

I took several women's studies classes, still searching for these man-hating feminists who are supposedly politicizing education and intimidating students. But all I found were classrooms full of discussions, not politically correct sermons. And I never encountered any classes in other departments that had such a dramatic impact on the lives of the students. I suppose some "politically incorrect" topics were off-limits — we never had a debate about the equality of women — but I saw far more openness there than in most of the other courses I took.

I remember economics classes where the students never argued about economics but instead answered test questions and homework assignments according to the assumptions of a free-market model that even the teachers admitted was inaccurate. I also took large lecture classes in many departments where hundreds of students copied down identical notes (or purchased them from professional note takers) in preparation for the upcoming multiple-choice test. I finished one fill-in-the-ovals final exam in fifteen minutes while proctors patrolled the lecture hall and checked IDs. Curiously, no one called this "indoctrination," even though it was far more oppressive to me than any women's studies class I took.

I never saw a conservative student silenced or insulted or punished in any class for expressing politically incorrect ideas. As a columnist for the student

newspaper, I never heard of any conservative being prevented from expressing controversial views by the supposedly ubiquitous "speech codes." The idea
that leftist students and faculty dominate American colleges and universities
seemed like a joke in view of the general apathy on campus.

The most student activism I ever saw came during the Persian Gulf War
in 1991, when students marched in protest against (and some in support of)
the war. Perhaps the funniest moment occurred during a small antiwar rally
held in a park across the street from a fraternity. Some fraternity members
tried to drown out the speeches by playing music on their stereos full blast. To
my amusement, the songs they played were Bruce Springsteen's "Born in the
USA" and Jimi Hendrix's Woodstock rendition of "The Star-Spangled Ban-
ner"—these two antiwar songs were the most patriotic music they could find
on their CD racks. But strangely, trying to silence an antiwar rally didn't count
as political correctness.

As I began to examine the stories about political correctness, I noticed a
curious double standard. Whenever conservatives were criticized or a leftist
expressed some extreme idea, the story quickly became another anecdote of
political correctness. But when someone on the Left was censored—often with
the approval of the same conservatives who complained about the PC police—
nobody called it political correctness, and stories of this right-wing intolerance
were never mentioned in articles and books on PC totalitarianism. My own experience made me question the existence of the "PC fascism" I had read about.
And as I began to study the terrifying tales of leftist McCarthyism, I found
that the truth was often the reverse of what the media reported. While some
stories about PC are true and deplorable, the scale of censorship is nowhere
near what most people think.

What startles me most about the PC scare is that the critics are so uninter-
ested in what is really happening on college campuses. The anecdotes have
become more important than the reality. By force of repetition, these anecdotes have been woven into the tale of a "victim's revolution" on campus.
When closely examined, however, these anecdotes unravel under the strain
of exaggeration, deceptive omission of key facts, and occasional outright invention. What matters to critics is not the truth but the story—the myth of
political correctness. Every PC anecdote retells this myth by ritualistic invoca-
tion of the image of leftist thought police. The myth of political correctness
is a powerful conspiracy theory created by conservatives and the media who
have manipulated resentment against leftist radicals into a backlash against
the fictional monster of political correctness.

The Myth of Political Correctness

The Myth of Political Correctness

In 1991, a new phrase began to be heard across America. *Political correctness,*
PC for short, quickly became one of the hottest terms in the country, spawn-
ing a flood of books, magazine articles, and editorials describing a reign of
terror at American universities, led by radical students and faculty and supported by acquiescent administrators. Within the span of a few months, the
media produced a barrage of articles, each a variation on a single theme: that
leftist totalitarians had taken control of universities and were intimidating professors, censoring conservatives, politicizing curricula, and imposing a new
"McCarthyism of the Left" on higher education.

"Political correctness" became the rallying cry of the conservative critics
of academia, the phrase behind which all of their enemies — multiculturalism,
affirmative action, speech codes, feminism, and tenured radicals — could be
united into a single conspiracy. The mythology of political correctness declares
that conservatives are the victims of a prevailing leftist ideology in American
universities, oppressed by radical students and faculty determined to brain-
wash them. But the conservative attacks on these politically correct "thought
police" have distorted the truth about what goes on in colleges and universities. Instead of condemning the excesses of a few extremists and abuses of due
process by administrators, critics have declared that the mere presence of radical ideas has corrupted the entire system of higher education. Instead of telling
the truth, the forces against political correctness have used exaggeration and
distortion to create the mythology of PC, a myth that bears little resemblance
to what is really happening on college campuses.

Conservatives manufactured the political correctness crisis and skillfully
pushed it into the national spotlight. This does not mean that all examples
of political correctness are pure invention; leftists do sometimes show intol-

erance toward those who fail to toe the party line. But leftist intimidation in universities has always paled in comparison with the far more common repression by the conservative forces who control the budgets and run colleges and universities.

My claim is not that American universities are perfect defenders of free expression, or that political correctness is pure invention with no basis in reality. When I describe political correctness as a myth, I do not mean that everything about it is false or every anecdote is fraudulent. Walter Lippmann once noted that "the distinguishing mark of a myth is that truth and error, fact and fable, report and fantasy, are all on the same plane of credibility."[1] Without doubt many students and faculty have been wrongly punished for their views. And there are some leftists who would not hesitate, if given the power, to oppress conservatives. But generally they do not have the power, and few have the inclination to create their own ideological monarchies. The greater power is held by the status quo, which often enforces conservative doctrines without ever gaining the publicity devoted to leftist PC.

The myth of political correctness has created the illusion of a conspiracy of leftists who have taken over higher education and twisted it to serve their political purposes. Attacks on political correctness have misled the public and unfairly maligned a large number of faculty and students. Worse yet, the crusade against PC has silenced the deeper questions about quality and equality that our colleges and universities must face, and a greatly needed debate has been shut down by the false reports and misleading attacks on higher education. The myth of political correctness has made every radical idea, no matter how trivial or harmless, seem like the coming of an apocalypse for higher education, complete with four new horsepeople—Speech Codes, Multiculturalism, Sexual Correctness, and Affirmative Action.

The conservative backlash against universities has been funded by right-wing foundations and supported by liberals and journalists who dislike the academic Left. Using a long list of inaccurate anecdotes, endlessly recycled in conservative and mainstream publications, the right-wingers have distorted and manipulated the debates about higher education. Presenting conservative white males as the true victims of oppression on campus, they have convinced the public that radicals are now the ones who threaten civil liberties. This is the myth of political correctness that conservatives have created and successfully marketed to the media and the general public.

Not only are most of the anecdotes purporting to prove political correctness badly distorted by conservative propaganda, but the litany of scattered examples fails to demonstrate the critics' central claim: that these stories are not isolated incidents but a national pattern of repression under the control of a secret cabal of leftist professors. These conspirators are called by many names—the thought police, the PC totalitarians, the new McCarthyists, and tenured radicals—but the threat is always the same: conservatives silenced, Western culture trashed, academic standards discarded, and classes turned over to politicized teaching and ethnic cheerleading.

The refusal of conservatives to see anything but a conspiracy of malicious leftists in recent efforts to broaden the college curriculum has created the very atmosphere of intellectual intimidation that critics blame on the Left. Although the attacks on political correctness have helped to stimulate some debates about higher education, they have mostly silenced discussion. Critics frequently make no effort to argue about the ideas they deride, and opposing views are mocked rather than refuted—with "PC" itself being an unanswerable form of ridicule. By criticizing anyone who dares to discuss race, class, and gender, by attacking all multiculturalism as political indoctrination, by misrepresenting the facts about the PC controversy, and by failing to consider the arguments of the other side, the conservatives and the media distorted what might have been (and what still can be) a productive debate about our universities.

The myth of political correctness has become accepted as gospel when describing the state of American universities. But the myth did not appear out of nowhere. It is the product of a conservative movement that undermined higher education throughout the Reagan-Bush years, honing its skills and funding the attacks that led to the PC bashing. The story of how "political correctness" began, and how conservatives used the myth of political correctness to appeal to liberals and journalists, reveals how little of the truth has really been told.

The Origins of Political Correctness

In only a few years, the term *political correctness* has grown from obscurity to national prominence. The words first appeared two centuries ago in the 1793 Supreme Court case *Chisholm v. Georgia*, which upheld the right of a citizen to sue another state. Justice James Wilson wrote an opinion in which he objected to the wording of a common toast: " 'The United States' instead of the 'People of the United States' is the toast given. This is not politically correct."[2] Wilson's use of the term was quite literal. He felt that the people, not the states, held the true authority of the United States, and therefore a toast to the states violated the "correct" political theory. Supporters of states' rights did not concur, and the Eleventh Amendment was passed to overturn the *Chisholm* decision. And the phrase *politically correct* quickly faded from memory.

Although no one is sure when or where *politically correct* was revived, nearly

everyone agrees that it was used sarcastically among leftists to criticize themselves for taking radical doctrines to absurd extremes. Roger Geiger notes that
political correctness was "a sarcastic reference to adherence to the party line
by American communists in the 1930s."[3] Herbert Kohl "first heard the phrase
'politically correct' in the late 1940s in reference to political debates between
socialists and members of the United States Communist Party," where "politically correct" was "being used disparagingly to refer to someone whose loyalty
to the CP line overrode compassion and led to bad politics."[4] Ruth Perry traces
PC to the late 1960s and the Black Power movement, perhaps inspired by Mao
Tse-tung's frequent reference to "correct" ideas. "Politically correct" was used
not by extremists on the left to describe their enemies but by more moderate
liberals who objected to the intolerence of some leftists. Perry says that "the
phrase politically correct has always been double-edged" and "has long been
our own term of self-criticism."[5]

During the 1980s, conservatives began to take over this leftist phrase and
exploit it for political gain, expanding its meaning to include anyone who expressed radical sentiments. Conservative writer Robert Kelner first heard of
"political correctness" in the fall of 1985 as "a bit of college slang bandied about
by young conservatives."[6] And the conservatives not only appropriated *politically correct* for their own attacks on the radical Left, they also transformed it
into a new phrase — *political correctness.*

The liberals' original "I'm not politically correct" was an ironic defense
against those who took extremism to new extremes, who demanded absolute
consistency to radical principles. The conservatives warped this meaning to
convey the image of a vast conspiracy controlling American colleges and universities. *Politically correct* referred to the views of a few extreme individuals;
political correctness described a broad movement that had corrupted the entire
system of higher education. By this transformation the conservatives accused
universities of falling under the influence of extremist elements. For conservatives, "I'm not politically correct" became a badge of honor, a defense against
a feared attack — even though no one had been seriously accused of being
politically incorrect.

Politically incorrect is now used as a marketing device. The Madison Center for Educational Affairs recently published *The Common Sense Guide to
American Colleges,* with "politically incorrect" proudly emblazoned on the top
right-hand corner; Berke Breathed's collection of cartoons is titled *Politically,
Fashionably, and Aerodynamically Incorrect;* and Rush Limbaugh's newsletter is
advertised as an "absolutely politically incorrect publication."[7] A *National Review* book is titled *The Politically Incorrect Reference Guide.* A company adver-

tises "politically incorrect" bank checks printed with conservative cartoons.[8] Another company sells T-shirts with "Politically *In*correct" on the front and "Free Minds, Free Markets, Free Society" on the back.[9] The power of PC has even reached into mainstream culture: a radio commercial for AT&T features a reference to the "PC police." A commercial for Haggar Wrinkle-Free Slacks shows a man who says, "I'm not politically correct."

Perhaps the most amusing example of how economically powerful the term *politically incorrect* has become is the federal lawsuit filed on 2 November 1993 by the Comedy Central cable channel for its talk show *Politically Incorrect*. Comedy Central sued comedian Jackie Mason to stop him from naming his one-man Broadway show "Jackie Mason, Politically Incorrect." According to Comedy Central, "People could get confused. It tends to dilute the rights to the name that we've built up and spent a lot of money on."[10] Ironically, Mason proved quite adept at using the PC language of victimhood: he filed suit after his "Politically Incorrect" show was not nominated for a Tony Award, claiming that it was "an abridgment of my rights as a human being" and discrimination against him for being a "guy with a big mouth."[11]

Many critics overlook the self-critical origins of the phrase. Dinesh D'Souza, for example, writes, "The term 'political correctness' seems to have originated in the early part of this century, when it was employed by various species of Marxists to describe and enforce conformity to preferred ideological positions. . . . The revolutionary ideologues of that period were serious people, and there is no indication that they spoke of political correctness with any trace of irony or self-deprecation."[12] Carol Iannone claims that PC, "long a designation of approval by the hard Left, . . . suddenly became a pejorative description for the political agenda of those on the Left who were claiming to speak for certain groups defined by race, gender, class, selected ethnicity, and sexual behavior, and who were attempting to intimidate and silence anyone trying to question their own orthodoxy."[13] In the views of D'Souza and Iannone, political correctness is an ideology so repressive that leftists celebrate their intellectual conformity by calling each other "politically correct." The self-critical leftists who actually used the term are ignored. The conservatives' distaste for radicals is such that they refuse even to acknowledge stealing *political correctness* from leftists; to admit this would suggest the presence of critical elements (and a sense of humor) on the left.

While claiming to be silenced, conservatives now use PC to silence their opponents. In August 1993, Joe Rabinowitz, news director of WTTG-TV, the Fox station in Washington, D.C., wrote a memo to the chair of Fox Television, urging the firing of "politically correct" employees. To hunt down these employees he consulted with conservative media critics like L. Brent Bozell III, chair of the Media Research Center, and Reed Irvine, head of Accuracy in Media.[14] As the American Association of University Professors (AAUP) observed, "Charges of 'political correctness' . . . have a way of taking on their own coercive tone."[15] If an opponent could be dismissed as politically correct, there was no need to reply to any substantive arguments. Anthony DePalma observes that "P.C., or political correctness, has evolved into a catch-all campus putdown."[16] And Catharine Stimpson of the MacArthur Foundation reports that "the accusations of campus malfeasance have taken hold, to such a degree that the label, 'You're P.C.,' can now be slapped on like a gag."[17]

By expanding the meaning of *political correctness* to include *any* expression of radical ideas, conservatives distorted its original meaning and turned it into a mechanism for doing exactly what they charge is being done to them—silencing dissenters. Michael Bérubé points out that "the term 'PC' is doing the work that the term 'liberal' did for Bush in 1988: it's trying to dismiss large potential constituencies for cultural activism, and to narrow the bounds of permissable political debate."[18] Critics who attacked leftists' alleged use of insults and ridicule to suppress unorthodox views showed no hesitation in using exactly the same tactics against their radical opponents. The genius of using a term like *political correctness* was that people would never declare themselves politically correct, so it was virtually impossible to counter the conservative attacks when a culture of soundbites defied the kind of analysis needed to refute the presumption that political correctness existed.

The Making of the Myth

Today, "political correctness" permeates our culture like no other soundbite of recent times. Although the debate in the universities has subsided somewhat, the phrase *politically correct* regularly appears on T-shirts and in newspaper headlines, TV shows, comic strips, and everyday conversations. The fear of being PC often reaches ridiculous proportions. In 1994, the Wilmette, Illinois, village board decided not to put a drawing of four children of different races on its village vehicle sticker because "it would take 'political correctness' too far" and would be "forcing people to promote diversity" in that nearly all-white suburb of Chicago.[19]

"Political correctness" is a label slapped on an enormous range of liberal views—from environmentalism to multiculturalism to abortion rights. According to one writer, "It is P.C. to be in favor of affirmative action" and to "profess a belief in environmentalism, Palestinian self-determination, third-world revolutionaries, and legalized abortion."[20] By this definition, 90 percent of America is politically correct, which makes one wonder who's listening to Rush Limbaugh. Speaking of Rush, you can't read his books without being inundated with the phrase—he calls political correctness "the greatest threat to the First Amendment in our history," transcending wartime censorship and McCarthyism.[21] Altogether, Rush invokes PC at least twenty-five times in his book *See, I Told You So*, including in two chapter titles. In "Political Correctness and the Coming of the Thought Police," Rush calls PC "political cleansing" akin to Serbia's "genocidal scorched-Earth policy against the Muslim population in Bosnia."[22]

Political correctness even gets blamed for the censorship committed by its worst enemy, the religious Right. *Time* warns us that "under the watchful eye of the p.c. police, mainstream culture has become cautious, sanitized, scared of its own shadow. Network TV, targeted by antiviolence crusaders and nervous about offending advertisers, has purged itself of what little edge and controversy it once had."[23] But virtually the only ones to protest TV shows and organize advertiser boycotts are right-wing groups who object to the depiction of homosexuality and other such "antifamily" material. The religious Right—not the PC Left—has been at the forefront of efforts to purge offensive elements from movies, music, and television, ranging from *The Last Temptation of Christ* to 2 Live Crew to *NYPD Blue*.

It isn't hard to learn that one can escape responsibility by yelling "PC" as loud as possible. James "Pate" Phillip, the Republican president of the Illinois Senate, said to a newspaper editorial board about black social workers, "Some of them do not have the work ethics that we have . . . they don't tend to turn on or squeal on their fellow minorities." Philip—who easily won reelection in his district and was reelected by the Senate GOP caucus as their leader—justified his remarks by proudly declaring, "I'm not politically correct, I don't try to be."[24] William Cash, who wrote a 1994 article about Hollywood's "Jewish cabal" in the British magazine *Spectator,* claimed it was "politically correct" to ignore this "Jewish influence." The *Spectator*'s editor defended his decision to run the anti-Semitic essay by observing that "American papers have a code of political correctness."[25]

People seem to cry "political correctness" whenever they want to disassociate themselves from supposedly radical ideas. President George Bush devoted an entire commencement address in 1991 to the blight of political correctness, and President Bill Clinton told Americans, "The time has come to stop worrying about what you think is politically correct."[26] Even God, it turns out, is against political correctness: John Cardinal O'Connor declared in a St.

Patrick's Day sermon that "neither respectability nor political correctness is worth one comma in the Apostles' Creed."[27]

In every newspaper someone is bound to be complaining about political correctness. Not even the sports pages are a refuge from attacks on PC. A *New York Times* college football columnist wrote that the University of Alabama Crimson Tide "won with a reliable defense and a conservative, politically incorrect offense."[28]

Although it is impossible to gauge its spread precisely, it appears that PC exploded into popular consciousness in 1991. A *Times Mirror* survey in May 1991 found that 48 percent of adults in a national sample had heard about PC.[29] And despite the reports of its imminent death, the attacks on political correctness have continued and show no signs of fading away. *Political correctness* is now a confirmed part of our vocabulary. A search of the NEXIS database found that the number of articles in the media mentioning political correctness has increased dramatically in the past few years: 1985, 0; 1986, 7; 1987, 7; 1988, 7; 1989, 15; 1990, 65; 1991, 1,570; 1992, 2,835; 1993, 4,914; and 1994, 6,985.

President Bush's speech about the dangers of political correctness at the University of Michigan's 4 May 1991 commencement was evidence that the slogan had grown to national stature. In his address, President Bush used the political correctness mythology to support his attack on unnamed radicals:

> The notion of political correctness has ignited controversy across the land. And although the movement arises from the laudable desire to sweep away the debris of racism, sexism and hatred, it replaces old prejudices with new ones. It declares certain topics off-limits, certain expressions off-limits, even certain gestures off-limits. What began as a cause for civility has soured into a cause of conflict and even censorship. Disputants treat sheer force — getting their foes punished or expelled, for instance — as a substitute for the power of ideas. Throughout history, attempts to micromanage casual conversation have only incited distrust. They've invited people to look for insult in every word, gesture, action. And in their own Orwellian way, crusades that demand correct behavior crush diversity in the name of diversity.[30]

Bush's speech is a classic display of conservative ideology, combining Reaganomics (the leftists "micromanage conversation") with a denial of prejudices (which are called "old" prejudices, as if no one believes them anymore) and a total dismissal of racism (which no longer exists except as "debris," since charges of prejudice are created by hypersensitive minorities who "look for insult"). Just as the Civil Rights Act of 1964 is a noble idea corrupted into quotas, "well-meaning" PC people have turned a good idea ("civility") into a crusade of repression.

Bush proclaimed that the danger to freedom comes not from racists (who can be dealt with using "reason") but from the "political extremists" who "roam the land, abusing the privilege of free speech, setting citizens against one another on the basis of their class or race." In this turnabout, it is not racists but leftists who abuse free speech (which has suddenly been transformed from a right into a privilege). When Bush said that "such bullying is outrageous," he referred not to those who use racial epithets to abuse other people but to the "extremists" who criticize racism. They, not racists, and certainly not George "Willie Horton" Bush, are responsible for the "boring politics of division and derision."

The double standard applied in Bush's speech is typical of the attacks on political correctness. While racists are to be treated with respect and reason, leftists are described as Stalinist threats to civilization. Though Bush attacked the use of "sheer force" to replace the exchange of ideas, he then went on to criticize leftists for expressing their ideas. In Bush's speech as elsewhere, it is when radicals openly state their beliefs to provoke a debate that they are most likely to be accused of political correctness.

Bush himself knew nothing about the phrase, which had suddenly popped into existence while he was busy being president. His speech was simple demagoguery, a routine jumping on the bandwagon to deliver the soundbite of the week. Like condemning Michael Dukakis for failing to violate the Constitution and force schoolchildren to recite the Pledge of Allegiance, Bush's attack on political correctness was an easy way to win popular approval. Who, after all, could be in favor of political correctness?

Bush's political correctness speech revealed the success of the conservative attack on universities. The day after his speech, *This Week with David Brinkley* focused on "Political Correctness on Campuses." On 13 May 1991, *Nightline* devoted a show to the subject, and on 22 May programs about PC on campus were featured on *Good Morning America* and *Crossfire*. This media attention was followed by a week-long series of interviews in June on the *MacNeil-Lehrer Newshour,* an *Evans and Novak* show in July, and a *Firing Line* debate in September 1991: "Resolved: Freedom of Thought Is in Danger on American Campuses."[31]

Not only was the presidential seal of approval given to the myth of political correctness, but the mere fact that Bush bothered to make such an attack showed how effectively conservatives had transformed the anti-PC movement into a popular political crusade. Within the span of a few months, PC went

from an obscure phrase spoken by campus conservatives to a nationally recognized sound bite used to attack political dissenters on the left.

The Conservative Backlash against Higher Education

Although political correctness seemed to appear out of nowhere in 1991, the
attacks on colleges and universities that propelled it had been organizing for
more than a decade. Much of the conservatives' resentment stemmed from
their opposition to the 1960s civil rights and antiwar movements which they
felt had become entrenched in the universities. For the conservatives (and
even some liberals), the 1960s were a frightening period on American campuses; students occupied buildings, faculty mixed radical politics into their
classes, administrators acquiesced to their demands, and academic standards
fell by the wayside. Conservatives convinced themselves that the 1960s had
never ended and that academia was being corrupted by a new generation of
tenured radicals.

In reality, American professors are not nearly as liberal as is often asserted.
A 1984 survey of faculty members found that a majority were moderate or conservative: only 5.8 percent described themselves as leftists, 33.8 percent were
liberal, 26.6 percent were middle of the road, 29.6 percent were moderately
conservative, and 4.2 percent were strongly conservative.[32] Yet throughout the
1980s, conservatives portrayed themselves as fighting a Marxist conspiracy in
the universities. A 1982 *U.S. News & World Report* cover story warned that "a
small but fervent group of radical leftist professors is expanding its foothold
on the nation's campuses."[33]

The Young America's Foundation called itself "a resource for advice and
support for students who face an ideological struggle against what *U.S. News
and World Report* has estimated are 10,000 Marxist professors."[34] A 1983 article
in *Conservative Digest* declared that a "Marxist network" giving students "the
heaviest dose of Marxist and leftist propaganda" had "over 13,000 faculty
members, a Marxist press that is selling record numbers of radical textbooks
and supplementary materials, and a system of helping other Marxist professors receive tenure."[35] In a 1986 *Commentary* article, Stephen Balch and
Herbert London—who would soon become the leaders of the National Association of Scholars—warned that "whereas in the 1960s only a handful of
courses in Marxist philosophy were being taught, today there are well over
400 such courses offered on American campuses."[36] In 1987, London declared
that Marxism was "thriving on American campuses" and attacked those who
believed it was "a legitimate form of scholarship."[37] Contrary to their recent

stance as defenders of free speech on campus, the Right has always wanted to get rid of Marxist professors.

A direct attack on academic freedom came in 1985 when Accuracy in Academia (AIA) was formed. Its founder, Reed Irvine, ran Accuracy in Media—a conservative organization that exposes bias in the "liberal" media—and he hoped to create a similar watchdog group to examine liberal bias in college classrooms. Accuracy in Academia's Les Csorba claimed that "in greater numbers than ever before, Marxists, neo-Marxists, quasi-Marxists, and other assorted revolutionaries have crept onto the college campuses—some even into the classrooms."[38] But AIA failed in its efforts to expose this Marxist "conspiracy" because it tried to mount an external attack on universities. The organization was ridiculed in *Doonesbury* and the media for having students spy on professors and for its criticism of an Arizona State University professor for spending "excessive" time "teaching about all the dangers and horrors of nuclear power."[39] One ominous ad at the University of Chicago for an AIA speaker superimposed a picture of an eye and the words "We Are Watching You" over the names of liberal professors on campus.[40]

Most of all, AIA alienated its most important allies, the moderate professors who were alarmed by the radicals on their campuses. These professors feared being criticized by students and other faculty, and the last thing they wanted was students spying on their classes, an image that evoked the old fears of McCarthyism. National Association of Scholars leaders Stephen Balch and Herbert London admitted that "among [AIA's] shortcomings" was "a certain surreptitiousness invariably associated with 'whistle-blowing' enterprises."[41] Even conservative Midge Decter criticized AIA as "wrong-headed and harmful" and urged in a *New York Times* op-ed piece that conservatives within the academy should be the ones to launch the attack on radicals.[42]

The AIA policy that "academic freedom permits professors to research whatever they please but it does not give them license to give biased lectures in the classroom"[43] threatened to intrude on the academic freedom of classroom teaching and alarmed many liberals. Even Sidney Hook, who condemned the bias in universities "against American policies and institutions" and sympathized with AIA's aims, nevertheless criticized the group for "unwittingly damaging the cause of academic freedom."[44]

Despite its initial failure to gain a popular following, in 1995, bolstered by the wave of attacks on political correctness, Accuracy in Academia announced that it would return to its old practice of spying on liberal professors. Peter LaBarbera, the new executive director of AIA, promised to "rededicate *Campus Report* to the cutting edge, no-nonsense investigative journalism that first characterized its debut in 1985. In that regard, I will focus on stories that *expose the teachings of individual professors in their classroom*—so that at least radical instructors know that there is someone out there scrutinizing what they teach."[45]

By the mid-1980s, conservatives had failed to convince the public of a crisis in higher education. Dinesh D'Souza was ignored when he wrote in 1986 (long before any of the incidents he describes in *Illiberal Education*) that "the most pervasive form of censorship in America today is not exercised by backwater fundamentalists, but by distinguished intellectuals in the academy and government."[46] The conservatives' attack on the universities was so ineffective in 1986 that Jon Wiener published an article in the *Nation* titled "Why the Right Is Losing in Academe," in which he declared that "neoconservatives in academia are not only on the defensive; they are steadily losing ground."[47]

But within a few years, Wiener would be proved wrong. In the late 1980s and early 1990s the attacks began to come from inside the university rather than outside it. One key group in this attack was the National Association of Scholars (NAS), the leading organization of academics opposed to multiculturalism, affirmative action, and political correctness. Scott Henson and Tom Philpott trace the origins of the NAS to the Campus Coalition for Democracy (CCD), which was founded in 1982 with the help of Midge Decter's conservative group, the Committee for the Free World. The leaders of the CCD were Herbert London, dean of New York University's Gallatin Division, and Stephen Balch, a professor of government at City University of New York. In late 1987, the CCD transformed itself into the National Association of Scholars. Initially, the NAS did not present itself as the defender of academic freedom. Instead, London attacked academic freedom as "a defense for intolerant positions and those hostile to free inquiry." The NAS became the central organization in the attack against multiculturalism, affirmative action, sexual harassment codes, and the so-called politicization of higher education. And London's early attacks on academic freedom faded as the NAS increasingly presented conservative professors as the victims of leftist indoctrination.[48]

By the late 1980s, leading conservatives had raised their accusations to new extremes, building on Allan Bloom's blockbuster about the decline and the fall of the university, *The Closing of the American Mind.* Sidney Hook wrote in 1987 that "there is less freedom of speech on American campuses today, measured by the tolerance of dissenting views on controversial political issues, than at any other recent period in peacetime in American history."[49] In a 17 April 1988 speech, Secretary of Education William Bennett declared that there was a "rising tide of left-wing intolerance" on campus and added, "Some places are becoming increasingly closed, increasingly conformist, increasingly insular and in certain instances even repressive of the spirit of the free marketplace of ideas."[50] In 1988, Alan Charles Kors urged NAS members to "become the monasteries of a new dark ages, preserving what is worth preserving amid the barbaric ravages in the countryside and towns of academe."[51] Charles Sykes's 1988 book *Profscam* blamed the problems in higher education on professors who ignored teaching, filled unread journals with trivial and jargon-filled research, and politicized the university with their bizarre beliefs.[52] This last charge was emphasized by Roger Kimball in 1989 when he wrote *Tenured Radicals,* which ridiculed radical papers delivered at academic conferences and published in academic journals. Kimball attacked one essay, Eve Sedgwick's "Jane Austen and the Masturbating Girl," before it had even been written. Based solely on the title, it became the most famous example of politically correct scholarship, although apparently none of Sedgwick's critics ever bothered to read it.[53]

The breakthrough for the conservatives came near the end of 1990 and in the first months of 1991, when a large number of mainstream newspapers and magazines repeated the stories about political correctness that the right wing had been circulating for years. These articles were almost uniformly critical of the Left and accepted the conservatives' attacks without questioning their accuracy or their motives. By using a few anecdotes about a few elite universities, conservatives created "political correctness" in the eyes of the media, and in herdlike fashion journalists raced to condemn the "politically correct" mob they had "discovered" in American universities.

The first articles on the politically correct appeared in the *New York Times,* written by Richard Bernstein, who would later write a book attacking PC, with funding supplied by conservative foundations. An article by Bernstein written in 1988 compared a conference on liberal education at Duke University to the tyrannical "minute of hatred" described in George Orwell's *1984.* Bernstein called the professors "uncivil libertarians" with an "enemies' list."[54]

Two years later, in 1990, Bernstein wrote an article that helped set in motion a wave of attacks on higher education. The *National Review* called it "an exceptionally important piece," probably as much because it appeared in the pages of their eternal enemy, the *New York Times,* as for the information it conveyed. Both the title ("The Rising Hegemony of the Politically Correct") and the subtitle ("Academia's Fashionable Orthodoxy") reveal Bernstein's one-sided perspective and set the tone for the articles that followed.[55]

These accusations about political correctness received confirmation in the 24 December 1990 issue of *Newsweek,* which had "Thought Police" emblazoned on its cover. An article by Jerry Adler titled "Taking Offense" asked in a subtitle, "Is this the new enlightenment on campus or the new McCarthyism?" Readers who passed over the obvious answer on the front cover found an article inside telling them that political correctness "is, strictly speaking, a totalitarian philosophy," that "students censor even the most ordinary of opinions," that "PC represents the subordination of the right of free speech to the guarantee of equal protection under the law," that "politically, PC is Marxist in origin," and that all of these elements create the "tyranny of PC." [56]

The *Newsweek* story made "PC" a derogatory adjective and used it twenty-nine times to condemn anyone with vaguely liberal views. According to *Newsweek,* anyone who wears a prochoice or anti-Bush button is PC, anyone who favors multiculturalism is PC, and anyone who wears a tie-dyed T-shirt and sandals is a "PC person." "Politically correct," once a reference to extremists who enforced their views on others, was transformed by conservatives and the media to a term describing anyone who advocates progressive ideas.

As the PC bandwagon attracted the attention of the major newsmagazines, each invoked the same tired list of anecdotes. A special issue of the *New Republic* on 15 February 1991 was devoted to the PC scare. While American troops prepared to invade Kuwait, the *New Republic* found a new Saddam Hussein in the visage of the tenured leftist who controlled American universities and sought to destroy traditional learning with the same totalitarian vigor Hussein had used in ransacking his neighbor. At the same time the *New Republic* supported a war to destroy Saddam and free Kuwait, it also seemed to call for a war to free American education from the radical professors who had invaded it.

But it was Dinesh D'Souza's *Illiberal Education* that brought the PC backlash to its peak. By having his book excerpted in the *Atlantic Monthly,* a liberal-moderate magazine, D'Souza consciously avoided the label of "conservative" writer. D'Souza even erased his right-wing past, omitting mention of his first book—a fawning biography of Jerry Falwell—and claiming that he was an editor at the notorious *Dartmouth Review* "long before the newspaper's most notorious showdowns." [57]

In fact, during D'Souza's time as editor, the *Dartmouth Review* published an interview with former KKK leader David Duke in an issue that featured a staged photo on the cover of a black man hanging from a tree on campus. D'Souza's paper also ran a parody of Black English called "Dis sho ain't no jive, bro" in the voice of a black Dartmouth student who says: "Dese boys be sayin' that we be comin' here to Dartmut an' not takin' the classics. You know, Homa, Shakesphere; but I hea' dey all be co'd in da ground, six feet unda' and whatchu be askin' us to learn from dem?" [58] D'Souza personally "outed" gay students in 1981 by printing "personal letters from students confessing their gay sentiments," taken from the files of the Gay Student Alliance. The *New York Times* reported that one student "outed" by D'Souza became depressed and considered suicide. Another student's grandfather learned about his grandson's homosexuality by reading the *Dartmouth Review*.[59]

The reviews of D'Souza's book were important in promoting it as a supposedly moderate and truthful account of what was happening on college campuses. When leading liberals like C. Vann Woodward wrote favorable reviews of *Illiberal Education* in the *New York Review of Books*, the image of D'Souza as an objective journalist reporting on a national crisis was confirmed. Woodward concluded, "There is reason for hope that the current aberration in the academy may be halted before it is too late" and said that the time has come for scholars to "stand up, be counted, and speak out."[60] The success of conservatives at spreading the myth of political correctness can be attributed largely to the willingness of liberals to believe them. D'Souza noted the importance of the positive "strong reaction from this liberal intelligentsia" to his 1991 article in the *Atlantic*. D'Souza also reported the significance of C. Vann Woodward's endorsement, which, he said, made it "evident that the P.C. issue had deeply fractured the liberal intellectual mainstream."[61]

But Woodward's initial enthusiasm faded after the many flaws in D'Souza's account were pointed out. Even Woodward has admitted that, caught up in the fervor of D'Souza's message, he accepted the evidence presented in *Illiberal Education* without adequate criticism: "When I first wrote on the book, I accepted its purely factual statements as true." While Woodward thought "the investigation seemed reasonably thorough, the rhetoric comparatively temperate, and the documentation fairly detailed, . . . unfortunately, the book turned out to contain some serious and irresponsible factual errors." When his essay was reprinted in the anthology *Beyond PC,* Woodward went to the trouble of revising it to remove his errors of credulity, criticizing D'Souza's "occasional stretching of evidence and logic to score a point."[62]

It might be considered newsworthy that a major liberal supporter of D'Souza's claims had repudiated much of his positive review, but Woodward's quasi retraction received much less attention than his initial praise, and the paperback edition of *Illiberal Education* uses Woodward's original words as the sole quotation on its back cover.

The Myth of the Conservative Victim

The conservatives gained a major strategic victory in the culture wars when they declared themselves to be the oppressed rather than the oppressors. Instead of attacking Marxist professors and urging students to become spies as

Accuracy in Academia did, conservatives in the 1990s present themselves as the victims of false charges of racism and sexism, victims of the repressive thought police, and victims of reverse discrimination. The critics of political correctness invert reality by declaring themselves oppressed by feminists and minorities. While sarcastically attacking "the victim's revolution" of minorities on campus, D'Souza and other critics have created their own victim's revolution with a new victim: the oppressed conservative white male. *Illiberal Education* tells the stories of various conservatives victimized by tenured radicals and student activists, including the ultimate victims of PC: the Dead White European Males of Western Civilization.

The conservatives' self-declared "victimization" is displayed by Robert Weissberg, a political scientist at the University of Illinois. Weissberg, writing to his fellow conservatives, declares: "We are the queers of the 1990s." Continuing his analogy, Weissberg says conservatives try to "pass" and fear a "public outing" of their views, since being called a conservative is "not all that different than, say, 'Richard Speck, Mass Murderer.'"[63]

Even the rhetoric of the Left is being taken over by these "victimized" conservatives. "Young white men feel oppressed," the editor of *Reason* magazine says. "They have spent their entire lives officially marked 'undesirable.'"[64] A conservative newspaper announced an "Oppressed Faculty Contest" sponsored by the Young America's Foundation, to award the $10,000 Engalitcheff Prize to a "college faculty member who swims against the prevailing stream of political correctness and intolerance."[65] *American Spectator* founded a public service group, Amnesty in Academia, to defend the rights of faculty and students. It established a toll-free hotline to "report human rights violations on your campus" such as "the brutal interrogation of a student caught whistling the National Anthem on campus."[66] Russell Jacoby, who examined the "human rights violations" Amnesty in Academia protested, concluded that they were merely "fictitious tales of fired university professors."[67]

"Since our newfound sensitivity decrees that only the victim shall be the hero," Robert Hughes notes in *Time*, "the white American male starts bawling for victim status, too."[68] Hughes would have us give up the idea of victims altogether and ignore the women who face sexism, the minorities subjected to racism, and the gays and lesbians vilified and attacked. Removing victims erases both American history and current realities, replacing them with a myth of justice and equality, in which bland declarations of our ideals conceal the fact that the noble aim of equal opportunity has never been achieved. The difference between the old victims and the new conservative white male victims is that the conservatives aren't really victims. They are still the same privileged people they have always been.

What conservatives are demanding is not simply the right to speak, but the right, as victims, to be free of criticism and harassment — ironically, the same right that the politically correct are said to invoke when they support restrictive speech codes. But by using their own invented status as victims, conservatives were able to gain the sympathies of the liberals.

The poster child of the conservative victim's revolution is Stephan Thernstrom, a social historian with a progressive reputation who co-taught "The Peopling of America" at Harvard and who has become one of the most often cited victims of leftist orthodoxy. D'Souza's chapter on Harvard in *Illiberal Education* uses Thernstrom as the key example of PC, and John Taylor's 1991 *New York* magazine article (reprinted in *Reader's Digest*) begins with this story about Thernstrom:

> "Racist."
> "Racist!"
> "The man is a racist!"
> "A racist!"
> Such denunciations, hissed in tones of self-righteousness and contempt, vicious and vengeful, furious, smoking with hatred — such denunciations haunted Stephan Thernstrom for weeks.[69]

But these hissing, smoking words were never spoken. The only thing they haunted was Taylor's vivid imagination. Even Thernstrom said he was "appalled" at reading Taylor's words, explaining that "nothing like that ever happened."[70]

In 1988, Thernstrom was criticized by some of his students, who anonymously accused him in the student newspaper of racial insensitivity and then complained to Harvard's Committee on Race Relations. One of the students, Wendi Grantham, claimed that Thernstrom "said Jim Crow laws were beneficial" and "read aloud from white plantation owners' journals" that provided a positive view of slavery. Thernstrom was also attacked for using the words *Oriental* and *Indian,* for mentioning that some regarded affirmative action as preferential treatment, and for endorsing the view that the breakup of the black family was a cause of black poverty.[71] Another student, Paula Ford, claimed that "he said black men beat their wives, and then their wives kicked them out."[72] Soon these criticisms by a few students were being described as an attempt to suppress Thernstrom's free speech.

Thernstrom said it was a "McCarthyism of the left" that would have a "chilling effect." He believed that the Harvard administration's response had been too weak, and he made his status as an oppressed victim clear: "I felt like a rape victim, and yet the silence of the administration seemed to give the benefit of the doubt to the students who attacked me. . . . I could not even defend myself, because the charge of racism or racial insensitivity is ultimately unanswerable."[73] But except for a vague statement condemning "prejudice, harassment and discrimination" (issued weeks before the controversy began) and praise for the "judicious and fair" students who had "avoided public comment," Harvard officials never took the side of the students, and a month later the dean of the faculty announced that no disciplinary action would be taken against Thernstrom. While Thernstrom may have objected to the administration's neutrality, even Eugene Genovese — a critic of political correctness — admitted that "the Harvard administration more or less upheld Thernstrom's academic freedom."[74]

Thernstrom decided not to offer the class again: "The result of being smeared in the campus paper for two months was that I decided to stop teaching *The Peopling of America*. When it was time to decide whether or not to give the course the following year, I found myself thinking that I should try to defend myself against a repeat witch-hunt by taping all my lectures." Thernstrom concluded, "It just isn't worth it. Professors who teach race issues encounter such a culture of hostility, among some students, that some of these questions are simply not teachable any more, at least not in an honest, critical way."[75] By saying that his ideas were "not teachable" and that the attacks on him were "unanswerable," Thernstrom placed his critics beyond the realm of intellectual discourse and into the position of doctrinal enforcers.

Thernstrom depicts himself as the victim of a witch hunt comparable to the ones seen in the McCarthy era: "This seemed to me very much like being named a subversive by Senator McCarthy, and indeed somewhat worse in that McCarthyism was external to the academy and had very little support from within it. Being the target of a witch-hunt by one's students, with precious few sympathetic and encouraging words from one's colleagues, was perhaps more painful."[76] But Harvard law professor Randall Kennedy found "not the least bit of evidence . . . that the students who criticized Professor Thernstrom sought to hound him out of the university as real McCarthyists sought in the fifties to hound communists and their sympathizers."[77]

At no point did any of the students who criticized Thernstrom suggest that he ought to be fired or that his class should be eliminated. Grantham wrote in response to Thernstrom's letter, "I do not charge that Thernstrom is a racist."[78] Nor was Ford happy about Thernstrom's decision to stop teaching the class: "That was not our goal. Our goal was to point out areas in his lecture that we thought were inaccurate and possibly could be changed. To me, it's a big overreaction for him to decide not to teach the course again because of that."[79]

These students made no threats and interrupted no classes in their efforts to address important public issues. Controversy is an essential ingredient of debate in the university, yet Thernstrom recommends that "scholars with views like mine had best be very careful addressing ethnic issues and are best off avoiding them altogether." [80]

Thernstrom's case became a major weapon in the attack on PC, one of the "most notorious attempts to suppress thought and expression," in National Endowment for the Humanities chair Lynne Cheney's words. [81] But academic freedom does not include a right to be free of criticism, even if that criticism includes unfair accusations of racism. Classes involving controversial issues are "not teachable" only when professors refuse to teach them. It is far easier for these "victims" of PC to give up and gain another legend to use in the attack against political correctness than to admit that their freedom to speak is not threatened. If anyone now feels reluctant to express their views, it is the students who were attacked as politically correct censors, not the tenured Harvard professor hailed as an anti-PC hero. Rebecca Walkowitz, president of the student newspaper, observed: "It's important to remember who has the power here, because it's not students. Who would dare criticize a professor for political reasons now? In addition to fearing for your grade, you'd fear being pilloried in the national press." [82]

Nadine Strossen, president of the American Civil Liberties Union (ACLU), notes, "Putting aside the fairness of the criticism to which Thernstrom and other members of academic communities have been subjected, it is clear that such criticism itself is protected free expression, and often necessary, or at least desirable, to effect social reform. Therefore, it is problematic to invoke free speech principles, as some have done, to challenge this facet of the PC controversy." [83] Free speech requires both the freedom of professors to express their views and the freedom of students to criticize them, even if the criticisms are misguided or offensive.

While no other stories about Thernstrom are as dishonest as John Taylor's account, many writers distorted what happened to Thernstrom in order to fit him into the myth of the conservative victim. Referring to "prohibitory speech codes," the National Review declared: "Thus a distinguished Harvard historian will no longer give his course on slavery because some black students claimed to have been offended." [84] Patrick Garry wrote in a book on censorship, "A Harvard professor, Stephan Thernstrom, was sanctioned after having used the terms 'Indians,' instead of 'Native Americans,' and 'Oriental,' with its imperialistic overtones, in class." [85] William Bennett claimed that "Professor Stephan Thernstrom, a distinguished professor of history at Harvard, was forced to drop an undergraduate course after he was harassed because he used the term 'Indian' instead of 'Native American.' "[86] The Thernstrom incident had nothing to do with speech codes. Thernstrom was never punished, and Thernstrom himself chose—against the wishes of everyone involved—to stop teaching the class. But these facts are ignored in favor of promoting the myth of political correctness.

Mythmaking by Anecdote

The need to sustain the myth of political correctness and the victimology of conservatives has led to the invention of incidents that support the new oppression ideology. For example, the conservative newspaper *Heterodoxy* reported that the women's studies program at Wellesley College sent letters to students planning to major in modern European history, accusing them of "perpetuating the 'dominant white male' attitudes and behaviors that have been oppressing women for generations." But this was not true: there is no modern European history major at Wellesley.[87]

Many charges of leftist indoctrination turn out to be baseless after further examination. Lynne Cheney's 1991 NEH report *Telling the Truth* repeats a former student's allegation that the College of Wooster's freshman seminar program was a "re-education camp."[88] Ironically, Cheney herself had been invited the previous year to speak in a lecture series associated with the program but declined. A *Chronicle of Higher Education* reporter who went to Wooster, Ohio, to investigate the charge found no basis for it. The reporter interviewed students in one section of the class and discovered that "virtually all" of the students "describe the atmosphere as positive, allowing students to discuss controversial issues without feeling shut out." The reporter also found that "none of them said they felt that they could not speak out or disagree about politics." This concurred with evaluations for the entire program, in which 94 percent of students said that instructors encouraged "independent thought and disagreement."[89]

One particularly disturbing example of how political correctness gets invented was promoted in a 10 April 1991 *Wall Street Journal* editorial titled "The Return of the Storm Troopers." The article describes, in an ominous first-person narrative, a "mob" at the State University of New York at Binghamton that intimidated and disrupted a speaker from the National Association of Scholars. "The threat of violence is clear and soon fulfilled," wrote the *Wall Street Journal*, as "the mob disrupts the talk, jeers the speaker." But David Beers's *Mother Jones* article reveals that only one student caused a short dispute and acted offensively. These actions were certainly reprehensible: the student threw a picture that the speaker had passed around to the audience, and exchanged obscenities with him. The student also threw a piece of gum at a professor and then blew his nose and put the tissue in the lecturer's water glass. But there was no mob. The faculty member leading the group of black and Hispanic students (attracted by a false rumor that a KKK member would speak) who was accused of being the mob's leader told them "to refrain from disruption." A campus police investigator concluded, "It was just one case of disruption by one individual."[90] Even Saul Levin, one of the speakers, told a student reporter that "other than the one person who misbehaved, the meeting had gone well."[91]

There was no violence, the talk was completed peacefully after a four-minute disruption, and the student was disciplined by the university for his actions and placed on probation. Not only is there no sign of Nazi storm troopers around the corner, there is also no evidence of any improper action by the university or the vast majority of its "politically correct" students. Only in the myth of political correctness can the actions of one individual be used as evidence of a totalitarian "mob."

Yet the misinformation about what happened at Binghamton is frequently repeated by conservatives. "A mob of 200 students, apparently under the impression that a white-supremacy rally was going on, invaded a lecture hall, brandishing sticks and canes," John Leo declares. "They harassed the speaker, calling him a 'white dork devil,' broke a framed picture he was showing to the audience, and punched a student outside the hall."[92] The conservative newspaper *Heterodoxy* claims that "members of the BSU, some brandishing sticks, verbally abused and physically intimidated the participants."[93] Herbert London, head of the NAS, concludes that "in permitting hooligans to threaten both the speaker and the audience, academic freedom was irreparably harmed."[94]

As is the case with any mythology, certain stories about political correctness have achieved the status of canon and are recited religiously in almost every piece of writing on the subject. When it comes to PC horror stories, conservatives are more devoted to recycling than the most committed environmentalist. One anecdote alone, which first appeared in a *Wall Street Journal* column by Alan Charles Kors in 1989, has reappeared in at least thirty-five articles and books about political correctness.[95]

Kors had described a "courageous female undergraduate" member of a committee examining diversity at the University of Pennsylvania who wrote a memo in which she declared, "The desire of the committee to continually consider the collective before the individual is misconceived. At Penn we should be concerned with the intellect and experience of INDIVIDUALS before we are concerned with the group. . . . The desire of this subcommittee to dictate what to think regarding groups or individuals does not constitute education; it is merely a process of thought homogenization." A university administrator on the committee responded by circling the word "INDIVIDUALS," and commenting: "This is a 'RED FLAG' phrase today, which is considered by many to be RACIST. Arguments that champion the individual over the group ultimately privileges [sic] the 'individuals' belonging to the largest or dominant group." Probably no other note scribbled on a memo has ever attracted this much attention.

According to Roger Kimball, "What this alarming development portends is nothing less than a new form of thought control based on a variety of pious new-Left slogans and attitudes."[96] It is hard to discern what Kimball's "new form of thought control" is. The administrator did not take any action to punish the student, did not control what the student thought, and did not even make a public statement condemning the student's view. Instead, the administrator made a private comment about a memo, which the student herself then publicized. Even someone who finds the comment stupid (as I do) must recognize that it is hardly significant enough to be called "the most notorious incident" of political correctness or to deserve thirty-five retellings. If this "red flag" is the epitome of political correctness, then there is no threat to anybody's freedom of speech.

Many conservative critics see the mere declaration of liberal ideas as evidence of a secret conspiracy to destroy freedom of speech. Dinesh D'Souza, quoting four college presidents on diversity, writes that "they all employ the characteristic vocabulary of the revolution, which we must learn to recognize as a kind of code language for the changes to which they point."[97] This hidden "code language" includes praise for subversive ideas like "a more diverse and pluralistic community" and the need to "engage intolerance." Richard Bernstein calls multiculturalism "a code word for a political ambition, a yearning for more power."[98] President Stephen Balch of the NAS says that " 'diversity' has attained a dubious status as the most widely used 'code word' in academe."[99] Roger Kimball imagines a hidden conspiracy of "tenured radicals" who use *diversity* as "a favorite code word."[100] George Will also condemns *diversity* as a conspiratorial "code word" under which "radicals cluster to advocate academic spoils systems — racial, ethnic, sexual — and politicized curriculums."[101] But viewing *diversity* as a code word for "thought control" is as absurd as treating *individual rights* as a code word for "racism."

The use of code words is not the only charge made against this alleged

PC "conspiracy." It is virtually impossible to read any conservative attack on higher education without finding numerous references to Stalin, Hitler, fascism, and Orwell's Thought Police. Alan Charles Kors, for example, compares the University of Pennsylvania to the "University of Peking," as if American universities were centers of totalitarianism.[102] Roger Kimball refers to "liberal fascism," while Terry Teachout claims that "tenured radicals are turning America's institutions of higher learning into stalags of state-subsidized sensitivity fascism."[103] *Heterodoxy* editor David Horowitz writes, "The strategy of today's radicals is a strategy invented by the old Communist left in its heyday as a fifth column for Josef Stalin."[104] Columnist Walter Williams sees "the equivalent of the Nazi brownshirt thought-control movement" on college campuses. Noting that "much of Hitler's initial intellectual backing came from university students and professors," Williams urges private donors to "de-fund pre-Nazi universities."[105]

When conservatives are not busy imagining PC Nazis goose-stepping to class, they depict political correctness as an illness in the body of the university, a cluster of cancerous cells that must be surgically removed in order to return higher education back to health. William Bennett says, "Our common culture serves as a kind of immunological system, destroying the values and attitudes promulgated by an adversary culture that can infect our body politic."[106] Bennett is not the only one to compare dissenting ideas to a sickness. Stephen Balch wonders whether the "disease" of the "diversity campaign" can be "halted or reversed even in its more advanced stages"; and David Horowitz declares, "The radical left is a fascist force with a human face, the carrier of an ideological virus as deadly as AIDS."[107] Roger Kimball warns: "A swamp yawns before us, ready to devour everything. The best response to all this—and finally the only serious and effective response—is not to enter these murky waters in the first place. As Nietzsche observed, we do not refute a disease. We resist it."[108] By dehumanizing their intellectual opponents and regarding liberal views as viruses to be destroyed rather than ideas to be debated, these conservatives reveal that their aim is not free inquiry but ideological control. One does not argue rationally with a sickness or admit that it has some validity; one destroys it and inoculates the body against further invasions.

Winning the Culture War

What turned the tide for the conservatives in their war against political correctness was not their own organizing strength, or even the failure of academics to respond to the attacks, but the distrust of liberals and moderates in the media and academia for the Left. Without the support of liberals, the conservatives' attacks would have been dismissed as the same old complaints of those who resented the existence of radicals in universities. But by the late 1980s, liberals too were becoming increasingly concerned about the state of higher education.

One group of liberals within academia were alarmed by the rise of radical theories such as deconstruction, Critical Legal Studies, women's studies, and cultural studies, especially since the radicals who espoused them often focused their attacks on liberal ideas about rationality, free speech, and objectivity. Liberals were also concerned at the intolerance of leftists who did not accept liberal notions about the marketplace of ideas. President Derek Bok of Harvard, in his spring 1991 report to the Harvard Board of Overseers, declared: "In recent years, the threat of orthodoxy has come primarily from within rather than outside the university." [109]

Another important group of liberals came from the media. Dinesh D'Souza reports that a prominent liberal newscaster told him "Many of us here are concerned about the thought police who are roaming our nation's campuses." Even D'Souza admits, "This was a more strident formulation than anything I had said, but such is the way of the media." [110] Robert Kelner thinks that "the media have become enthralled by the notion that a political orthodoxy is entrenched on campus." [111] Why did the attacks on political correctness appeal so much to the so-called liberal media? The mainstream media have always been suspicious of academia, and most of the leading commentators and journalists had had no exposure to the new radical theories that proliferated after the 1960s. Journalists resent the academic Left and delight in ridiculing their jargon-filled writings (articles appear annually about the bizarre titles of papers delivered at the MLA convention) and attacking their cushy jobs at elite universities. Journalists are also, in D'Souza's words, "sensitive to threats to the First Amendment." [112] Most journalists are out of touch with what actually goes on at college campuses, and so they became a conduit for information delivered through the pipeline of conservative newspapers and organizations devoted to spreading stories of political correctness. Sympathetic to the carefully crafted anecdotes of oppression told by conservatives, reporters had little concern for finding the truth.

Part of the blame for the inaccurate depiction of higher education must be given to the academic Left itself, which allowed political correctness to become a public relations fiasco through its inability to tell the other side of the story to the general public, and its lack of interest in doing so. D'Souza notes that "a national debate raged about political correctness, with virtually no response from the leading advocates of racial preferences and multiculturalism and a kind of deafening silence from university administrators." Because no powerful reply came back from academia, many people assumed that the conservative stories had a great deal of validity. People found it "hard to avoid the suspicion that they could not make an effective public defense of their policies and thus made a tactical decision to lie low until the storm clouds of criticism passed."[113] Whether it was because of their jargon-filled writings, their preoccupation with their own research and teaching, or the unwillingness of the media to listen to them, academics on the left never made a sustained rebuttal to the conservative attacks.

Another key to the conservatives' triumph at promoting the myth of political correctness is their ability to link themselves to public dissatisfaction with universities. James Carey, former dean of the College of Communications at the University of Illinois, says that "while much of the political correctness literature is a disinformation campaign designed to discredit higher education, it could never be politically effective and the academic Left never forced into the role of a scapegoat except for one overriding fact: Public resentment against higher education is real."[114]

A number of factors in the 1980s led to strong resentment among students and their parents. The first of these was the increasing cost of higher education. Tuition and fees at public four-year colleges and universities rose 141 percent during the 1980s, much more than the increase in inflation of 63.6 percent. The financial crisis in many states exacerbated this problem in the 1990s. Public universities increased tuition and fees by 12 percent in 1991–92, while the inflation rate was only 3.2 percent.[115] Meanwhile, financial aid to students, especially the Pell grant program, was being cut drastically by the Reagan administration.

At the same time, students complained bitterly that the quality of their education was declining because of large lecture classes and courses taught by untrained graduate students. Worse yet, many college graduates in the 1980s and 1990s had difficulty finding good jobs, which for most of them was the sole purpose of getting a degree. Top universities were also blamed for emphasizing research at the expense of teaching, which added to the problems of inadequate education and skyrocketing tuition. Not surprisingly, the attack on political correctness has not cured these problems, although leftists continue to be blamed for them.

The Money behind the Myth

The attacks on political correctness did not arise from a grassroots movement of noble individuals resisting leftist totalitarians; instead, they were carefully developed over many years by well-funded conservative groups. The conservative movement against the universities has been organizing since the early 1980s, working to create the institutional framework and compiling stories of oppression by radicals to be used in their attack on political correctness.

Nearly every critic of higher education in the past decade has been supported by a conservative foundation or think tank. Allan Bloom was funded by the John M. Olin Foundation and until his death served as director of the Olin Center at the University of Chicago, which receives nearly $1 million per year from the foundation. Dinesh D'Souza received a $30,000 grant from the Olin Foundation via the Institute for Educational Affairs to write *Illiberal Education*, $20,000 to help promote the book, and in 1991 held a $98,400 Olin research fellowship at the American Enterprise Institute.[116] Charles Sykes wrote *The Hollow Men* after being hired by conservative Dartmouth alumni to investigate disturbing liberal tendencies at their alma mater. Roger Kimball's book *Tenured Radicals* appeared first as essays he wrote as an editor for *New Criterion*, a conservative art criticism journal, which began in 1982 with office space and a $100,000 start-up grant from the Olin Foundation and which received a total of $1,425,000 from the Olin, Scaife, and Bradley Foundations from 1984 to 1988.[117] Martin Anderson, author of *Impostors in the Temple*, is a fellow at the Hoover Institution, as is affirmative action critic Thomas Sowell.[118] The Olin Foundation gave $350,000 in 1989 to the Second Thoughts project of Peter Collier and David Horowitz; the money helped them to sponsor conferences and write *Destructive Generation*, their critique of the 1960s.[119]

Even supposedly neutral journalists have been the beneficiaries of right-wing largess for projects attacking political correctness. *New York Times* reporter Richard Bernstein thanked the Smith-Richardson Foundation and the Lynde and Harry Bradley Foundation for making his research possible.[120] In 1991, the Olin Foundation granted $20,000 to Christina Hoff Sommers for an attack on academic feminism, $25,000 to Linda Chavez for research on multiculturalism, and $18,000 to Carol Iannone—the rejected nominee to the National Endowment for the Humanities Council—for a book attacking multiculturalism. Sommers, in her book *Who Stole Feminism?*, acknowledges three conservative foundations which spent more than $100,000 supporting her attacks on feminism—the Lynde and Harry Bradley Foundation, the Carthage Foundation, and the Olin Foundation—and observes, "I could not have written this book without their aid and cooperation."[121]

Yet Sommers denies that conservative groups like the National Association of Scholars are heavily supported: "The NAS has an office in Princeton, New Jersey, with a staff of six (two part-timers), a budget of $900,000, and a national membership of fewer than three thousand." Sommers claims that "the NAS operates entirely on its own; no university supports it or offers it facilities."[122] This image of an impoverished NAS is amusing to those involved with its liberal counterpart, Teachers for a Democratic Culture, whose newsletter I edit. We have no office, no staff, a budget far less than 2 percent of what the NAS spends, and unlike the NAS—which received more than $682,000 in grants in 1991 from four conservative foundations—we have no foundation or university support.[123]

The Olin Foundation spends $15 million annually on grants to practically every conservative magazine, including *American Spectator, Crisis, National Review, Business Today, Encounter, Public Interest,* and the *Journal of Democracy.* Money is also provided to conservative think tanks like the American Enterprise Institute, which received $400,000 in 1989. Robert Bork is now writing a book on the culture wars with the leisure provided by his $167,000 post at the institute. The Olin Foundation also is an important promoter of the conservative law and economics movement, providing more than $5 million in 1989 to nine leading law schools to fund programs. A program at UCLA funded by the Olin Foundation was rejected after one year because the university thought that the faculty should design a program of its own and that the Olin Foundation was "taking advantage of student's financial need to indoctrinate them with a particular ideology."[124]

Conservative foundations also fund the proliferating lawsuits filed by "politically incorrect" professors and students. In the past, students and faculty who objected to campus policies or disciplinary proceedings often accepted the results quietly and the media rarely paid attention to their complaints. But litigation proved an effective way to attack campus programs like affirmative action and sexual harassment and to publicize incidents of political correctness. The Center for Individual Rights, a leading defender of conservatives on campus, has received nearly $2 million from right-wing foundations since it was founded in 1989.[125]

Perhaps the most important money in the culture wars on campus has gone to conservative student newspapers. In 1991, the Olin Foundation gave $114,000 to the Madison Center for Education Affairs, which provides small but important grants to the Collegiate Network of conservative college newspapers.[126] The center spends more than $300,000 each year on a network of sixty-five campus papers, providing workshops on publishing and attracting advertisers, suggestions for help through a monthly newsletter and a toll-free telephone line, and an advertising consortium to sell ads for the papers.[127] The *Dartmouth Review* is an example of how powerful this support can be. Founded in 1980, the *Dartmouth Review* received a $10,000 grant in its first year and quickly became one of the most important (and most controversial) conservative student newspapers in the country. In 1982, under editor Dinesh D'Souza, it became too controversial for the Madison Center, which cut off its funds after the interview with David Duke. But the *Dartmouth Review* eventually returned to the good graces of conservatives, who have defended it in many recent confrontations with Dartmouth officials. The Olin Foundation gave the paper $295,000 to pay for legal expenses in its disputes with Dartmouth administrators.[128]

What this support shows is not a conspiracy but a well-organized and well-funded network that gives conservative voices an opportunity to be heard in the media. The importance of these newspapers to D'Souza and other conservative collegians is difficult to underestimate. The subsidized papers gave them a supportive environment in which to sharpen their skill at complaining about liberal bias. The papers provide a network of contacts and editorial internships that have led to jobs in the White House, Republican congressional offices, and conservative publications. William Cattan, a *Dartmouth Review* editor, became a speechwriter for Vice President Bush; after graduation, D'Souza became the editor of *Prospect,* a conservative Princeton alumni magazine (as did another *Dartmouth Review* editor, Laura Ingraham), and then managing editor of the Heritage Foundation's *Policy Review.*[129]

Most of all, these conservative student newspapers, along with two national conservative newspapers—*Campus,* which is distributed to 1,200 colleges by the Intercollegiate Studies Institute, and Accuracy in Academia's *Campus Report*—help spread stories about political correctness. Thomas Sowell, a fellow at the Hoover Institution, says that "the whole apparatus of campus thought control known as 'political correctness' was first exposed" by the conservative newspapers. He adds, "Only after their many horror stories began to be picked up by journalists in the mass media did this become a public issue." He praises these "unsung heroes" for risking cries of "fascist," death threats, academic punishment, and social ostracism to tell us about "the internal corruption of American higher education."[130]

But liberals and leftists on campus have no support network to provide subsidized newspapers and free legal assistence. Jon Wiener, a history professor at the University of California at Irvine, says about the conservative foundations, "It's a great system. I wish those on the left had the resources to do the same."[131] There are no comparable left-wing think tanks in which diatribes can be composed; no left-wing foundations handing out big checks to scholars who write articles and books on the crisis in education; no left-wing alternative newspapers receiving grants to support their publishing; no left-wing old-boy networks to hand out well-paid jobs to radicals after graduation.

The conservatives often claim that mainstream foundations favor leftists. Heather MacDonald writes in a *New Criterion* article that "millions of dollars of support" for "curricular transformation projects" have been provided by groups such as "the Mellon, Ford, and Rockefeller foundations, the National Endowment for the Humanities, the MLA, and the Fund for the Improvement of Postsecondary Education, and individual colleges."[132] But none of these agencies is devoted to funding a leftist ideological agenda, unlike the clearly conservative aims of the Olin Foundation. The most "radical" group MacDonald mentions, the Modern Language Association, does not give any grants. The major foundations generally support mainstream projects such as curriculum reform rather than radical critiques of society or academia. And the National Endowment for the Humanities explicitly funded a conservative agenda under the leadership of William Bennett and Lynne Cheney.

The fact that conservatives' attacks on political correctness have been well funded and carefully organized in no way refutes their ideas. Nor is there any conspiracy here. But the large amount of money given to conservative organizations to promote the attack on higher education helps explain why there have been so many books and publications devoted to "exposing" political correctness and so little response from the other side. The myth of political correctness has been sustained not by a careful examination of the evidence but by the fact that large amounts of money and support are available to only one side in the culture wars.

There was no crisis of "political correctness" on college campuses in the 1980s. Alexander Astin, the country's leading expert on student attitudes, reports, "There's no thought-control occurring." Astin did a massive survey on diversity: "If anyone would have been the target of pressure for political correctness," he says, "it would have been me. I felt none."[133] A survey of 210 faculty by Lionel Lewis and Philip Altbach found that "political correctness had relatively little salience among our respondents." More than two-thirds of the professors felt "vulnerable and buffeted," but the cause was budget cuts, not political correctness.[134]

A 1991 survey by the American Council on Education found that only 10 percent of colleges and universities reported controversies of any kind involving campus speakers during the previous year, and only 3 percent of all institutions experienced battles over textbooks or classroom information. Even these numbers exaggerate the amount of political correctness involved, since they include controversies over leftist speakers as well as campus debates where free speech was fully protected and no one urged censorship. By contrast, 36 percent of all institutions—and 74 percent of the research institutions—reported incidents of intolerance involving race, gender, or sexual orientation. Elaine El-Khawas, who conducted the survey, concluded that "reports of widespread efforts to impose politically correct thinking on college students and faculty appear to be overblown." [135]

Academic freedom is more protected today than at any other time in the history of higher education. A study of investigations by the American Association of University Professors found that in the 1970s, fifty-five faculty were involved in civil liberties or political ideology cases, compared with only two in the 1980s—and in almost every case it was leftist faculty whose rights were violated.[136] While the crusade against political correctness has inspired a new wave of censorship against leftist views during the 1990s, the AAUP has reported virtually no attacks on the academic freedom of conservatives. But not one of these facts contributed by neutral observers of colleges and universities has affected the myth of political correctness.

➤ 2 Conservative Correctness

On 18 November 1994, vandals struck at feminist, gay, and lesbian journals in the Zimmerman Library at the University of New Mexico. Five shelves of bound periodicals were stolen and replaced with Nazi books moved from another part of the library. The few remaining volumes had their call number labels and title pages defaced with swastikas and phrases like "Bitch propaganda." A title page of the journal *Lesbian Ethics* had the title crossed out and "God's Ethics" written above it, with "God made women for men" and a swastika drawn on the same page. On 29 November, the missing journals were finally discovered inside the library, hidden behind other journals on the highest shelves in a little-used area of the library. It was not the first hate crime on that campus; two weeks earlier, a mural of American Indians in the student union was defaced by a swastika, and the month before that, three youths carrying white supremacist literature were arrested on campus for possession of explosives.[1]

Bigotry on college campuses isn't unusual. Within a month of the vandalism at the University of New Mexico, student leaders at Pacific Lutheran University in Tacoma, Washington, received threatening hate mail with derogatory comments about minorities, feminists, and homosexuals. Trancey Williams, the coordinator of African American programs at Moorhead State University in Minnesota, received a series of threatening calls from a Ku Klux Klan supporter, who asked for Williams's measurements to have a coffin prepared.[2]

But racism isn't considered as newsworthy as political correctness. No major newspapers picked up the University of New Mexico story, while much more trivial examples of political correctness made front-page headlines. To judge from the news, most people thought the "PC police" posed a greater threat to free speech than neo-Nazi vandals.

Contrary to the common media image of cowed students and professors terrified by radical feminists, sensitivity police, and PC extremists, most of the attacks on freedom of expression on college campuses still come from the Right. Complaints about political correctness reflect a small number of incidents, usually misreported, while the large number of attacks by conservatives on academic freedom and free speech on college campuses are often ignored or defended.

When free speech is endangered on campus, the correct response is not to attack a mythical leftist "domination" of the university, but to demand strong and consistent principles of academic freedom everywhere, applied with equal vigor to conservatives and leftists alike. Yet the Right rejects this goal, demanding a censorship of its own. Conservative Robert Kelner admitted in the *Wall Street Journal*, "The irony is that many conservatives actually want a politically correct campus. It's just that right now campuses are politically 'incorrect' as far as we can see. Conservatives never sought parity with the campus liberals. We sought — and still seek — ascendancy.... I think it's fair to say that freedom of speech was not the rallying cry of the movement."[3]

The conservatives' attacks on political correctness have included open contempt for academic freedom, which they condemn for protecting PC faculty. Les Csorba of Accuracy in Academia says that "academic freedom on college campuses is nothing more than a useful device which gives license to some people and silences others."[4] Columnist Thomas Sowell sees academic freedom as an obstacle to the elimination of tenured radicals: "Tenure and academic freedom have not protected individual diversity of thought on campus but instead have protected those who choose to impose the prevailing ideology through classroom brainwashing of students and storm trooper tactics against outside speakers who might challenge this ideology."[5] Herbert London, one of the founders of the National Association of Scholars, declares: "Academic freedom has become a refuge for radicals."[6]

Thomas Short of the NAS explicitly demands that universities monitor and censor leftist teachers: "We need to explain that academic freedom, which ordinarily requires independence from outside interference, calls for just such interference when that freedom is being subverted from within."[7] Short adds, "Academic freedom is not free speech for professors: in particular, it is not freedom for political speech. It is the freedom to do research and to teach as one sees fit to teach *within* the discipline or disciplines in which one has proven competence."[8] In Short's view, "political" ideas are not protected by free speech, nor are "political" departments like women's studies or minority studies, because they supposedly lack any "disciplinary" basis.

The aim of the *National Review College Guide,* Brad Miner informs his readers, is to show parents the "safe" schools where "your kids are not going to go as a Young American for Freedom and come back after a semester a Marxist." Not surprisingly, the *National Review College Guide* praises the Franciscan-run University of Steubenville in Ohio because "professors who use their positions to propagate Marxism, secular humanism, lesbianism and feminism 'as a priority over a Christian commitment' have been eased out."[9] This is hardly the free examination of ideas without indoctrination; it's a call for right-wing indoctrination.

The Right's hypocritical defense of free speech is exemplified by Hillsdale College and its outspoken president, George Roche. Hillsdale, a small liberal arts college in Hillsdale, Michigan, recommended by the *National Review College Guide* for "its commitment to academic excellence and intellectual integrity," is a darling of the conservatives.[10] Thomas Sowell praises colleges like Hillsdale as the ones with "backbone" who have "fought the lonely fight for traditional academic values and standards."[11]

In 1991, however, four former Hillsdale College professors, all members of the NAS, dared to criticize Hillsdale and its president: "For years the Hillsdale administration has neglected its academic program to pay for 'outreach' activities designed to promote Dr. Roche, maintained a curriculum that requires no appreciable knowledge of Western culture, and used every possible means, including dismissals and threats of lawsuits, to silence dissent of any kind among faculty and students." According to these professors, in 1986 "the administration began to attack the student newspaper, the *Collegian,* for its disagreements with college policies, threatening lawsuits and other reprisals against the student staff and any faculty who defended it."[12] The editor of the *Collegian* was forced by the administration to resign, and the rest of the student staff resigned in protest.

Roche also urged a student, Mark Nehls, not to publish the *Hillsdale Spectator,* an independent newspaper. When Nehls went ahead with his plans and began criticizing Roche in editorials, Roche forbade distribution of the paper on campus and then expelled Nehls. One editorial in the banned *Hillsdale Spectator* claimed that "Hillsdale is a cult of personality and not of principle. Roche is the divine monarch."[13]

Faculty at Hillsdale have also been victims of Roche's conservative correctness. When a dean sued a faculty member, accusing him of committing slander in a private conversation with another administrator, assistant history professor Warren Treadgold was one of sixteen faculty who signed a letter to the student newspaper protesting the use of lawsuits. Three months later, Treadgold was dismissed. Hillsdale officials reportedly said that Treadgold did not "fit in" at Hillsdale and called his letter "unwise, unbecoming, and unprofessional." Hillsdale, which has no appeals or grievance procedures, refused to give any reasons for Treadgold's dismissal.[14] Treadgold said: "I am a conservative, and my disagreements weren't with their politics. Basically Hillsdale is a feudal manor run by George Roche."[15]

An investigation by the AAUP found that Treadgold was one of the top scholars at Hillsdale. He had a Ph.D. from Harvard and had written a book that was being published by Stanford University Press. A 1987 evaluation of Treadgold at Hillsdale declared that "his scholarship is of the highest quality as well as of superior quantity" and called his teaching "clearly above the average." The AAUP concluded that the letter he signed "was the determining factor in the administration's decision to issue notice of nonreappointment when it did."[16] All this is a far cry from the *National Review College Guide*'s description of Hillsdale as a utopia where "top-notch" faculty "express a sense of joyful release at their departure from the stifling atmosphere of the official ideologies of their old schools."[17] Yet, the conservatives who condemn the PC thought police fail to mention Hillsdale, except as a model college in the fight against political correctness.

John Silber at Boston University

Another idol of conservatives is Boston University president John Silber, who for two decades has led efforts to remove faculty he dislikes. For this, Silber is celebrated by conservatives as a model president and rewarded by his board of trustees as America's highest-paid college president. He received $776,963 in total compensation in 1993.[18]

English professor Julia Prewitt Brown was denied tenure by Silber in 1980, despite the fact that the English department voted 22 to 0 in favor of granting tenure and the College of Liberal Arts' Appointments, Promotions, and Tenure (APT) Committee voted 9 to 0 for tenure, calling her a "first rate" scholar. Even after the dean of the College of Liberal Arts advised granting only a three-year probationary extension to reevaluate her work, the university-wide APT committee nevertheless voted 9 to 2 for immediate tenure. But Silber recommended to the board of trustees that Brown be denied tenure, and they agreed.[19]

A jury and an appeals court concluded that Silber was guilty of sex discrimination and found that many of his comments "reflected a patronizing attitude towards women"; Silber had called the English department "a damn matriarchy" (six of the twenty faculty were women) and had told a female professor that she didn't need job security because "your husband is a parachute, so why are you worried?"[20]

Silber has sought to remove leftist faculty and troublemakers like Brown, who had openly picketed in front of Silber's office during a 1979 faculty strike.[21] Elizabeth Rapaport, Roslyn Feldberg, and Seyla Benhabib, all active in union work and feminist studies, were also denied tenure in the early 1980s, despite receiving overwhelming support from their departments and from faculty committees. Rapaport said that "the President does not recognize the legitimacy of feminist inquiry."[22]

Silber reportedly said of Henry Giroux, a well-known education theorist: "It would be a pleasure to rid Boston University of Henry Giroux."[23] Although deans and committees unanimously recommended Giroux for tenure in 1983, Silber appointed conservatives Chester Finn and Nathan Glazer to an *ad hoc* committee reviewing his tenure and used their objections to get rid of Giroux, despite the positive endorsements for him at all the major university tenure-review levels.

Silber has a long record of obstructing academic freedom and civil liberties. In 1976, the National Labor Relations Board found that Boston University had "unlawfully discharged" four women at the university health clinic for having a meeting to complain about working conditions. They were rehired and then fired again. In 1978, Silber's administration delayed the publication of the student yearbook and had some objectionable political material removed. In 1979, the Massachusetts chapter of the ACLU reported that it had "never, in memory, received such a large and sustained volume of complaints" about one institution, and concluded that "B.U. has violated fundamental principles of civil liberties and academic freedom." A student newspaper critical of Silber had its student funding vetoed by the Boston University administration, but eventually won an out-of-court settlement. The director of the campus radio station was fired for refusing to delete a joke about Silber from a tape.[24] In 1985, an honors student being interviewed for a university brochure was told she could not refer to Howard Zinn, a Silber critic, as one of the school's best professors. In 1986, the Silber administration threatened to evict a student from a dormitory because he put a sign with the word "Divest" in his window; a judge ruled in the student's favor, criticizing "B.U.'s desire to prevent the exercise of free speech rights."[25] In 1987, a *New York Times* report said that "in one recent case Mr. Silber called the candidate for tenure into his office and grilled him for several hours about his leftist political views. . . . He asked that his name not be used, because he said he felt 'scared and intimidated.' "[26]

Boston University faculty member Patricia Hills claims that people who dis-agree with the administration have had their salary increases lowered.[27] James Iffland, chairman of the Faculty Council, reports that faculty members are pressured to reject certain dissertation topics proposed by doctoral students.[28] A *Newsweek* article also notes Silber's repressive tendencies: "He broke B.U.'s faculty union and has targeted faculty he considers too left-wing."[29]

In a report to the board of trustees on 15 April 1993, Silber praises Boston University (and himself) for being "highly resistant to political correctness and to ideological fads." According to Silber, "We have resisted the fad toward critical legal studies. In the English Department and departments of literature, we have not allowed the structuralists or the deconstructionists to take over. We have resisted revisionist history." Silber also reports that the university resisted the "official dogmas of radical feminism," the "fad of Afrocentrism," and had "not fallen into the clutches of the multi-culturalists."[30] When Silber describes how Boston University has "resisted" all of these intellectual move-ments, he means that he and his handpicked administrators have stopped the appointments of these radicals.

Political scientist Frances Fox Piven left Boston University in 1982, saying to Silber in an open letter that her move was "because your administration has created a situation where good academic work is no longer possible." One anonymous faculty member reports, "As a tenured person and as one who believes in free speech and unpopular causes—I am quite literally afraid to go public in my opposition to this dangerous and vindictive man."[31] Silber's intolerance has been recognized by people who cannot be dismissed as radi-cals. Historian Richard Freeland notes, "One of the B.U.'s stars during the Silber years, literary critic Helen Vendler, ultimately became disillusioned with her president for forcing out a significant number of dedicated teachers who were contributing greatly to the quality of undergraduate education but lacked scholarly luster."[32] Vendler left in 1979, saying: "In this University, everyone's personal and professional lives are subject to harassment: we are spied on and photographed from behind parked cars. . . . Rational speech with him [Silber] is impossible; he does not listen, and he resorts to vilification without provocation."[33] Silber called her "Henry the Eighth with tits."[34]

Silber has been at the forefront of the attacks on PC. He tries to suppress leftist views at the same time that he says, "Today, there is virtually no inter-ference or restriction on the actions or opinions of professors by politicians, boards of trustees, or influential businessmen. Sadly, it is now more likely that groups of students led by faculty will attempt to suppress the academic free-dom of a professor or a visiting speaker whose views they oppose."[35] But one need only look at Silber's own administration to contradict this absurd statement. Silber is the model of an ideological and authoritarian leader, hounding out liberal faculty while hypocritically complaining about the tyranny of the liberal thought police.

Conservative Correctness in Law School

The emergence of Critical Legal Studies (cls), a group of leftist scholars who argue that the legal system of the United States is not a neutral, fair system, has caused outrage among conventional legal thinkers. Many conservatives have expressed a belief that cls scholars should be excluded from law schools because they challenge the foundations of the law. In 1981 Judge Richard Posner called the Critical Legal Studies movement "unassimilable and irritating foreign substances in the body of the law school."[36] In 1984 Paul Carrington condemned cls in the *Journal of Legal Education,* arguing that "the nihilist who must profess that legal principle does not matter has an ethical duty to depart the law school." If the cls "nihilist" would not leave, Carrington said, then the university has "a duty to constrain teaching that knowingly dispirits students."[37] The attack against cls scholars around the country grew so intense that Susan Praeger, president of the Association of American Law Schools and dean of the ucla Law School, worried that "faculty members at self-proclaimed prestigious schools and more modest ones alike express determination that no Critical Legal Studies adherent will find a place on their faculty."[38]

Harvard Law School has been a center for cls and for the backlash against it. In 1986, the *Wall Street Journal* editorialized, "Harvard Law will sink or swim with its ability to quiet the Crits."[39] Harvard law professor and former solicitor general Charles Fried claims that cls "tried to colonize the law school."[40] Julius Getman reports that "serious accusations were made in the late 1980s that professors were denied tenure and appointment because of their adherence to the philosophy of the critical legal studies movement."[41] Because tenure requires a two-thirds vote of the law school faculty, the conservative faction at Harvard had enough power to block cls-connected professors. Fearing that additional leftists on the faculty might soon overwhelm them, the conservatives began a campaign in 1986 to block radicals, beginning with Daniel Tarullo, a cls thinker and the first junior professor denied tenure in seventeen years.[42]

The most extreme example of the conservative backlash occurred in 1987 when Clare Dalton, another professor associated with cls, fell four votes short of the two-thirds majority needed for tenure. Although Dalton received the highest possible ratings from twelve out of fourteen outside reviewers, had published an article in the *Yale Law Journal,* and had a book ready to be published by Oxford University Press, the conservatives at Harvard engaged in a smear campaign against her (led by Robert Clark, who claimed she didn't "meet the standards that we ought to have") that included one professor's eighty-nine-page memo criticizing her scholarship.[43] The five male assistant professors up for tenure all received tenure offers. Robert Gordon, a Stanford law professor, called it "red-baiting" and "hysteria" about CLS, and more than two hundred law professors petitioned President Bok to reconsider the politically motivated rejection of Dalton; Bok refused. However, when another CLS adherent, David Trubek, was approved for tenure in 1987 by a 30-to-8 vote of the faculty, Clark and the conservatives went to Bok and convinced him to interfere in the process and deny tenure to Trubek—an unprecedented intrusion into the law school's hiring decisions.[44]

Soon, the ideological battle lines were such that virtually no tenure candidate was acceptable. President Bok's "solution" to this ideological division was to appoint the leader of the conservative bloc, Robert Clark, dean of the law school in 1989. Clark, a Republican and faculty adviser to the school's right-wing Federalist Society, had called CLS "deeply pernicious," accused the group of a "ritual slaying of the elders," and urged that they be "combatted in legal education."[45] In a *Wall Street Journal* article L. Gordon Crovitz says that Clark was appointed "to break the grip that the establishment of tenured radicals has on the school."[46] For the first time in its history, Harvard had selected the dean of its law school for the purpose of controlling its radical elements and preventing additional leftists from joining the faculty.

The ideological battles in the law school have not ended; leftist and conservative faculty simply reached a standoff. In 1991, the Left and the Right at Harvard Law School reached an agreement to appoint four white men with tenure.[47] But conservatives at Harvard still exert tremendous power. In 1993, Dean Clark and Alan Dershowitz successfully led the fight to keep Catharine MacKinnon off the faculty.[48] Clark himself reports that on fundraising trips, alumni ask him "what are you doing to get rid of the radicals on the faculty?"[49]

Dinesh D'Souza devotes three pages of *Illiberal Education* to discussing the plight of Ian Macneil, a Harvard law professor accused of sexism by some students for quoting Byron's *Don Juan* ("A little still she strove, and much repented, / And whispering, 'I will ne'er consent'—consented") to illustrate a point in contracts law. Although Macneil was never charged with anything, was never criticized or punished by the Harvard administration, and voluntarily left to take a job at Northwestern University, Macneil and D'Souza warn about those who would "destroy academic freedom." [50] But the successful effort at Harvard Law School to get rid of radical professors goes unmentioned in D'Souza's book. The conservative campaign to stop leftist appointments has been strongly supported at every turn by the Harvard administration, but none of the numerous books and articles about political correctness bother to discuss this disturbing example of ideological enforcement at America's leading university.

The Myth of Leftist Control of Higher Education

Although the radicalism of professors is often painted in alarming terms, a 1984 survey found that only 5.8 percent of faculty were self-described leftists, and only 33.8 percent called themselves liberals. Compared with 1969 numbers, the proportion of self-described liberals had dropped 6.8 percentage points. The greatest increases from 1969 to 1984 were among self-described moderate conservatives (29.6 percent) and strong conservatives (4.2 percent). Even those who called themselves leftist or liberal showed a considerable moderation of attitudes from 1969 to 1984; among leftists, the proportion who opposed relaxing standards in appointing minorities jumped from 39.4 percent in 1969 to 71.7 percent in 1984. [51]

The attacks on PC obscure these facts by focusing on elite universities and colleges (where the proportion of liberals is somewhat higher) and by examining selected departments (such as sociology, political science, English, and history) where liberals and leftists tend to be in the majority. Critics ignore the "political bias" of business professors, even though business schools have more majors than all the humanities combined. Fewer than 1 percent of business school faculty are self-described leftists, and fewer than 16 percent call themselves liberal. [52]

Russell Jacoby notes that "nothing is said of the conservatives who control most departments of economics or philosophy or political science or psychology." [53] Economics is one example of a field in which a conservative orthodoxy is seen as normal and is even celebrated. An article in the Heritage Foundation's *Policy Review* praises the fact that market capitalism "flourishes in economics departments," which have developed an "immunity" to "diseases" like "the creeping rot of multiculturalism, feminism, deconstructionism, and other fashionably radical intellectual trends." [54] Alice Amsden, professor of economics at the New School for Social Research, notes that the "economically correct" orthodoxy requires "believing in the superiority of the free market to achieve the highest efficiency, fastest growth and greatest welfare. It means championing market liberalization, deregulation, and privatization. Free trade is 'in.' Industrial policy is way 'out.' "[55]

One Marxist economist observes that many radical economists have left the academy: "You can't get tenure if you don't publish in the mainstream journals. If you have views that don't correspond to the mainstream point of view, you won't get published."[56] This view is shared by those on the right. Stephen Balch and Herbert London, the founders of the NAS, note with approval that "in the case of economics, for instance, the Left is relatively small and somewhat intellectually isolated."[57] "As long as dissent is labeled not economics and suppressed," Diane Strassmann writes, "critique of standard economic assumptions remains taboo."[58] Challenging the conservative status quo, not being politically incorrect, creates the greatest threat to a student's grade or a professor's career in many fields.

There are many examples of leftist professors being punished or censured by authorities, although this kind of political correctness is never questioned by the new defenders of free speech. Law professor Patricia Williams notes that when a student complained that Williams's class on property made her uncle seem like a slumlord, Williams received a memo from an associate dean telling her to stop "trumping moves" used to "silence the more moderate members of the student body."[59] While mere complaints from leftist students are the basis of anecdotes attacking political correctness, a reprimand from a dean is ignored (or even applauded) when it is directed against a leftist.

Conservatives complain that accusations of racism "intimidate" professors, but little is said about the far more repressive intimidation frequently directed at radicals. Asoke Basu, a professor of sociology at California State University, Hayward, received a letter from a person falsely claiming to be enrolled in his sociology class who wrote: "While you have not openly advocated Soviet Communism as a way of governance for America, your implication of this idea has caused students to question this notion." The letter writer continued, "Our group wishes to inform you that your lectures have been and are being taped. We hope there will be some improvement on the above items. If there is not, we are preparing our tapes and specific instances to support our observations."[60]

David Abraham was a young historian teaching at Princeton whose prospects for tenure looked promising. But then he was accused of fabricating parts of his first book because, as a beginning graduate student, Abraham did research in Germany and mistakenly used a paraphrase as a quotation, misattributed one document, and mistranslated another document. Historians Henry Turner of Yale and Gerald Feldman of Berkeley led a crusade against

Abraham, accusing him of intentionally fabricating documents to serve the Marxist conclusions of his book, which they sharply disagreed with. Feldman accused Abraham of "egregious errors, tendentious misconstruals, and outright inventions" and called the book "a veritable menace to other scholars."[61] Turner urged the University of Chicago to revoke Abraham's Ph.D., and Feldman asked Princeton University Press to withdraw the book as "fraudulent."

Feldman began phoning and writing historians across the country. Whenever Abraham was being considered for a job, Feldman made unsolicited calls to faculty and administrators attacking Abraham and threatening to take his case to that university's board of regents if Abraham was approved. At Catholic University, a dean rejected the history department's recommendation of Abraham after numerous calls from Feldman. Princeton history professor Lawrence Stone reported, "I've never seen a witch hunt like this in forty years in two countries." University of Chicago president Hanna Gray and Princeton history professor Stanley Katz protested Feldman's interference to the American Historical Association as a violation of professional norms, as did thirteen professors at the University of California, Santa Cruz, where Abraham was considered for a job. But for Abraham, it was too late. Feldman and Turner successfully ruined his reputation and intimidated everyone who considered hiring him. Prevented from getting a history job, Abraham instead went to law school and in 1991 became a law professor at the University of Miami.[62]

In some extreme cases, attacks on radicals include physical threats. At Syracuse University, English professor Mas'ud Zavarzadeh periodically receives threatening postcards, most recently on 13 October 1993. A 1992 postcard included a poem, "Roses are red / Violets are blue / Marxism-Leninism is dead," and concluded with a physical threat to Zavarzadeh if he did not leave town. Zavarzadeh discovered that "when a Marxist is harassed, no one is willing to raise a voice."[63] Jeff Grabmeier, after asking an Ohio State University professor about political correctness, noted: "Another faculty member said he wouldn't comment because he had received death threats after he supported politically correct ideas in a public forum."[64]

English professor Susan Gubar and her friends at Indiana University have witnessed or directly encountered a number of intolerant acts, including hate mail addressed to "Nigger-Lover," being called a "Kike-Dyke" on a home answering machine message, a note put on an office door threatening to disrupt a women's studies symposium on sexual violence, a student protesting a single lecture on women's issues as "too much about feminists" and ripping up his course pack in front of the class, and a graduate student receiving notes from a freshman threatening to stalk her.[65]

Art is a frequent target of the conservatives' attacks. In 1991, Southwestern Michigan College in Dowagiac cut theater instructor Patrick Spradlin to a part-time position (after which he quit). People for the American Way reported, "When he submitted a proposal for the 1990–91 [theater] season, his second year with the college, the administration informed him that the treatment of sex in [a] scheduled musical, *Baby,* was inappropriate for the audience, citing, among other things, the word 'spermatozoa' in a song lyric." [66] Ohio State University considered disciplining three art students who fooled the local media with a press release for a group called, "Arm the Homeless," which aimed to help the homeless "regain their Second Amendment birthrights." [67] At Idaho State University, an art gallery exhibit featured paintings of partially clothed women. Campus officials covered the gallery's windows with brown paper and excluded people under seventeen. [68] At Baylor University, the regents voted unanimously to prohibit nude models in art classes where physicians were to lecture to art students about anatomy and muscle structure. [69] At the University of Michigan, Flint, Vice Chancellor Dorothy Russell removed a Lawrence Ferlinghetti poem, "Repeat after Me," from the wall of an eatery in the University Center after parents complained that the parody of the Lord's Prayer attacked their religious beliefs; Russell overruled the governing board's decision not to remove it. [70]

At the University of Pittsburgh, art student David Brown was not allowed to show his surrealistic painting *There's No Place Like Hollidaysburg* because the vice chancellor of student affairs considered it "offensive" and "not in good taste." [71] At McKendree College in Lebanon, Illinois, the board of trustees supported President Gerrit TenBrink's ban on the play *Acts of Passion* because "profane and vulgar words will not be allowed in any cultural artistic production." [72]

The administration at San Francisco State University destroyed a controversial mural in 1994. The ten-foot-square mural depicted the face of Malcolm X along with dollar signs, Stars of David, skulls and crossbones, and the phrase "African blood." Jewish students complained that the mural was anti-Semitic because of the Stars of David. The artist, Senay Dennis, refused administration requests to alter it, claiming that the Stars of David represented Malcolm X's criticism of Israel, not anti-Semitism. President Robert Corrigan ordered the entire mural removed. When students twice scraped off paint used to cover the mural, Corrigan ordered it sandblasted off. The ACLU refused to defend the mural because the university had commissioned it. [73]

If free speech is to be defended and bigotry condemned—and both ought to be our goals—then there should be no more double standards, no more demands that every black intellectual and political leader stand up to condemn every racist who happens to have a black face, no more accusations of political correctness when white bigotry is challenged, and no more attacks on those who defend the free speech of black bigots. If academic freedom means anything, it means we have to defend the right to speak of those we hate and condemn.

The Ivory Closet: Heterosexual Correctness in Academia

While colleges and universities often espouse principles of freedom of expression and tolerance, they are frequently the source of intolerance and repression of gays and lesbians, the most common targets of conservative correctness. Openly gay teachers are often denied appointments and passed over for promotion. When Sue Brown invited three lesbians to speak at her "Psychology of Women" class at Aims Community College in Greeley, Colorado, and used a "non-academic text" (*Our Bodies, Our Selves*), she was fired for incompetence.[74] In 1981, an instructor at the University of Texas at Austin was "reassigned" away from teaching after students complained that she had invited a group of gays and lesbians to speak to her sociology class. A faculty grievance committee concluded that the reassignment was a "political attack on her teaching," but the president overruled their decision.[75] When a Berkeley academic sent out two groups of résumés to colleges in the 1980s, only the one that excluded his gay-related work brought invitations for interviews.[76]

Historian John D'Emilio notes, "Responses from the heads of 640 sociology departments early in the 1980s revealed that 63 percent held reservations about hiring a known homosexual and 84 percent about hiring a gay activist. Almost half reported barriers in promotion, and the figure jumped to two-thirds in the case of activists. Of the gay sociologists surveyed, half told of obstacles placed in the way of their doing research on homosexuality and of advice that it would hurt their careers."[77] A recent survey of gay and lesbian historians by the American Historical Association found that 70 percent had faced prejudice from students and colleagues, and 43 percent had experienced some form of discrimination.[78] Although fewer gays and lesbians are closeted than in the past and discrimination is less severe than it once was, coming out is still a risk to a teacher's career.

Students are also subject to persecution, both formal and informal, if they are openly gay on campus. Although some courts have upheld the right of gay and lesbian student groups to exist, the Supreme Court has supported sodomy laws, and Justice William Rehnquist praised bans on campus homosexual organizations in the 1970s, reasoning that gay student groups were "likely to incite a violation of a valid state criminal statute" and presented a "danger" that is "particularly acute" for a university full of students "still coping with the sexual problems which accompany late adolescence and early adulthood." Rehnquist compared homosexuality to a disease, asking "whether those suffering from measles have a constitutional right, in violation of quarantine regulations, to associate together and with others who do not presently have measles, in order to urge repeal of a state law providing that measle sufferers be quarantined."[79] Ironically, Rehnquist recently attacked political correctness and the "suppression" of dissent on college campuses in a 1993 commencement address at George Mason University, saying that "ideas with which we disagree—so long as they remain ideas and not conduct which interferes with the rights of others—should be confronted with argument and persuasion, not suppression."[80]

The fight for the right of gay and lesbian students to associate is not over. In 1993, the Gonzaga University Board of Trustees refused to recognize a gay and lesbian student group. In view of the university's Catholic affiliation, Gonzaga president Bernard Coughlin declared, "such a movement clearly is a betrayal of the university's tradition and mission."[81] At Saint John's University in 1993, the student government voted to end official recognition of a gay and lesbian student group, claiming that the group was incompatible with that Catholic school's moral teachings.[82] In 1995, the University of Notre Dame banned a gay and lesbian student group from meeting in the University Counseling Center because the group advertised its gatherings in the student newspaper.[83]

In 1993, the student senate at Ohio Northern University voted to deny recognition to the Gay, Lesbian and Bisexual Alliance. University officials said that they could do nothing to overturn the decision, which prevents the group from being covered by the university's liability insurance, receiving school funding, or being listed in the student handbook.[84] At North Idaho College, the student senate denied official recognition to the Lesbian, Gay and Bisexual Alliance in 1994 because the student body president claimed that "a club based solely on sexual orientation is not needed on this campus." The conservative newspaper *Campus* applauded the decision against "the arrogant organization," although the university twice overruled the senate.[85]

At Stephen F. Austin State University in Nacogdoches, Texas, the student government tried in 1994 to cut off funding for the Gay & Lesbian Student Association, arguing that its members were breaking the state's sodomy law. Although the university rejected the attempt, Jared Wylie, president of the student government, promised to continue antigay efforts: "Students want to see traditional values served at the university." Protests against support for gays and lesbians have often been successful. When the University of Texas at Austin planned to spend $882 on workshops for gay and lesbian students, campus conservatives threatened to disrupt the workshops and a state representative tried to cut the university's budget. When the Office of Gay, Lesbian, and Bisexual Student Support Services was created at Indiana University, in response to incidents of antigay harassment, a state representative proposed a $500,000 cut in the state appropriation to the university. In both cases, the university decided to use private funding instead of state money to fund gay and lesbian activities.[86]

At the University of Alabama in the 1991–92 school year, members of the university senate sponsored a resolution asking the state attorney general to rule on whether it was legal to fund the gay and lesbian alliance in view of the state law prohibiting sodomy.[87] A 1993 Alabama law prohibits the use of state funds to "sanction, recognize or support" any group that "promotes a lifestyle or actions prohibited by the sodomy and sexual misconduct laws" of Alabama. A representative of the ACLU said that "Alabama has tried to legislate away the free speech and association rights of lesbian and gay college students."[88]

Auburn University started forcing student groups in 1992 to sign a form pledging compliance with Alabama sodomy and sexual misconduct laws. Although university officials eventually stopped the practice, in 1993 a three-member committee set up by the board of trustees began investigating the conduct of student groups in an attempt to destroy the Auburn Gay and Lesbian Association.[89] One gay professor says that he "is not openly gay because Auburn is too hostile." As part of this antigay backlash, a group of gay students was shot at with a pellet gun in 1992.[90]

Gays and lesbians have always been victims of harassment and intimidation on the streets and in the quadrangles, but the late 1980s and early 1990s witnessed a surge of antigay violence on campus. At Columbia University, two leaders of the Gay and Lesbian Alliance received death threats in the mail; a .38 bullet was taped to one letter.[91] At Jamestown College in North Dakota, a student beat up a gay man because he looked at him and touched him on the shoulder.[92] At Mount Vernon College in Washington, D.C., a black lesbian student found notes on her door such as, "Die Dyke!" and "You Need Dick."[93] At Ohio State University in 1990, death threats and repeated harassment were aimed at two gay students on campus.[94] At Ohlone College in Fremont, California, flyers that announced a Gay Student Union were torn down and defaced with swastikas and slogans such as "Gays must die."[95]

At the University of Delaware in 1988, more than forty antihomosexual slogans were chalked on campus sidewalks, including "A Warrior Needs to Kill Homos Badly," "Gays = Aids," and "Fags are going to die from AIDS," by a group calling itself the Anti-Homosexual Federation.[96] The message "Another dead faggot" was left by the Homophobic Liberation Front next to a chalk body outline with raw meat splattering the head.[97]

A 1986 study of 166 gay and lesbian students at Yale University found that 98 percent had overheard antigay remarks, 65 percent had been verbally insulted, 25 percent had been threatened, and 19 percent had had objects thrown at them. Ninety-two percent of those surveyed anticipated being victimized in the future.[98] A shocking number of straight students favor outlawing homosexuality. A 1990 national survey of incoming freshmen found that 56 percent of men and 35 percent of women believe it is important to legally prohibit homosexual relationships.[99]

Even at a liberal college like Oberlin—where only 5 percent of the students oppose the presence of gays and lesbians—gays and lesbians are silenced. Contrary to the claim that a politically correct orthodoxy controls liberal campuses, 44 percent of gays, lesbians, and bisexuals at Oberlin reported feeling the need to censor themselves when addressing gay and lesbian issues, compared to only 20 percent of the heterosexuals. More than 80 percent of the students had heard derogatory comments about gays and lesbians on campus, and 75 percent had seen graffiti degrading them. One lesbian received threats through a closed door from men who said, "That dyke just needs a good fuck. Who's going to give it to her?"[100]

Discrimination is also directed against people with AIDS and those who seek to stop its spread. In 1994, Loyola Marymount University in Los Angeles forced a benefit dance for Caring for Babies with AIDS to be moved off campus because the organizers distributed condoms along with candy to advertise the event.[101] Campbell University, in Buies Creek, North Carolina, fired an instructor of weight training, aerobic dance, and sports management for having AIDS. The instructor, who was in good health, had worked for more than two years, with good job reviews, before he was found to have AIDS. Student body president David Lewis had "no doubt in my mind that our school must maintain its image of being a purely Christian university, and I think that the unfortunate stigma that is attached to the AIDS virus was a major player in the school's decision."[102]

At some religious institutions, simply talking about homosexuality with less than complete condemnation can be grounds for dismissal. At Bethel College in Minnesota, Kenneth Gowdy—a straight professor—was fired after twenty-one years of teaching because (outside of class) he suggested that homosexual sex should be allowed in lifelong relationships.[103] At Nyack College, in New

York, English professor June Hagen was fired in 1993 after a student complained that she was "tolerating" homosexuality because a button on her briefcase said "Support Gay Rights." A local pastor wrote to the college, "A professor who advocates 'gay/homosexual rights' has no place at Nyack College." Administrators reminded Hagen of the school's policy on sexuality, which says that the college promotes a biblical lifestyle that "precludes premarital and extramarital intercourse, homosexual practice, and other forms of sexual behavior incompatible with the conservative Christian life-style. Any student violating these principles will be subject to dismissal." Hagen declared that she was a "wholehearted supporter" of this statement and removed the button, explaining that it represented only her concern about violence against homosexuals, not acceptance of homosexual behavior.

Rexford Boda, the college's president, interrogated Hagen and was satisfied with her answers, although he also asked about her membership in the American Civil Liberties Union and said, "In terms of your future I am wondering if the campus can tolerate a liberal Democrat." Despite Boda's support, three months after she removed the controversial button from her briefcase Hagen was dismissed by the board of trustees without an explanation. And because President Boda had defended Hagen at a chapel service, he was also fired by the board of trustees.[104]

At Converse College in Spartanburg, South Carolina, a group of conservative alumnae and trustees forced out President Ellen Wood Hall in 1993 for being too liberal. The right-wing newspaper *Campus* reported, "Hall's radical feminist agenda has included a watering down of the curriculum, the formation of a lesbian support group, and inviting Molly Yard to campus."[105] Homophobia, such as fears about a "lesbian support group" (which in fact was an informal meeting of some students with a counselor to talk about lesbianism), was behind many of the attacks on Hall and her administrators. Hall's dean of students was forced out for being "intemperate" while arguing with an alumna who wanted to ban lesbians from the school.[106]

In 1991, Lee Griffith, the campus minister at Elmira College in New York, was fired after writing an open letter to President Thomas Meier expressing concern about "gay-bashing" incidents on campus and urging the administration to enforce a faculty statement of nondiscrimination based on sexual orientation. The administration responded by firing Griffith for promoting his own "social action program." The administration also retaliated against faculty members who criticized the college and led a vote of no-confidence against the president, calling these actions "grave misconduct" and "tantamount to sabotage."[107]

At the Montana College of Mineral Science and Technology in Butte, English professor Henry Gonshak proposed a summer course on gay and lesbian studies. A fundamentalist pastor in a local church wrote a letter to the local newspaper protesting the class title. Although the pastor admitted he was "unclear" about the content of the class, he warned about "radical gay agendas" and urged readers to contact the college to oppose having their tax money "tossed away." [108] Gonshak reports that "the alumni soon began besieging Tech administrators with letters and telephone calls. They threatened to withdraw thousands of dollars in contributions unless the class was dropped." Gonshak said that he would let students "express themselves and no one will be intimidated into not having their opinion," and he even invited the pastor to make his views known in the class. Under pressure, Gonshak reluctantly agreed to drop the class, but then changed his mind and fought for its reinstatement; however, the college's president refused to reauthorize it (fearing alumni reaction) until Gonshak agreed to "repackage" the class under the new title "Differing Views on Alternative Lifestyles." [109]

Conservatives frequently urge restrictions on academic freedom when gay and lesbian topics are involved. After Richard Rhoads discussed gay issues in an introductory sociology class, some students accused him of "indoctrinating students to be gay." And at Kent State University in Ohio, the College Republicans led efforts to prevent "Sociology of Gays and Lesbians" from being taught. Accuracy in Academia's report of the incident says, "The class drew the immediate ire of campus conservatives who feared that offering it is tantamount to University sanctioning of the gay lifestyle." [110]

Openness about homosexuality is still suspect. Christopher Phelps reports one example at the University of Oregon in 1990 on National Coming Out Day: "A law instructor, during a discussion of Supreme Court verdicts on gay rights, told his class he was gay and read a poem. Conservative students complained, and the law school administration reprimanded the instructor and demanded he apologize to his class. The instructor complied, apparently out of fear for his career." [111] A 1992 article on gays and lesbians on campus in the *Chronicle of Higher Education* concludes, "Some gay and lesbian academics interviewed said that they had decided to keep a lower profile after receiving hate mail and phone calls, and a few wondered whether their sexual preference had kept them from getting promotions and grants." A lesbian professor in the SUNY system is "planning to be more open when I get tenure, because it will be safer then." [112]

William Tierney found that a large number of gay professors fear having their sexual orientation revealed. One gay man noted the dangers of entering a gay bar near campus: "You don't know the consequences if someone sees you going in—a student, or your department chair, or someone on the promotion and tenure committee." An untenured humanities professor at a small liberal arts college in the Southwest said, "I teach in a conservative school, and if some people found that I was gay I could lose my job."[113] Sometimes the reaction to gays and lesbians is more than academic: When University of Colorado president Judith Albino announced the first gay and lesbian studies conference on the campus, she received death threats and had to wear a bullet-proof jacket to the opening.[114] But not one of the articles about "leftist intolerance" and PC on campus contain a word about homophobia and discrimination against gays and lesbians.

Unusual and Unexpected Censorship at the University of Iowa

A good example of how homosexual content in college classes is censored comes from Iowa. In October 1993, the Iowa Board of Regents imposed a policy on the University of Iowa requiring professors to warn students before presenting any materials, "graphic, still photo, motion film form, or otherwise," that included "explicit representations of human sexual acts that could reasonably be expected to be offensive to some students." These students, the board ruled, must be allowed to skip class without penalty and complete an alternative assignment, or drop the course without penalty.[115]

The policy was prompted by an optional film, *Taxi zum Klo,* shown as part of the German Film and Video Series for German conversation classes in 1991 at the University of Iowa. The flyer promoting the film included the disclaimer, "Don't come near this film if the world of homosexuality upsets you in any way." Although students in German conversation classes were told that attendance was optional, Iowa president Hunter Rawlings quickly condemned the showing of the movie: "I find it difficult to believe that it was appropriate to use this film in this course, and I have conveyed this concern to the College of Liberal Arts."[116] In response to the film, then board of regents president Marvin Pomerantz said, "We hope we don't see this kind of thing again, and we're going to make sure everyone involved hears that from the regents." Pomerantz did not believe the instructors would be fired, but only because "it would be difficult to make the dismissals stick."[117]

The University of Iowa tried to stop further showings of *Taxi zum Klo.* The codirector of the Bijou student film theater dropped plans to include the film in a gay and lesbian series the next semester out of fear for the group's survival. When two student groups, the International Socialist Organization and the Committee for Multiculturalism and Affirmative Action, announced a public screening of *Taxi zum Klo,* Dean Philip Jones prohibited the showing. The University of Iowa administration continued to refuse to allow permission for the movie to be shown until a few hours before its screening on 21 November 1991, when the Iowa attorney general informed university officials that they had no legal authority to prevent it.[118]

After the controversy over *Taxi zum Klo,* the board of regents ordered the development of policies regarding sexually explicit materials at Iowa public universities. While the faculty debated regulations, two additional incidents occurred at the University of Iowa.

In February 1993, teaching assistant Megan O'Connell was reprimanded and ordered to apologize to students for showing offensive material in a class and failing to inform students of their right to leave. An eight-minute video by Iowa City artist Franklin Evans that depicted two men engaged in oral sex was shown to her art colloquium of 150 students. The video consisted of a collage of images altered by various technical tricks, including three short segments totaling fifteen seconds that contained the offensive material.[119] A first-year student who objected to the video called her mother, who attacked the video as "pornographic" and declared, "For a man to be having oral sex with another man is objectionable." The student said, "To me, it wasn't art at all because this guy was trying to push his way of life on other people. I don't think that's right, showing a sexual act in class and condoning it."[120] Former board of regents president Marvin Pomerantz warned in a board meeting: "Somebody is going to get fired around this university if they don't follow the rules."[121]

In April 1993, a teaching assistant for an "American Cultures" class was reprimanded for showing *Paris Is Burning* to a class, even though the film, which is about transvestites, has no graphic sex scenes, and despite the fact that the teaching assistant had warned the class beforehand about its content. Nevertheless, three students complained to university officials about being shown a film on drag queens. Only when the teaching assistant fought back and protested the decision was a letter rescinding the reprimand put in his file. The original letter was not removed, however, and the retraction was issued only because the policies "were not readily available or widely known."[122]

While the board of regents worried about any mention of homosexuality on campus, they did not object to homophobia. Jeff Renander, editor of the University of Iowa's conservative *Campus Review,* brags that during a 1990 Gay Pride Rally, "my friends and I demonstrated against the abuse of gerbils by certain segments of the gay community. (We had a gerbil graveyard with 50 little white crosses, and our infamous gerbil quilt.)"[123] Again, in September 1993, when the AIDS Quilt was exhibited at the University of Iowa, the *Campus*

Review staff brought out the gerbil quilt. Accuracy in Academia reported the event with approval: "The 'Gerbil Quilt,' consisting of 25 patchwork squares each depicting a gerbil, was put on display in a glass case in the student union along with a copy of *The Myth of Heterosexual AIDS* by Michael Fumento and displays of statistics from the Centers for Disease Control which showed that AIDS ranks only twelfth among the leading causes of death in the United States. Gerbils were chosen for this quilt because of the role they play in certain homosexual practices."[124]

After the University of Iowa (unlike the other Iowa universities) failed to pass a sexually explicit materials policy that satisfied the board of regents, a policy was unilaterally imposed that required instructors to warn students of potentially offensive sexual materials and to consult with the offended students to offer alternative assignments or the option of dropping the course.[125] In 1994, the university's president imposed a "compromise" version of the rule requiring teachers "to give students adequate indication of any unusual or unexpected class presentations or materials."[126] While the new rule eliminates specific attacks on issues of sexuality, it broadens the policy to cover any material that any student might feel is "unusual or unexpected." There is little doubt that discussions of sexuality, especially homosexuality, have been stifled as a result.[127]

A professor in a French literature class had to warn students that one book on the syllabus praised women's bodies and sexuality. The instructor of "Greek and Latin for Vocabulary Building" spent ten minutes explaining that certain explanations of word roots might offend students, and apologized in advance. Rebecca Biron, a graduate student teaching "Latinos in the U.S.," gave students an assignment to research the effects of NAFTA on the Mexican-American community. A student objected that NAFTA was too political an issue for the class and therefore "unusual and unexpected."[128] Many teachers are likely to discard thought-provoking but potentially "offensive" materials rather than stigmatize their class by having to warn students about anything "unusual" and wondering what might happen if someone complains.

A growing conservative crusade against homosexuality is increasing its attacks on gays and lesbians in higher education. Accuracy in Academia's former executive director, Mark Draper, wrote an editorial entitled "Hooray for Homophobia!" in which he declares that "homosexuals have been able to silence any criticism of their sexual perversion" and invokes many key phrases of the antigay movement: "Gay activists want special rights for their bizarre sexual practices. They want to rub your nose in the filth and make you like it. They want to flaunt their disgusting sexual practices, purposefully offend you with their dirty, dangerous, and diseased 'lifestyle.' " Draper concludes, "Homophobia for you or homosexuality for your kids. You choose." Accompanying Draper's editorial was a list of the home addresses and phone numbers of the Lesbian, Gay, and Bisexual Student Caucus of the U.S. Student Association, and a recommendation that readers "drop 'em a line." [129]

Draper is accurate in pointing out that gays and lesbians have no protection under the law: "You do not have to take it. It is clear that it is entirely legal for you to discriminate against homosexuality. There is no federal law prohibiting you from discriminating against them. In fact, the majority of states have valid laws on the book that make homosexuality a crime. . . . In most parts of the country, therefore, governments, employers, and individuals are legally free to treat homosexuals differently." [130] Draper's comments show how deceitful the conservatives' campaign against "special rights" for gays has been, since homophobes like Draper readily admit that gay and lesbians still do not (and, according to them, should not) have equal rights. Draper's call for a campaign of homophobia and discrimination against gays and lesbians is one of the few honest explanations of the antigay movement's goals.

In *Illiberal Education,* Dinesh D'Souza (after condemning the recognition of a lesbian sorority at UCLA because it made heterosexuals "suspect") describes the official response of Yale University to a 1987 *Wall Street Journal* report that the university had a "gay" reputation: "Concerned that this flagrancy would upset alumni donors, President Benno Schmidt of Yale promptly sent a letter to two thousand volunteer fund-raisers, denying that Yale was a 'gay school' and concluding, 'If I thought there were any truth to the article, I would be concerned, too.' " Amazingly, D'Souza immediately follows this description with the statement, "As these examples suggest, an academic and cultural revolution is under way at American universities." [131] In fact, Schmidt's statement is typical of the official and unofficial discrimination against gays and lesbians that continues to run rampant on college campuses.

University officials who do speak out against homophobia are attacked by conservative groups and politicians. After the conservative magazine *Peninsula* published an issue condemning homosexuality in 1991, Harvard's Memorial Church chaplain Peter Gomes — who had led prayers at the inaugurations of Ronald Reagan and George Bush — announced he was gay; a group of students called Concerned Christians for Christ promptly demanded Gomes's resignation.[132] While complaints about political correctness regularly fill the pages of magazines and newspapers, the continuing repression of gays and lesbians on college campuses goes on virtually unnoticed.

Political Correctness: The Myth and the Reality

The title of this book may lead some people to think that because I call politi-cal correctness a myth, I must be denying the existence of leftists who censor conservative views. Not so. I fully acknowledge that political correctness does exist and should be condemned. There are leftists who are intolerant of other viewpoints. As Harvard law professor Randall Kennedy says, "Politically pro-gressive academics are by no means immune to failings and misdoings. Some of those who are part of 'politically correct' academic circles have taken ac-tions or displayed attitudes for which they should rightly be criticized." But, Kennedy adds, "the campaign against political correctness has blown its com-plaints out of all sensible proportion in a propaganda offensive that is, to a significant extent, part of an ongoing ideological war against the Left." [133]

Although most stories of political correctness are gross exaggerations of cases in which conservatives have been criticized, not censored, restrictions on conservatives, when they do occur, should be strongly condemned. How-ever, condemnation of such censorship should not lead us to accept the myth of political correctness and ignore the censorship directed against leftists and liberals on a regular basis.

In 1991, the University of Delaware refused to allow two researchers to ac-cept grants from the Pioneer Fund, whose charter, written in 1937, declares that consideration for grants "shall be especially given to children who are deemed to be descended predominantly from white persons who settled in the original 13 states prior to the adoption of the Constitution of the United States." In 1985, the reference to whites was deleted, but the Pioneer Fund remains devoted to supporting scientific research whose aim is to show the mental inferiority of blacks. [134]

When the Pioneer Fund offered $174,000 to education professors Linda Gottfredson and Jan Bilts for their research on racial differences in intelligence, the University of Delaware decided that faculty could not accept funding from organizations "incompatible with the University's mission." [135] By banning this funding, the university was clearly restricting scholars' ability to do research freely, intellectually dubious and offensive as that research may be. The idea that research funds are a privilege subject to university approval merely be-cause they are channeled through the university, is ridiculous. Universities should not restrict professors' sources of funding, so long as those sources do not impose impermissible guidelines or limits.

In the end, free speech was not endangered at the University of Delaware. When the two scholars threatened to sue, the university agreed to an out-of-court settlement that allowed them to receive grants from the Pioneer Fund, provided a year's paid leave of absence for both, and assured that a monitor would ensure fairness in one professor's promotion decision.[136]

The culture wars sometimes bring out the intolerant side of leftists. In September 1990, Stanley Fish — at that time the chair of Duke University's English department — denounced the NAS as "racist, sexist, and homophobic." Fish also wrote to the provost that "members of the National Association of Scholars should not be appointed to key university committees . . . dealing with academic priorities and evaluations," because "you wouldn't want on a personnel or curriculum committee somebody who had already decided, in terms of fixed political categories, what is or is not meritorious. You wouldn't want, say, somebody who believes that all work done in the past 15 years under new methodologies is to be held in deep suspicion." [137]

But Fish obviously has his own political categories and holds certain methodologies in "deep suspicion," so it is implausible for him to accuse conservatives of being "political." Though it could have posed a serious threat to academic freedom, Fish's misguided attempt to exclude his political opponents from key committees was never taken seriously, and there is no evidence that Fish's suggestion affected the department he used to chair. One of the traditionalists in Duke's English department, Victor Strandberg, has high praise for Fish, calling him "fair-minded and open-minded" and applauding his work as chair.[138]

Other examples of PC are more alarming. At Dallas Baptist University, a professor and a dean were fired in 1992 for indefensible reasons. David Ayers, an assistant professor of sociology, had criticized feminism, and another professor attacked his position at a faculty lunch. Ayers then distributed copies of both papers to students, calling his critic's paper the "razor-sharp sword of the assassin." Dean John Jeffrey refused to investigate Ayers on the grounds that his actions were protected by academic freedom and was fired, along with Ayers, for failing to follow orders.[139] While Ayers deserves criticism for advocating "the universality of patriarchy," certainly neither he nor Jeffrey should have been fired or punished in any way.[140]

It is important to recognize, however, that Ayers was fired from a small liberal Christian college, not a leading secular university. And while PC was part of the reason for the firings at Dallas Baptist University, the main cause was simply the administration's desire to control the faculty and get rid of embarrassing "troublemakers," combined with its failure to respect basic principles of academic freedom.

Unfortunately, some on the left do try to censor views they dislike instead of refuting them by argument. During the 1980s, conservative speakers were

occasionally shouted down by crowds, including Jeane Kirkpatrick at Berkeley, Casper Weinberger at Harvard, and William Rehnquist at the University of
Indiana.[141] At Harvard Law School, Contra leader Adolfo Calero was attacked
by a person shouting "Death to the Contras." When it was announced that
Calero would not speak, some members of the audience applauded and one
declared, "Calero has nothing to do with free speech and exchange of views."[142]

While the shouting down of speakers occurs less often now (although cries
of "political correctness" have grown more and more strident), not all leftists
are willing to listen to opposing voices. In one deplorable and highly publicized example, former Pennsylvania governor Robert Casey (who is opposed
to abortion) was prevented from speaking at Cooper Union in 1992 by dis-
ruptive protestors who chanted, "Racist, sexist, antigay, Governor Casey go
away."[143] But conservatives on campus can be equally intolerant of views they
dislike. James Brady, the Reagan administration press secretary disabled by an
assassin's bullet, was booed off the stage along with his wife, gun control activist Sarah Brady, when they appeared in 1992 at the University of Nevada at Las
Vegas. She was heckled and booed throughout her speech and finally had to
cut her lecture short.[144]

Linda Chavez, the director of the U.S. Commission on Civil Rights under
President Reagan, was invited to give the commencement address at the University of Northern Colorado in 1990, but the decision was protested by some
students. President Robert Dickeson retracted the invitation, noting that the
university had issued it "to be sensitive to cultural diversity" and now decided
that it was "both uninformed and gave the appearance of being grossly insensitive" because students who disagreed with her views on bilingual education
were opposed.[145] Chavez had a speech at Arizona State University canceled for
the same reason. The lecture series director wrote to Chavez: "I was impressed
by your résumé and career in Civil Rights, I was unaware however that your
stand on the issue of bilingualism and the state is so controversial an issue
among our minority students. The Minority Coalition has requested that we
cancel this engagement and bring other speakers whose views are more in line
with their politics."[146]

Intolerance is not a monopoly of the Left, however. In 1986, Harvard followed the demands of Assistant Secretary of State Elliott Abrams and disin-
vited Robert White, U.S. ambassador to El Salvador under Jimmy Carter, from
a foreign policy forum. Conservative professor Harvey Mansfield (who mod-
erated the forum) defended the exclusion of White on the grounds that he was
a "representative of the far left." The forum was to be a debate "between liberals and conservatives," and Mansfield did not want "the liberal point of view
to be drowned out by the far left."[147] In 1994, the trustees of Southwestern

Theological Seminary in Fort Worth rescinded an invitation to Rev. R. Keith Parks because he had left the Southern Baptist's Foreign Mission Board after clashing with conservatives.[148]

Daniel Maguire, a leader of Catholics for a Free Choice, found that invitations to speak at Catholic colleges were canceled because of his unorthodox views, even when abortion was not the subject of his speeches.[149] The president of Saint Martin's College in Lacey, Washington, wrote to Maguire: "The Board [of Trustees] determined that the Saint Martin's religious studies program should avoid the hiring of personnel who advocate teachings that may be contrary to the tenets of the Roman Catholic Church," which included hiring Maguire to deliver a speech. Maguire's lecture at the College of Saint Scholastica in Duluth, Minnesota, was canceled by the president because of Maguire's "association with Catholics for a Free Choice." Similar cancelations occurred at Villanova University and Boston College.[150]

Abortion rights supporter Bill Baird was scheduled to participate in a debate at Catholic University of America in Washington, D.C., with Sandra Faucher, director of the National Right to Life Political Action Committee. But the program board canceled the debate, claiming that Baird was "overemotional." The move was protested by the Catholic University Students for Choice, a group that is not officially recognized by the university because of its political views, and which is prohibited from holding functions on university property.[151]

While conservatives are sometimes protested as commencement speakers, the same intolerance also happens to controversial figures on the left. In 1994, University of Rhode Island president Robert Carothers rejected a committee's selection of Patricia Ireland, president of the National Organization for Women, as commencement speaker. Saying that Ireland was "too controversial," Carothers instead chose National League baseball president Leonard Coleman. When students and faculty protested, Coleman withdrew and Carothers finally agreed to invite Ireland.[152]

Conservative and mainstream political figures are almost always the ones chosen to give commencement speeches, a bias that is never criticized by those who complain about political correctness. In 1993, students at Harvard chose Marian Wright Edelman, president of the Children's Defense Fund, to deliver the commencement address, but a committee of faculty and administrators instead selected General Colin Powell to speak.[153]

It is time for both the Left and the Right to end the fear of controversy that silences intellectual debate. While the selection of campus speakers creates dilemmas, it is essential to allow the greatest possible debate of serious ideas. And it is on this point that extremists on both the Left and the Right have often fallen short.

The leftist PC I have described here, and other examples that could be cited, are serious violations of academic freedom. But the situation is nowhere near as grim as the attackers of PC claim in their alarmist tracts. There is no national conspiracy of leftists to suppress ideas they disagree with. No one can plausibly maintain that leftists exert powerful control over higher education. The problem, instead, is that universities have never attained their ideal of a marketplace of ideas. Administrators on college campuses are equal opportunity offenders when it comes to academic freedom. Intent on avoiding controversy, they are rarely staunch defenders of free speech for anyone, and pressure to get rid of troublesome faculty most often comes from conservatives, not liberals. Violations of due process rights and efforts at outright censorship are common on college campuses.

But the critics of political correctness show a curious blindness when it comes to examples of conservative correctness. Most often, the case is entirely ignored or censorship of the Left is justified as a positive virtue. Even centrist critics of PC ignore these facts; like Nat Hentoff, they blame conservatives only for censoring ideas in the public schools, never in colleges and universities. The idea that left-wingers control higher education and are never censored by anyone goes mysteriously unquestioned as the central dogma of the myth of political correctness. The censorship of leftists is said to have ended in the ancient times of McCarthyism, and everyone assumes that nothing similar could ever happen in today's "leftist-dominated" universities. Phrases like "McCarthyism of the Left" conceal the reality that an old-fashioned McCarthyism of the Right still prevails on many campuses.

By reporting only acts of censorship against themselves, conservatives were able to strengthen the myth of political correctness. The notorious examples of leftists being censored were conveniently ignored. A balanced perspective was lost, and everyone missed the fact that people on all sides were sometimes censored. Violations of academic freedom, due process, and fundamental fairness are common on college campuses among people of all ideologies. But the victims of conservative correctness do not have a network of well-funded foundations, newspapers, lawyers, and a sympathetic media to whom they can turn for help and publicity. Even when a case of censorship by conservatives reaches the pages of the *Chronicle of Higher Education* or the *New York Times,* it is quickly forgotten; meanwhile, conservatives churn out books that constantly resurrect these anecdotes of PC oppression, creating the false impression that there is a crusade against conservatives in academia.

The National Endowment for the Conservatives

The publicity given to incidents of political correctness has obscured the rising power of conservatives in the national government, where the doctrines of conservative correctness are enforced with virtually no criticism. The people who shout "political correctness" the loudest — such as Lynne Cheney and the *Wall Street Journal* editorial board — are also the leading enforcers of conservative correctness.

While the controversies in the National Endowment for the Arts sparked headlines during the Reagan and Bush administrations, a quiet ideological revolution was occurring at the National Endowment for the Humanities. Under the leadership of William Bennett in the early 1980s and then Lynne Cheney, the NEH became the model conservative agency in Washington, carefully avoiding controversy while systematically preventing leftists from receiving NEH grants.

The fight to control the NEH reached its zenith in July 1991, when by a vote of 9 to 8 the Senate Labor and Human Resources Committee killed the nomination of Carol Iannone to the NEH Advisory Council. It was an example of liberals winning a battle but losing the war, a culture war at the NEH in which the conservatives have been victorious for a decade.

For years, the Reagan administration stacked the nonpartisan NEH Advisory Council with conservative nominees, and these efforts intensified during the Bush administration. While previous candidates were always conservatives and moderates of high reputation and integrity, this changed with the appointment of Carol Iannone to the council. Iannone was a scholar of little note who had written short book reviews for *Commentary* magazine and had never published in a scholarly journal. Her work had been cited by other scholars only eight times, compared with hundreds of citations for other members of the council, who were serious scholars.[154] Iannone's main claim to fame was an article claiming that Alice Walker received the National Book Award for *The Color Purple* only because of her race and gender.

In Iannone, liberal groups finally saw the opportunity to strike back against conservative control of the NEH. They resented the domination of conservatives on the NEH Council, and they especially resented Iannone, who seemed to have been appointed solely because of her political views and her membership in Scholars for Reagan-Bush.[155] But when liberal groups attacked Iannone for her lack of qualifications, Senator Patrick Moynihan (D-New York) accused critics of "introducing political terminology where it has no role." Lynne Cheney called Iannone's rejection "character assassination," "liberal

McCarthyism," and "a case of political correctness." But Iannone's appointment itself was manifestly political, since no leftist with similarly weak credentials would ever have been considered for the job. Cheney accused Iannone's
critics of demanding that "the opinions of NEH council members ought to fall
within a certain range—one that would exclude Carol Iannone," even though
liberals had supported the nomination of eminent scholars with similarly conservative views. Michael Malbin and Harvey Mansfield, both noted conservative thinkers, were approved without any opposition at the same time that
Iannone was rejected, and the MLA praised conservative NEH council member
Robert Hollander.[156]

Iannone's rejection was depicted as a classic case of political correctness
and leftist totalitarianism. Nat Hentoff declared that "one of the most repellent
such attacks I've seen for a long time is being directed against Carol Iannone."
The *Wall Street Journal* accused liberals of creating "ideological and partisan
struggle" and heard "the building roar of an ideological mob." The extent to
which conspiracies were seen in the liberal opposition to Iannone was reflected
by the bizarre accusations of Senator Moynihan, who declared: "I very much
fear Professor Iannone's troubles arose not from the quality of her work, but
from her genes, social and otherwise. She is an Italian, Catholic ethnic with a
working class background."[157]

Although liberals were able to stop the appointment of Carol Iannone, they
failed to end the packing of the NEH Advisory Council with conservatives.
Even worse, the liberals lost the public relations war, for while their opposition to Iannone was perceived as political, they failed to bring out the issue
of conservative bias at the NEH. *Time* reported, "Score one for the politically
correct" and "Carol Iannone loses a round to political correctness."[158]

In 1992, President Bush announced eight nominees to the council, four of
whom belonged to the National Association of Scholars. One writer observed
that the NAS "has become a kind of breeding ground for the NEH council."[159]
As a result of these appointments, a third of the NEH council was made up
of NAS members (an organization with fewer than three thousand members),
a far cry from Congress's original mandate of "comprehensive representation
of the views of scholars."[160] Bush also appointed people with close ties to his
administration, including Joseph Hagan, the president of Assumption College
and an active Republican supporter and Bush campaign contributor.[161]

Members of the NEH Advisory Council have always been political appointees, but before the 1980s ideology was not the primary focus for appointments.
During the Reagan and Bush administrations, however, nominees were increasingly selected on the basis of their ideological views. Even more alarm-

ing, there was strong evidence that the NEH was no longer evenhanded in its evaluation of grant applications. With the help of a council stacked with conservatives, the NEH regularly rejected grants for projects it deemed too liberal.

After giving $100,000 to help plan *1492—A Clash of Visions,* a television miniseries about non-Western cultures in the fifteenth century, Cheney vetoed the recommendation of a panel of historians and denied the $500,000 needed to finish the project because of "a lack of even-handedness in the film's approach, with distressing aspects of Aztec culture being minimized, while the excesses of the Spanish are emphasized."[162] Cheney objected to the proposal because it suggested that "Columbus is guilty of—and this word is used in the proposal—genocide."[163] In Cheney's view, "Media projects must be balanced. Skepticism must be applied evenhandedly. . . . Because we are such a diverse culture, it is all the more important the projects exhibit a balanced approach to all groups."[164] Rather than funding a variety of projects reflecting different views, Cheney rejected controversial ideas and instead demanded a "balanced" perspective that conformed to her own views.

Carlos Fuentes's documentary about Spanish America, *The Buried Mirror,* was also rejected by Cheney because of its supposed "imbalances." Celeste Colgan, an NEH staffer, said that the Fuentes film was "dull" and "tedious," "a five-hour flogging" of U.S. policies in Latin America.[165] When *The Buried Mirror* appeared on the Discovery Channel, sponsored by the Smithsonian Institution rather than the NEH, it drew widespread praise. Robert Royal, a scholar who strongly defends Columbus against today's critics, praised the miniseries as "a basically evenhanded approach to the history of the Americas" and noted, "it provides a remarkably balanced account of how two civilizations coalesced into one new civilization across vast religious, cultural, and material divides." Royal applauded Fuentes because he "admires native cultures but does not indulge in non-historical idealizations" and points out the "positive developments" of contact, such as Christian influences replacing the harsh Aztec religion. By contrast, Royal criticized the NEH-sponsored series *In Search of Columbus* because "the encounter's potential for good and the roots of very definite evils are obscured by what can only be squeamishness about provoking controversy." In Royal's view, anyone who attacked Fuentes's documentary "must contemplate history through very thick ideological lenses indeed."[166] But leading NEH officials often wore ideological lenses, as did the members of Congress who make funding decisions. Senator Ted Stevens (R-Alaska) attacked the Smithsonian Institution for funding the project, calling Fuentes a "Marxist Mexican" and charging the series with accusing Columbus of genocide.[167]

The NEH's open opposition to any truly critical viewpoint was also expressed by Celeste Colgan, who declared: "Taxpayers do not want their dollars spent on projects that harangue them. Therefore the NEH must not support a film that seeks to persuade its viewers of particular political, philosophical, religious, or ideological points of view, or that advocates a particular program of social action or change." Yes, Colgan admitted, people can turn off their television sets, but "why should they have to pay for the thing that offends them?"[168] While Senator Jesse Helms (R-North Carolina) was fighting to force the NEA to stop funding projects he found offensive, the NEH under Cheney accepted this principle without an argument and actively used the grant process to eliminate funding for views the conservative leaders disliked.

One former NEH staffer claimed that the evaluation panels were filled from "lists that include some reputable scholars and some with a definite conservative tilt. Program officers are told to choose panelists from this list." As a result, "projects dealing with Latin America, the Caribbean, some women's studies, and anything appearing as vaguely left wing are seen as suspect. Controversy is a central issue: will this cause a headline and get us in hot water with our conservative constituency."[169] Cheney rejected proposals with an "undesirable, leftist scholar," and in one case she rejected a project because it "included a 'leftist' in its bibliography." By keeping these actions behind the scenes, Ellen Messer-Davidow notes, "the restriction of NEH funds from ideological (meaning feminist and Marxist) projects goes unremarked."[170]

One former staffer said that as many as 10 percent of applications were "flagged" for political content and that staff members were making "tactical instead of intellectual" decisions. Representative Chester Atkins (D-Massachusetts), noted that under Cheney there was "a slow process at the NEH of granting the far right ideological veto power." Atkins said this violated the NEH's "history of being isolated from political considerations and supporting scholarship, whether it is scholarship from the left, right or center."[171]

People whose views were criticized by conservatives became reluctant to apply to the NEH. A director of research at a university in Massachusetts recommended to the head of the women's studies department that other funding should be sought because a feminist research proposal would "never fly" at the NEH.[172] Indeed, only 2 percent of NEH project funding went to studies of women, gender, and feminism.[173] A former NEH staff member says that applicants were warned, "Don't talk about deconstruction or about feminism," and University of Louisville political science professor Mary Hawkesworth was told by a program officer not to include feminist phrases in her proposal to examine new questions raised by the study of women (one conserative panelist still opposed her project as "indoctrination into feminist dogma").[174]

The most persuasive evidence for right-wing control of the NEH comes from conservatives who celebrate this censorship as a model for the NEA. Former NEA chair John Frohnmayer writes that Cheney was "the darling of the conservatives in Congress and the White House. With her emphasis on 'balance,' which basically meant that she deep-sixed any grant she didn't like, she was the epitome of a 'responsible' administrator."[175] Harvey Mansfield, an NEH council member, declared, "Conservatives have to use politics to rid the campus of politics."[196] The *New Criterion* noted with approval that NEH critic Stanley Katz "was entirely correct" when he said Cheney had "packed her advisory council with critics of multiculturalism and women's studies."[177] George Roche praised Cheney's "concerted effort" to "battle the 'political correctness' and unabashed socialist propaganda found in a number of previous NEH-funded projects."[178] Irving Kristol wrote in the *Wall Street Journal:* "The NEH may get as many zany proposals as the NEA, but Lynne Cheney, its chairman, along with her staff and her Advisory Council, cull them more intelligently and more bravely."[179] The "culling" (elimination) of "zany" (leftist) proposals was a key activity of the Reagan-Bush NEH, which explains why ideological control of the council and review panels was essential for Cheney: By using people critical of leftist ideas to denigrate their quality, Cheney was able to avoid the unpleasant duty of overruling her advisers. The quietest and most effective form of censorship was performed at the lower levels of the bureaucracy.

In her resignation letter to her staff after the 1992 elections, Cheney all but admitted her efforts at ideological control as head of the NEH. She declared that the NEH's only role should be to emphasize "traditional scholarship, and traditional approaches to traditional scholarship."[180] In an interview with Catharine Stimpson, Cheney asked, "You don't think that there is a bias in favor of innovation and the cutting edge? I see it in panels here all the time, frankly."[181] Cheney obviously regarded her contempt for multiculturalism, feminism, and similar ideas as a counterbalance to the "cutting edge," and thought a bias in favor of traditional scholarship (rather than good scholarship, whether traditional or not) was necessary in NEH funding decisions.

Now that Cheney no longer exerts ideological control over the NEH, she is urging its elimination. After voluntary national standards for teaching U.S. history were published in 1994 (developed with an NEH grant given during Cheney's reign), she led the attack on them in the *Wall Street Journal,* accusing the standards of being "politically correct" and failing to have a "tone of affirmation" for American traditions. Cheney made no contention that anything in the national standards is inaccurate; her sole objection was ideological: "We are a better people than the National Standards indicate, and our children deserve to know it." [182] Some of Cheney's objections were ridiculous. She complained that George Washington "is never described as our first president," even though a guidebook for history teachers shouldn't treat them like idiots or waste space by listing the basic facts of American history. Other objections were simply inaccurate, such as her accusation that "not a single one of the 31 standards mentions the Constitution." [183]

The national standards included several elements that conservatives should have cheered, including a strong emphasis on religion and the use of stories to educate students. The standards urged discussion and debate of issues rather than memorization of facts. But for Cheney, neutrality and truth were not enough: the national standards, like the NEH, ought to indoctrinate students with a positive view of American society and its history. And when the NEH failed to champion Cheney's values and no longer reflected her ideology, she urged Congress to abolish the agency altogether. [184]

An NEH council member, Gertrude Himmelfarb, has also urged the elimination of the NEH — because it failed under Cheney's reign to remove all leftist views. The NEH, she says, "was swamped with applications for Marxist, neo-Marxist, feminist, deconstructionist, and other modish projects," so Cheney and her staff devised a program to teach high school teachers to "concentrate on the traditional works of philosophy, literature, and history." Yet this attempt to promote a conservative agenda was not successful enough for Himmelfarb ("the books were being Marxized, feminized, deconstructed, and politicized"), who concludes that the failure of the NEH to "counteract" the "dogmas of academia" is "a good argument against a publicly funded Endowment." [185]

During Cheney's reign, George Will praised her by comparing the leftists threatening academia to Saddam Hussein, and her role to that of the secretary of defense: "In this low-visibility, high-intensity war, Lynne Cheney is secretary of domestic defense. The foreign adversaries her husband, Dick, must keep at bay are less dangerous, in the long run, than the domestic forces with which she must deal." [186] Cheney seemed to confirm this view when she said, "I'm behind enemy lines most of the time." [187] While she was secretary of cultural defense, Cheney was careful not to give any comfort and support to the enemy, and she controlled the NEH like a weapon to serve her cause in these ideological battles. Yet little of this remarkable story reached the American people because the mainstream media had no interest in conservative correctness at the National Endowment for the Humanities.

For many people, the decline of Western civilization was symbolized at Stanford University in 1988 when, as Dinesh D'Souza describes it, "Jesse Jackson led a group of protesting students who chanted, 'Hey, hey, ho, ho, Western culture has got to go.'"[1] This ominous chanting would be repeatedly cited by Stanford's critics, including Education Secretary William Bennett and NAS founder Herbert London (who, apparently mistaking Jackson for one of Snow White's seven dwarves, accused him of chanting, "Heigh-ho, Western civ has got to go").[2] However, Jesse Jackson never chanted anything—and the students who did the chanting were attacking not Western culture but the Stanford class called "Western Culture," which they wanted replaced with a class that would permit non-Western texts to be presented alongside traditional Western texts. Like the myth of the chanting reverend, the attacks on Stanford's curriculum reform and on multiculturalism across the country are based on imagined conspiracies and inaccurate information.

On 31 March 1988, the Stanford Faculty Senate voted 39 to 4 to replace its required "Western Culture" class with a new course called "Cultures, Ideas, and Values" (CIV). The vote was the culmination of a long debate that had attracted the attention of Bennett and many other critics. Stanford, said Bennett, was "trashing Western culture" under intimidation from radicals.[3] Stanford, said Dinesh D'Souza and a chorus of conservatives, was discarding the Western tradition and replacing it with "little more than crude Western political slogans masquerading as the vanguard of Third World thought."[4] But none of these "facts" were true.

In the late 1960s, Stanford dropped its traditional "History of Western Civilization" requirement, which had existed since the 1930s. But in 1980 the faculty senate established a new requirement called "Western Culture," which consisted of six different tracks. The course's shared core list of books, which became fixed by bureaucratic inertia, excluded non-Western works (and even marginalized Western texts). A 1986 report from the Western Culture Sub-committee on Gender and Minorities criticized "Western Culture" because "significant numbers of students now complain about the narrow conception of the tracks in the regular course evaluations."[5]

Seventy Stanford faculty members, including eleven instructors in the "Western Culture" course, expressed their support for the CIV program in a petition which noted that the CIV proposal, "while requiring few changes in existing tracks, allows for courses that examine other cultures on a fully equal basis with that of Europe and courses that fully recognize the multicultural character of the United States. Until now such tracks have been excluded from the program."[6] Plainly, the purpose of the CIV proposal was not to destroy "Western Culture" but to expand its horizons.

Rather than criticize the CIV plan on its intellectual merits (as did its opponents among the Stanford faculty), Bennett, D'Souza, and other conservatives distorted what was happening at Stanford, maligning CIV supporters as ideologues and extremists who censored their opponents. On 19 January 1988, before debate had even begun at Stanford on the CIV proposal, Bennett proclaimed: "There is no intellectual or academic defense for such a thing. . . . [W]hat's going on is that a very vocal minority is attempting to overpower a less vocal majority." Bennett declared that if the proposal to "drop the West" passed, "it probably will be an example not of academic freedom but of academic intimidation."[7]

The sheer volume of misinformation about CIV made it impossible for an informed debate to occur on a national level. Allan Bloom declared, "Everyone knows that the white, Western male hegemony in the curriculum was overthrown there."[8] *Time* perpetuated the false claim that Western texts were being discarded: "This fall the original 15 books, all of them written by white, Western males, will be pared down. Out goes Homer, as well as Darwin and Dante."[9]

By any factual account, traditional classics clearly remain dominant in the CIV course. In 1990, all eight tracks included the Bible, Freud, Shakespeare, Aristotle, and Augustine; six read Plato, Machiavelli, and Aquinas; only two read Confucius and Fanon.[10] Isaac Barchas, a 1989 Stanford graduate who opposed the CIV proposal, admits that the changes are not dramatic because "the people teaching CIV are more or less the same ones who taught Western Culture"; and "exactly three new teachers have entered the program, teaching exactly one new track." According to Barchas, "One new track on the native peoples of the Americas appears to be the only one likely to be offered any time soon that even vaguely conforms to the radicals' conception of what a CIV course should be like." Barchas says that even the "Europe and the Americas track" is no worse than most regular courses, "and, at least by all accounts, is well taught." [11]

Judith Brown, a professor at Stanford who teaches the History 1 quarter of one CIV track, reports the reading required for her class:

> They are required to read substantial segments of Aristotle's *Politics*, portions of the Old and New Testaments, the *Aeneid*, parts of Josephus's *History of the Jewish Wars* as well as of Augustine's *Confessions* and *City of God;* parts of the *Koran*, the *Hadith*, and Thomas Aquinas's *Summa Theologica*, as well as Maimonides' *Guide for the Perplexed* and al-Ghazali's *Deliverance from Error;* they read most of Dante's *Inferno* and large segments of the *Lais* of Marie de France, Boccaccio's *Decameron*, and Chaucer's *Canterbury Tales;* they also read much of Christine de Pizan's *City of Ladies*, Castiglione's *The Courtier*, Bernal Diaz's *Account of the Conquest of Mexico*, and Aztec accounts of the same event; Machiavelli's *Prince* and More's *Utopia* are read in their entirety. Like most introductory history courses, we also use a textbook, Kagan, Ozment, and Turner's *The Western Heritage.* [12]

This is a far cry from D'Souza's claim that Stanford is teaching "little more than crude Western political slogans masquerading as the vanguard of Third World thought." [13]

The CIV program did not discard the Great Books of the West, lower the intellectual quality of the course, or eliminate its primarily Western focus. Traditionalists argued that the uniform core list had allowed students to share a common experience and talk with each other about the same books. But a survey of students taking "Western Culture" found that the core list had little to do with student discussion. When asked, "Did you talk with students in other tracks about ideas encountered in the courses?" only 7 percent strongly agreed; 47 percent had never or almost never talked with students outside their track about the ideas they encountered. Ironically, the "Alternative View" track of "Western Culture" (which conservatives condemned because it had only one or two of the core list books) had the highest rate of discussion across tracks. [14] As Stanford anthropology professor Renato Rosaldo points out, "People do not have to read exactly the same books to engage in a conversation: Indeed, the reverse could be true, as it was in my undergraduate experience." [15]

From the perspective of critics like Secretary Bennett, it was inexplicable that most of the Stanford faculty supported the changes. If the new CIV program was really trashing Western culture and politicizing education, why would thirty-nine out of forty-three faculty senators—at least some of whom could not be dismissed as left-wing radicals—support the new course? The critics claimed that moderate faculty had been forced to support the CIV proposal through physical intimdation by hundreds of radical students who surrounded the building where the senate met and threatened to attack its members if they failed to pass it. Conservatives present the Stanford debate as a key example of political correctness: cowardly faculty and administrators, intimidated by the demands of radical colleagues and violent students, acquiesced to a radical plan of multiculturalism designed to exterminate Western culture.

This revisionist history of what happened at Stanford was promulgated by Bennett in a speech only a few weeks after the CIV plan was approved. In the speech Bennett condemned Stanford in extreme terms, declaring that the decision "was not a product of enlightened debate, but rather an unfortunate capitulation to a campaign of pressure politics and intimidation. . . . [A] great university was brought low by the very forces which modern universities came into being to oppose—ignorance, irrationality, and intimidation." [16]

Bennett gave five examples to support his extraordinary charges. The first was his claim that "if you disagreed with the proposal being pushed, you would be called a racist." According to Bennett, "the loudest voices have won, not through force of argument but through bullying, threatening, and name-calling." [17] But all reports indicate there was no bullying or threats of any kind, and almost all of the name-calling came from conservatives like Bennett, who accused anyone who supported the CIV proposal of trying to destroy Western culture. The only intimidation witnessed by biology professor Craig Heller was "the intimidation coming from outside the university of people making false accusations." [18]

The second act of "intimidation" described by Bennett was the 15 January 1987 protest with "Jesse Jackson leading a group of students in the now famous cry: 'Hey, hey, ho, ho, Western culture's got to go.'" Unfortunately, Bennett had his facts wrong, as he grudgingly admitted: "I suppose the students were chanting, and perhaps the Rev. Jackson was not chanting." When Jackson spoke, he declared that "the issue is not that we don't want Western culture. We're from the West." The Black Student Union quoted Bennett's remarks about needing to study Western culture, but added: "We would like to remind Mr. Bennett that we, too, are a part of Western culture." [19]

The third incident Bennett mentioned was a subcommittee meeting where "students disrupted the proceedings, chanting, 'Down with racism, down with Western culture, up with diversity.'" But English professor William Chace, a moderate, observes: "The facts are the committee was not disrupted, nor was it intimidated." [20]

The fourth event was a student protest in the spring at which, according to Bennett, "some members of the so-called Rainbow Agenda student group occupied President Kennedy's office for five hours and released a set of 10 demands, one of which was the adoption of the task force proposal. So far as I know, no one was punished or even censured for this occupation." [21] But Donald Kennedy explains, "The sit-in last spring, which lasted four hours and did not outstay the time at which they could legally be present in the reception area, was about 10 issues, one of which was this one, and it was never discussed and was plainly low priority at the time." [22]

Finally, Bennett claimed there were "200 angry CIV supporters waiting outside the meeting room" (Bennett later inflated the figure to 300) when the new course was passed, who "said if the faculty was going the wrong way they were going to march in." [23] Yet everyone involved in the Stanford debate denies that any intimidation occurred, and the vote was taken after an unprecedented amount of discussion and meetings. Faculty senate chair Gerald Lieberman "did not sense any coercion or intimidation whatsoever." [24] Kenneth Arrow, although he strongly supported Bennett's criticism of CIV, calls his remarks on this point "misleading," adding: "The presence of a large number of students outside the Senate during the final day of debate was not even known to me nor, I believe, to other members. The need for coming to a final vote on that date was recognized by everyone, with no regard for pressures from outside; the matter had been fully debated and the consensus arrived at would not have been changed by further arguments." [25]

Traditionalists like Sidney Hook had to see the CIV proposal as a conspiracy to impose race, class, and gender on students; otherwise, their reactions would be far out of proportion to the changes: "If it were not for this reorientation towards race, sex, and class, the claim that the changes in the basic curriculum were 'sweeping' or 'monumental' would be transparently disingenuous." [26] Hook himself had no evidence that sweeping changes were occurring, but he speculated that the "Europe and the Americas" track "presages the changes that may be introduced" and that it depended "on whether the obvious political bias and indoctrination in the track on 'Europe and the Americas' is to be reflected in the other tracks." [27]

Daniel Gordon, a Harvard professor who taught in the CIV program at Stanford, rebuts the inaccurate descriptions of the class: Even the "Europe and the

Americas" track "tries to instill appreciation for the European classics," he says, and any student could still take one of the more traditional tracks, which dominate the program. Gordon's direct experience as a CIV instructor contradicts the critics' condemnations. Gordon reports, "I was not given a political agenda," and adds that in his class, "I often formulated arguments in favor of absolute monarchy, aristocracy, male-dominance, and slavery." Gordon also notes that "the students themselves do not feel that they are being pressured to adopt a 'correct' ideology." Instead, the students describe the course favorably in their evaluations, writing that "homogeneous thought is not what this class is all about. We were expected to challenge ourselves and others." [28] Gordon's report has been confirmed by students in the CIV course like Raoul Mowatt, who notes: "As surveys of numerous works, thoughts, and paradigms, CIV courses pose little threat of indoctrination." [29]

Gordon is no radical—he praises conservatives for having "effectively raised doubts about the value of affirmative action and speech codes"—but he criticizes the "very low level" of debate about the Stanford program, concluding "Stanford has done a reasonably good job of creating a distinctive program in which this Socratic enterprise is enhanced by the addition of minority authors to the syllabus." [30] Yet, to this day, the truth about the CIV class has never been a concern of the conservative critics and the media, who could easily have discovered that the "ideological indoctrination" they feared was nothing more than a myth of their own creation.

D'Souza's Distortions

The story of Stanford's CIV debate received the widest attention (and the most distorted explanation) in Dinesh D'Souza's *Illiberal Education*. D'Souza's description of the events at Stanford is now widely acknowledged by both his critics and his allies as false, but that does not reduce its impact on the readers who accepted his report as accurate. D'Souza claims that "the new CIV sequence would substitute a multiple-track system" for what existed, when in fact "Western Culture" already had at least six different tracks. "To get an idea of how Stanford manages the new mixture," he says, "consider the university's outline for the CIV track on 'Europe and the Americas.'" [31] D'Souza then proceeds to use this one track to represent the entire CIV course, even though only 50 of the 1,500 first-year students were enrolled in it. [32] Finally, D'Souza's attack on CIV is reduced to a single book when he claims that "the text which best reveals the premises underlying the new Stanford curriculum is *I, Rigoberta Menchú*." [33] Not only does D'Souza make one book in one track representative of the entire CIV curriculum, but that book is also grossly misrepresented. Even if all of D'Souza's attacks on Menchú's book were true—and practically none of them are—his assertions would be irrelevant because *I, Rigoberta Menchú* is only one book in one class in one quarter of the CIV sequence.

Inaccuracies about Menchú's book can be found in nearly every paragraph of D'Souza's description. He claims, "Rigoberta's political consciousness includes the adoption of such politically correct causes as feminism, homosexual rights, socialism, and Marxism. By the middle of the book she is discoursing on 'bourgeois youths' and 'Molotov cocktails,' not the usual terminology of Indian peasants."[34] D'Souza is simply deceiving his readers. Menchú does not mention homosexual rights, and the only "Marxist" jargon occurs in phrases like, "we behave just like bourgeois families in that, as soon as the baby is born, we're thinking of his education, of his well-being." Menchú even defends her Christian views to a Marxist friend: "The whole truth is not found in the Bible, but neither is the whole truth in Marxism." Menchú is anything but "politically correct." On the very first page of the book, she says: "Our customs say that a child begins life on the first day of his mother's pregnancy." She calls family planning "an insult to our culture and a way of swindling the people, to get money out of them" and says, "to us, using medicine to stop having children is like killing your own children."[35]

D'Souza tries to depict Menchú as a radical feminist, pointing out that "one chapter is titled, 'Rigoberta Renounces Marriage and Motherhood,' a norm that her tribe could not have adopted and survived."[36] Menchú actually says, "I am human and I am a woman so I can't say that I reject marriage altogether, but I think my primary duty is to my people and then to my personal happiness." Menchú also says she "didn't want to go through all the grief" of watching loved ones die.[37] Had D'Souza been truly concerned about the survival of Menchú's Quiché Indian tribe, he might have looked into the Guatemalan government's attack rather than scorning Menchú's personal decision not to marry—a decision based on her devotion to political activism, not a "feminist" hatred of marriage, and one that hardly threatens the future of her people.

Rather than discuss Menchú's ideas, D'Souza simply dismisses her as "a mouthpiece for a sophisticated neo-Marxist critique of Western society" and a "quadruple victim." D'Souza seems to think Menchú is not a real human being at all, but the creation of a Marxist conspiracy led by her French feminist translator and "a projection of Marxist and feminist views onto South American Indian culture."[38] But Menchú is far from being the radical feminist caricature described by D'Souza. She says, for example, "We've found that when we discuss women's problems, we need the men to be present, so that they can contribute by giving their opinions of what to do about the problem." [39]

D'Souza consistently casts doubt on the accuracy and sincerity of Menchú's story. D'Souza says that "her parents are killed for unspecified reasons in a bloody massacre, reportedly carried out by the Guatemalan army." [40] The reasons are, in fact, clearly specified: Menchú's father was thrown in jail for more than a year because he opposed the landowners who tried to take the tribe's land. He was kidnapped and tortured, spent eleven months in the hospital, and then was killed during an occupation of the Spanish embassy. Menchú's sixteen-year-old younger brother was kidnapped and tortured for sixteen days: "They cut off his fingernails, they cut off his fingers, they cut off his skin, they burned parts of his skin. Many of the wounds, the first ones, swelled and were infected. He stayed alive. They shaved his head, left just the skin, and also they cut the skin off his head and pulled it down on either side and cut off the fleshy part of his face." Her mother was kidnapped and raped, and then slowly tortured to death. [41] Menchú's family was trying to organize the peasants to resist the brutal tactics of the landowners, who "reportedly" use the Guatemalan army to intimidate the peasants.

By D'Souza's no-win logic, one could exclude any book resembling *I, Rigoberta Menchú* from a class: If a book criticizes the "West," then it is an "uncritical examination" of non-Western culture; if it criticizes a non-Western culture, then it represents the "domestic prejudice" of "Western intellectuals" and could not possibly be a legitimate representative of that culture. If Menchú is a feminist, then she is a Western intellectual betraying her own culture; if she is not a feminist, then she is uncritically accepting the biases of non-Western cultures.

The same double bind appears in D'Souza's treatment of "values." On the one hand, he criticizes Stanford's "Cultures, Ideas, and Values" because "values suggested a certain relativism, in which various systems of thought would be considered on a roughly equal plane." On the other hand, D'Souza attacks minority students because, "like Rigoberta Menchú, they tend to see their lives collectively as a historical melodrama involving the forces of good and evil, in which they are cast as secular saints and martyrs." [42] Once again, Menchú is left in the lurch: If she says all values are equal, she is an evil relativist, but if she says that some things are right and some are wrong, she is being "melodramatic."

Dinesh D'Souza's distortions have, after the fact, been acknowledged. C. Vann Woodward recanted his earlier views of *Illiberal Education*, declaring that D'Souza's "account of the nature of changes in the Stanford curriculum, however, turns out to be seriously inaccurate"; and "whatever the shortcomings of this book [*I, Rigoberta Menchú*] as literature, there proves to be nothing in it to justify D'Souza saying that she turned against European culture, renounced marriage and motherhood, and became a feminist and a Marxist." However, Woodward goes on to say, "The unasked question is how to justify the attention demanded for this interview taped in Paris in one week and adapted by the writer to read like an autobiography. Ms. Menchú was then twenty-three, an illiterate peasant woman from Guatemala. Her story is indeed a moving one of brutal oppression and horrors. But I am left with some unresolved doubts about the place given it in the new multicultural canon."[43]

Woodward does not tell us what these doubts are, and the impression he leaves of his biases is rather disturbing. Apparently, illiterate Third World peasants (even if they win the Nobel Peace Prize) cannot be the source of good literature, particularly when their stories are merely "moving" accounts of "oppression and horrors." But Stanford anthropologist Renato Rosaldo says that books like Menchú's have led to "the most exciting teaching I've done in 19 years."[44]

The mythmaking about Stanford is typical of the techniques used to invent a crisis of political correctness: the most extreme views were misreported and then presented as representing the mainstream, and the facts were invented or selectively distorted to create the false impression that radicals were trying to destroy Western civilization and suppress traditional views. Years after the changes were made, CIV is still routinely cited by conservatives as evidence of political correctness, despite the fact that every single charge that Western classics have been discarded and replaced by leftist indoctrination at Stanford is contradicted by the truth.

Banning "Difference" at the University of Texas

The fear of leftist "political indoctrination" was also used to prevent reform of the freshman writing class at the University of Texas at Austin. Before a single class of "Writing about Difference" was ever taught, the new course was condemned by columnist George Will as "political indoctrination supplanting education," attacked by English professor Alan Gribben as "the most massive attempt at thought-control ever attempted on the campus," dismissed by the *Houston Chronicle* as "a new fascism of the left" run by "latter-day versions of the Hitler Youth or Mao Tse-Tung's Red Guards," and finally scuttled by the University of Texas administration.[45]

This condemnation was sparked by a decision within the English department to revise English 306, a required freshman rhetoric class, to focus on "argumentation around the social inequities raised by discrimination suits" and center the class on Supreme Court decisions.[46] Linda Brodkey, the director of the writing program, found that E 306 was receiving unfavorable evaluations from students and complaints from literature graduate students, who taught the rhetoric classes but felt unprepared to design their own courses.[47] Brodkey observed that "many students introduce issues associated with 'difference' into their discussions and essays even though it has not been the official topic" and that "many instructors would like the topic institutionalized, thereby authorizing the discussion of the topic and specifying the rights and responsibilities of students and teachers."[48] Even Richard Bernstein, a sharp critic of the proposed changes, admits that "many agreed that at Texas E 306 was taught without any consistent standard."[49]

In 1990, a faculty committee created to reform and standardize E 306 proposed that it should have a common syllabus that would include a traditional writing handbook written by two department members (who later opposed the course), a packet of Supreme Court opinions, and a book edited by Paula Rothenberg titled *Racism and Sexism: An Integrated Study* (soon dropped from the syllabus), which includes writings on the economic and social context of racism. At an 8 May 1990 department meeting the English department accepted the proposal, despite the resistance of a few professors.

After English professor Alan Gribben sharply attacked the proposal in public, the Texas affiliate of the National Association of Scholars placed an advertisement in the campus newspaper signed by fifty-six professors (out of a faculty of 2,200), expressing their fear that "the new curriculum for Freshman English distorts the fundamental purpose of a composition class—to enhance a student's ability to write—by subordinating instruction in writing to the discussion of social issues and, potentially, to the advancement of specific political positions." Ironically, the faculty were not concerned that standards were being lowered, but that standards might be set too high for instructors who "may have little or no training to prepare them to teach the complex legal, sociological, psychological, and historical issues of racism and sexism at a college level."[50]

Charges of indoctrination against the as yet untaught class became routine and the media onslaught increased. A philosophy professor declared that the course should be retitled Marxism 306, and syndicated columnist William Murchison wrote a series of columns in the *Dallas Morning News* attacking the course.[51] Pressure also came from the deans of engineering and biological science, who threatened to withdraw their students if the course was taught.[52]

In response to the negative publicity, in July 1990 Dean Standish Meacham of the College of Liberal Arts announced that the new course would be postponed—a euphemistic term for its permanent abolition. In doing this, the administration violated the freedom of the department to determine what should be taught in its classes, a curricular decision usually made without interference. Shortly before the decision was made, President William Cunningham had written a letter falsely stating that "after careful consideration the department has decided that the course will not be modified this fall." Cunningham refused to meet with the committee that had designed the course, refused to allow a field test of it, and proudly declared to the media, "I have not seen a syllabus."[53]

As University of Texas law professor Julius Getman observes, "Instead of protecting faculty decision making, it seems clear that the administration played a key role in overriding it." Getman, although critical of the course's proponents, notes that they "followed appropriate academic procedures at every step of the way," adding, "Nothing in the way English 306 was developed or structured suggests that Brodkey was intent on indoctrination. . . . Her primary purpose was to develop a sophisticated, intellectually respectable, and challenging course."[54]

The course had strong support from the professors and graduate students who would have taught it. In September 1990, the English department voted by secret ballot 46 to 11 in favor of the policy, and the graduate students (whose right to teach was supposedly infringed by the new plans) gave it a 52-to-2 vote of support.[55] The idea was exciting enough to inspire 10 percent of the English faculty to volunteer to teach a course that is normally taught only by graduate students.[56] The plans for E 306 certainly did not infringe on the academic freedom of teachers. All faculty were free to teach as they wished, and instructors (usually graduate students) could do the same after teaching the course once. Ironically, the much-heralded academic freedom of graduate students to design their own courses—a primary reason for objection to the revised syllabus—was revoked less than a year after the E 306 controversy when two courses with the word *lesbian* in the title were listed in the course catalog.[57]

What happened at Texas was grossly misreported. Richard Bernstein of the *New York Times*, for example, inaccurately claimed that "literary classics" were removed to include new materials, and that the new class was being taught.[58] Repeating Bernstein's error, Martin Anderson declares in his 1992 book *Impostors in the Temple*, "Beginning students at the University of Texas no longer will read the classics in their introductory writing class," apparently unaware that the proposed changes had been vetoed two years earlier.[59] Another *New York Times* article, this one by Anthony DePalma, describes the "attempt at the University of Texas to replace the standard readings for freshman English composition classes with a book of readings condemning the racism of white males"; *Newsweek* likewise reported that the Rothenberg book was the main text of the class, even though it had been dropped six months earlier.[60]

Lynne Cheney also repeats the errors while claiming to be "telling the truth" in her 1992 NEH report. Like many other critics, Cheney claims that all the classes would have used the Rothenberg book. In fact, as Brodkey and graduate student Shelli Fowler note, Rothenberg's book was dropped in June 1990 "when we realized we weren't going to use enough of it to justify asking students to buy it."[61] Conservatives repeatedly attacked Rothenberg's book long after it had been dropped from the class, falsely claiming that it formed the foundation of the E 306 course.

Alan Gribben, Conservative Victim

The attack on political correctness at the University of Texas at Austin also includes the inevitable tale of the victimized white male conservative. George Will, Richard Bernstein, and Lynne Cheney all tell the story of Alan Gribben, an English professor who publicly attacked the redesigned English 306. Cheney describes the case as follows: "It involves a professor who objected to turning the freshman composition class into a class on racism and sexism, and he has been hounded out of the university; he is now leaving."[62]

Gribben's troubles began with a seemingly insignificant incident in 1987, when the English department proposed to start a graduate program with a specialization in ethnic studies and Third World literature. Gribben supported the proposal with regard to the Ph.D. program but was the lone dissenter to its use in the M.A. program, believing that Master's students should focus on more "traditional" courses. After this event, Peter Collier notes, "a chill had entered his colleagues' attitude toward him. The hallway companionship he had come to depend on after 12 years at UT disappeared. Dinner invitations with other faculty couples ceased." Collier describes "the hits" as "subtle but palpable nonetheless," citing as an example a case where a colleague asked Gribben to move out of the way of the mailroom door "and then said, 'I said, please move!' when he didn't shuffle fast enough." These complaints seem trivial, even silly, but to someone like Gribben, who believes that "one of the reasons you get into this profession is for the collegiality," his colleagues' failure to be friendly became a form of repression.[63] "I was ostracized in such a systematic and cruel manner that I was eventually compelled to leave a tenured full professorship," [64] Gribben says.

But Gribben certainly did not endear himself to his colleagues when he wrote that the English department was dominated by a "highly politicized faction of radical literary theorists" and added, "our problems are so profound and likely to be longlasting that the English department should be placed in receivership indefinitely" to reorganize its intellectual priorities in a more conservative direction.[65] Gribben also urged the state legislature and board of regents "to consider abolishing required English courses." [66] Gribben accused his colleagues of the worst kind of unprofessional conduct and urged that the department's academic freedom be stripped away to ensure more conservative appointees. But Gribben's academic freedom was never violated. Gribben left voluntarily; no one demanded that he should be fired or that his teaching or research should be restricted in any way. If treating a colleague rudely is a violation of academic freedom, then thousands of professors (and Gribben himself) are guilty of it.

Yet Gribben presents himself as an innocent victim of totalitarian leftists, declaring about the writing class, "I just wanted to question a few features and my world fell apart." [67] But Gribben did not just question a few features; he condemned the entire idea of "Writing about Difference" as indoctrination and claimed that students would "inevitably be graded on politically correct thinking in these classes." [68] Nor did Gribben's world fall apart; having alienated most of his colleagues, he freely chose to leave for another job. But Gribben's story of victimization convinced many.

After his attacks on the course, Cheney says, Gribben was "vilified in campus speeches and receiv[ed] hate mail and anonymous late-night phone calls." [69] George Will notes, "He was shunned by colleagues, avoided by graduate students, effectively expelled from the life of the department, denounced as a racist at a campus rally. He received hate mail and anonymous calls." [70] The *National Review* says that "a distinguished English professor at the University of Texas was harassed into resigning because he voted against a freshman requirement of race and gender 'sensitivity' training." [71]

While anyone who writes threatening notes or makes threatening phone calls deserves to be punished, there is no evidence that Gribben's colleagues were responsible for anything like this, or for the "Salem witch hunt or a Stalinist-style purge" he claims oppressed him.[72] Moreover, the treatment of Gribben was certainly no worse than what happened to Linda Brodkey, who was condemned by conservatives as a Marxist propagandist seeking to indoctrinate her students. Brodkey also received hate mail and obscene phone calls from men who threatened, "I'm going to shoot your cunt off" and "I'm going to cut off your nipples, you dyke."[73] Abandoned by the administration and vilified in the media, Brodkey also left Texas to take another position.

Perhaps most alarming is Cheney's solution for dealing with the English 306 "problem." She criticizes the AAUP and the MLA for expressing concern that the English department lost its academic freedom in having its decisions overruled as a result of outside political pressure. Cheney tells us that academic freedom did not apply in this case because academic freedom only protects "disinterested inquiry" and "expertise." When the disinterested pursuit of knowledge is "hindered from within," as it was at UT-Austin, Cheney says, "academic freedom may well require those outside the department—and outside the university—to speak in its defense."[74] Cheney believes that liberals and leftists, because they are "politicized," must be controlled by the administration and outsiders in order to protect "objectivity." In Cheney's Orwellian version of academic freedom, we must restrict the freedom of radical professors in order to preserve the "disinterested" pursuit of truth. It is a curious kind of academic freedom that protects professors only when they agree with higher authorities (like Cheney) about the truth.

The true violation of academic freedom at UT-Austin came from the conservative forces inside and outside the university who sought to impose their ideological agenda on an English department that did not conform to their ideas. A few years earlier, the dean of liberal arts rejected the recommendation of the English department hiring committee and refused to hire two supposedly left-leaning American literature candidates on explicitly ideological grounds, according to conservative writer Peter Collier, because "they would further the growing political imbalance in the department."[75] Then the administration, with no concern for the quality of education, simply ordered the English department not to teach the revised E 306 class. In the few weeks left before the fall semester started, each teacher had to quickly develop a course syllabus—with the only requirement being that it could not follow the controversial E 306 proposal. When Dean Meacham failed to be aggressive enough at suppressing progressives, he was fired and replaced with a conservative more friendly to the administration's efforts to punish the English department.[76]

The story of what happened to English 306 at UT-Austin is a typical example of how the PC backlash works. A disgruntled professor criticizes curricular reforms. The attacks are picked up in the national media, first by conservative columnists and then by mainstream journalists. The facts are usually simplified or distorted to fit the event into the larger PC conspiracy. Then the story reaches the level of a myth and is repeatedly invoked by writers as evidence of political correctness. Cheney calls what happened at Austin "an almost classic example of what is happening on many campuses today" and contends that no one can deny the reality of political correctness: "There are too many examples of p.c. at work, powerful examples like that of Alan Gribben." [77]

The true story about E 306 shows not only that reports of politicization have been greatly exaggerated, but also that many of the facts are simply ignored or misreported in order to promote the backlash against political correctness. The UT-Austin example reveals how universities enforce conservative doctrines and censor liberal and leftist ideas under the guise of protecting professors and students from PC intimidation.

The Culture Wars

The opponents of multiculturalism depict these debates as nothing less than a war over the future of American culture. In 1992, Republican presidential hopeful Pat Buchanan, dubbed "the candidate of political incorrectness" by the *New York Times,* proclaimed that "our Judeo-Christian values are going to be preserved and our Western heritage is going to be handed down to future generations and not dumped into some landfill called multiculturalism." [78] At the 1992 Republican Convention, Buchanan declared, "There is a religious war going on in this country," and concluded, "we must take back our cities and take back our culture, and take back our country." [79] "While we were off aiding the contras," Buchanan said, "a Fifth Column in our own country was capturing the culture." [80]

Buchanan's call for a culture war is echoed by many conservative educators who have invoked the same militaristic rhetoric against multiculturalism. Hillsdale president George Roche claims that "PC professors have launched open war on religious values and the spiritual roots of Western civilization." [81] Midge Decter observes that "a culture war, as the liberals understood far better than did their conservative opponents, is a war to the death." [82]

In an article published in *Commentary,* Dinesh D'Souza says, "Although the fight against political correctness has so far gone well in the open air of public opinion, the fight on the ground has barely begun." [83] If America could vanquish the forces of Saddam Hussein in Kuwait, the PC critics seemed to be saying, surely they could force the "invading" feminists and multiculturalists out of our colleges and universities. Allan Bloom, in a 1991 speech to the U.S. Air Force Academy titled "Liberal Education and Its Enemies," began by praising the Gulf War and the cold war and declared that "the barbarians are not at the gate; they, without our knowing it, have taken over the citadel." Bloom warned of a conspiracy of "class, race and gender dominating the humanities," adding that "its adherents gradually take control of all tenured posts in the university humanities."[84]

Accuracy in Academia's former director Mark Draper also describes a "war against American culture" and claims that "we are losing this war for the soul of America."[85] Eugene Genovese, fearing the "repudiation of our Judeo-Christian heritage, the defilement of our national soul," declares, "We are today indeed engaged in a cultural war."[86] George Will warns of "a war of aggression against the Western political traditions and the ideas that animate it."[87]

Multiculturalism has many meanings, but none of them fits these conspiracy theories about a foreign enemy occupying American universities. *Multiculturalism* refers to the study of cultures outside the West—the "non-Western culture" part of the curriculum. It also refers to the study of the numerous minority cultures within Western culture and America that are not normally acknowledged by the dominant culture. But contrary to the allegations of conservatives like D'Souza, *multiculturalism* has never meant "the uncritical depreciation of Western classics as racist, sexist and homophobic, combined with ethnic cheerleading and primitive chic when the subject is minority or Third World cultures."[88] For example, writer Alice Walker, one of D'Souza's curricular villains in *Illiberal Education,* has led an international movement against the "unimaginable physical pain and psychological suffering" of female genital mutilation in African, Asian, and Middle Eastern countries. Walker's novel on clitorectomy, *Possessing the Secret of Joy,* along with her book and movie on the same subject, *Warrior Marks,* embody anything but "primitive chic."[89]

The only "ethnic cheerleading" to be found in the culture wars is in the writings of traditionalists who praise the West as eternally the best and condemn anyone who urges critical approaches to traditional books. The only ones advocating "uncritical depreciation" of certain texts are uninformed conservatives who regard any books other than the traditional classics as inferior, usually without even bothering to read them. This cult of Western culture sees any expansion of the curriculum as a betrayal of their values.

No one believes that the great books should be dismissed wholesale. Practically every advocate of multiculturalism has urged that the traditional canon continue to be taught. English professor Susan Fraiman says, "The goal, as I say, is not to stop reading the works of such canonical figures but to read them again."[90] English professor Stephen Greenblatt notes, "Like most teachers, I am deeply committed to passing on the precious heritage of our language, and I take seriously the risk of collective amnesia."[91] Conservative critics are quick to generalize about "multiculturalists" but rarely mention what any of them actually say. It is simply not true that multiculturalists want to destroy the traditional Western books or indoctrinate students. The editors of *Multicultural Teaching in the University* believe that "no one . . . devalues Western civilization or seeks its elimination from the curriculum."[92]

Critics commonly portray multiculturalists as being "obsessed" with issues of race, gender, and class to the exclusion of all other issues. A *New Republic* editorial, for example, claims that the goal of multiculturalism is "a unanimity of thought on campus" and that its advocates believe "accounting for sexual, racial, and political bias in texts" is "the only worthwhile intellectual exercise." The editors write that "racial dogmatists" proclaim a philosophy that "whispers in our ears that the barriers of race are unbridgeable."[93] But multiculturalists do not say that racial barriers are unbridgeable; they only state the obvious fact that these barriers have not yet been bridged.

Roger Kimball argues that "race, gender, and class" are "increasingly held to furnish the only appropriate criteria for determining the content of the curriculum and focus of pedagogical interest."[94] The *Wall Street Journal* declares that many in the humanities "think America can be explained only in terms of race, gender, class and, increasingly, 'sexual orientation.'"[95] But it is false to say that students learn about nothing but race, gender, class, and sexual orientation. No one declares that examining gender, race, and politics is the only worthwhile intellectual exercise, though, unlike the *New Republic*, "radicals" suggest that these topics should not be categorically dismissed. And even when teachers pay attention to race, gender, and class, they are not examining narrow issues, but instead are leading students into an exploration of fundamental questions about the human condition. No one should dismiss the works of Toni Morrison or Frederick Douglass as being only about race, because they explore universally human ideas as a part of understanding racism and oppression.

The critics of multiculturalism also accuse it of taking identity politics to new extremes. Berkeley philosopher John Searle claims that "most visibly in the humanities, it is now widely accepted that the race, gender, class, and ethnicity of the student defines his or her identity."[96] And William Bennett thinks "the new, divisive, ethnicity-is-identity multicultural curriculum is poison for these children."[97]

But these descriptions of multiculturalism are false. Barbara Ehrenreich explains: "When I say multiculturalism, I do not mean African American students studying only African American subjects; I mean African Americans studying Shakespeare (perhaps taught by African American professors). I mean Caucasian students studying African American history, Asian American history, and so on. That is my idea of a genuine multicultural education."[98] Multiculturalists do not claim that race, class, and gender determine everything, but they accurately observe that these categories have been neglected by traditional analysis. Certainly, race, gender, and class are not the sole determinants of a person's beliefs. But it would be wrong to claim that race, gender, and class have absolutely no influence, or to ignore the fact that members of oppressed groups (and their views) have historically been omitted from academia. The truth about how race, gender, and class affect us should be argued in a climate of free discussion, but the presumption that such questions are illegitimate and politically biased does not permit debate. Dinesh D'Souza, for example, complains that students are permitted to write papers about "latent bigotry in Jane Austen, or tabulate black underrepresentation in the university administration." He apparently believes that any analysis of "race or gender victimization" should be absolutely forbidden by all teachers.[99] The critics of multiculturalism, not its advocates, are the ones who urge a narrow and one-dimensional way of looking at literature and the world.

The Myth of a Curricular Takeover

Reports of the death of Western culture on American campuses are greatly exaggerated. Much of the alarm over multiculturalism has been sparked by an exaggeration of the extent of its growth. Roger Geiger claims, for example, "that by 1991, approximately half of all colleges and universities had established some requirement for students to take courses that treated material from the perspective of race, gender, or (often) social class. Nearly two-thirds had imposed multicultural additions to disciplinary courses."[100] *New York Times* reporter Richard Bernstein writes, "One report, issued by the American Association of Higher Education, found that as of July 1991 just under half (48 percent to be exact) of four-year colleges had a 'multicultural general education requirement.' . . . Now in what some critics have sardonically called a return to compulsory chapel, half the colleges in the country are saying, in effect, that a certain political attitude is also mandatory, since, as we have seen, multiculturalism is not so much a knowledge and appreciation of other cultures as it is an attitude toward the politics of race and gender."[101] This is an amazing leap in logic: taking the fact that about half of all colleges have multicultural requirements (mostly old-fashioned "non-Western culture" requirements supported even by conservatives like Lynne Cheney in her NEH "50 Hours" report) and concluding that every single one imposes a political agenda on students. Since Bernstein knows that *multiculturalism* is just a "code word" for leftist totalitarianism, he doesn't need facts or evidence to support his wild assertions.

But multicultural courses are not dominant. A 1991 survey by Alexander Astin found that while a third of college faculty thought that many courses included a minority perspective, only 11 percent actually used readings related to race or gender in their own teaching.[102] It is true that modest reforms have been made in recent years. By 1990, 46 percent of colleges required a class in international cultures, and 20 percent in racial or ethnic issues. But contrary to the claim that multiculturalism has caused the elimination of Western civilization classes (as Gertrude Himmelfarb asserts in writing that "most universities have abandoned the Western-civilization requirement"), the proportion of colleges requiring courses in the history of Western civilization actually rose from 43.1 percent in 1970 to 48.5 percent in 1985 and 53 percent in 1990.[103]

While curricular change is always occurring as a result of scholarly advances and increasing interest in the study of multiculturalism, it is not a change that eliminates traditional knowledge. Hunter College in New York City recently adopted a four-course "pluralism" requirement that makes students take courses focusing on non-Western cultures, American minority groups, gender or sexual orientation, and the intellectual traditions of Europe.[104] When SUNY-Buffalo created new requirements for arts and sciences majors, it required two semesters of Western civilization followed by a course on pluralism in American culture—yet a conservative newspaper warned that "it will almost certainly become a hostile environment for students who harbor more traditional values" and "risks replacing a liberal education with an illiberal one."[105] At York College, NAS president Barry Gross supported a new multiculturalism requirement—which included courses on multiculturalism in the United States, different regions of the world, and Western civilization—because it made the curriculum "more rigorous."[106] After the University of Massachusetts, Boston, put a new diversity requirement into effect in 1992, business teacher Peter Ittig attacked the requirement as "part of the political correctness party line." Two years later, Ittig conceded that the PC issue "doesn't seem to come up."[107] At most universities, the multicultural requirements condemned in the abstract by conservative critics are quite unobjectionable in practice.

When Berkeley decided to adopt a new American cultures requirement in 1989 by a 227-to-194 vote of the academic senate, many conservatives feared that it would be used to impose leftist views on students. "I fear that in practice, the course will lead to an unjust and unwarranted demonization of Western culture," said one Berkeley professor during the debate; John Searle, one of

Berkeley's most highly regarded professors, dismissed the proposed requirement as "political feelgood courses." [108] Columnist John Leo worried that "now
all Berkeley students are being required to take a course that looks more like
an expression of racial division than a cure for it." [109] Stephan Thernstrom
claimed, "If you don't have 'p.c.' . . . views, for example, you would be out of
your mind to teach one of the University of California's new required courses
in American cultures—which are designed to approach American history as a
study in racial oppression. Let slip a favorable reference to Moynihan or Glazer
or Sowell or Richard Rodriguez, I would bet, and your employment record
will have INSENSITIVE stamped in red all over it." [110]

But there is no evidence that Berkeley's requirement promotes political indoctrination or racial division. Nonradicals support the requirement, including the chair of the academic senate (a professor of business administration),
the former chancellor (a law professor), and the current chancellor of Berkeley,
a professor of mechanical engineering. Nor is there any sign that the hundred or so courses that can fulfill the requirement are politically biased. The
late Aaron Wildavsky, a member of the NAS Board of Advisers, developed and
taught a course called "Political Cultures" to fulfill the requirement. [111]

The attacks on multiculturalism at Berkeley echoed across the country. A
Houston Chronicle article noted, "Afraid of being labeled politically correct,
Texas universities are shying away from making students take courses in multiculturalism." [112] At Texas A&M University, the governing council of the College
of Liberal Arts voted to require liberal arts majors to take a class focusing
on ethnic, racial, and gender issues in the United States as well as a course
on foreign cultures. Students could satisfy the requirement from a long list of
courses, and there was no evidence of political bias. The proposed requirement
was condemned by the student newspaper, the State Republican Executive
Committee, the *Houston Chronicle,* and the *Houston Post,* which accused it
of being a "politicization of education" [113]—all of this before a single student
entered a classroom. The conservatives in this case and others are not object-
ing to leftist indoctrination, as this controversy shows; what they are opposing
is any proposal that says race, gender, and ethnicity deserve to be studied
and debated. And their attacks on multiculturalism often succeed. As one reporter observes: "Texas A&M faculty passed a plan, only to have hostile alumni
reaction cause the president to withdraw it." [114]

When the University of Wisconsin required students to take one class with
"an ethnic dimension"—which could be fulfilled by any of about a hundred
courses—the conservative newspaper *Heterodoxy* complained, "Courses like
Buddhist Theology and Hindu Mysticism which had a dozen or so students . . .

now have over ten times that many."[115] If the conservatives' real fear is that more students might study Buddhist theology and Hindu mysticism, it shows how dishonest and inaccurate most of the attacks on multiculturalism have been. Instead of examining what is taught in multicultural classes, conservative critics have relied on fear-mongering to successfully attack an intellectual revolution they refuse to study in depth or refute.

The critics of multiculturalism ignore how inadequate the study of non-Western cultures or minority cultures within the West has been. During his years as an undergraduate (1970–74) and as a graduate student (1974–78), William Cain "took twenty-five courses in English and American literature without ever reading a poem, play, story, novel, or critical essay by an African-American writer."[116] Michael Bérubé notes that only a decade ago, "throughout my undergraduate years, I never once heard Zora Neale Hurston's name — or Mary Wollstonecraft's, or Aphra Behn's. Even as an English major specializing in American literature, I was assigned one book by a black writer — American literature's number one crossover hit, *Invisible Man*." In graduate school, says Bérubé, "I was assigned a book by a writer of African descent only in my 14th of 14 graduate courses at Virginia, when the English department managed to hire someone who could teach courses in which 'American' was not automatically synonymous with 'white.'"[117] Rosa Ehrenreich, a 1991 Harvard graduate, observes: "I got through thirty-two courses at Harvard, majoring in the history and literature of England and America, without ever being required to read a work by a black woman writer, and of my thirty-two professors only two were women. I never even saw a black or Hispanic professor."[118]

Imaginary Revolutions

A casual observer of the conservatives' attacks on diversity might conclude that the universities are swarming with leftists who ruthlessly inculcate students with deconstructionist philosophy, pop culture, feminist theory, and Marxist proclamations masquerading as multiculturalism. Les Csorba of Accuracy in Academia claims that "Caldicott, Sagan, Dewey, Keynes, Galbraith are frequently required authors on reading lists while Shakespeare, Aristotle, Adam Smith, Max Weber, James Madison, Cicero and the Bible receive modern day intellectual punishment."[119] Herbert London asserts: "The names Foucault, Derrida, Barthes, and Lacan are better known to most undergraduates today than Augustine, Aquinas, Aristotle, and Milton. For many undergraduates the curriculum is barren of Shakespeare, Dante, and Plato and filled with fashionable thinkers." [120] The obvious falsity of these claims is clear to anyone who has looked in a college bookstore, but the myths circulating about multiculturalism make these absurd statements believable to many.

Perhaps the most famous inaccuracy was written by Christopher Clausen, chair of Penn State's English department, when he said, "I would bet that *The Color Purple* is taught in more English courses today than all of Shakespeare's plays combined." [121] Clausen's statement is cited by NAS member Thomas Short, who agrees that "it is possible that Walker's black lesbian saga is now assigned more often in college courses than all of Shakespeare's plays combined." [122]

My own survey of reading lists for English classes at the University of Illinois (Urbana-Champaign) in 1991 found that Shakespeare was the most popular author by a wide margin. In addition to five sections of "Introduction to Shakespeare," five sections of an advanced Shakespeare class, an honors seminar, and a graduate seminar, eight non-Shakespeare classes also included Shakespeare in their list of readings. Only one class read *The Color Purple*. Using a conservative estimate of eight plays assigned in each Shakespeare class, nearly one hundred Shakespeare plays were read for every copy of Alice Walker's book. [123]

As for Herbert London's assertion that Foucault, Derrida, Barthes, and Lacan are taking over English departments, those names do not appear at all on the University of Illinois reading list, and only one advanced class covers literary theory. The University of Illinois may not be the most radical institution in America, but if its English department is at all representative of others around the country, then the threat of political correctness to the curriculum is vastly overstated.

Most scholarship is equally traditional. Michael Bérubé did a study of the MLA Online Bibliography from 1981 through 1990, examining the works cited by scholars. By far the most popular author studied was Shakespeare, with 5,761 items. A distant second was Joyce, at 1,900; the remaining top ten was uniformly composed of Dead White Males: Chaucer, Milton, Faulkner, Dickens, T. S. Eliot, Melville, Lawrence, and Pound. [124] Since what is taught to students is more traditional than this "cutting-edge" scholarship, the conservatives' fear of multiculturalism replacing the classics of Western culture is obviously exaggerated. In one study of English professors, traditionalists selected fifteen books exclusively by white males for an introductory class, while revisionists advocated a syllabus that included seven of the same books (including *Macbeth*, the *Canterbury Tales,* and the *Iliad*) but also added less traditional works. [125] The Western classics continue to dominate what high school students read — and Shakespeare continues to be at the top of the reading lists. After comparing English courses in 1989 with those in 1963 and 1907, one researcher concluded that "the lists of most frequently required books and authors are dominated by white males, with little change in overall balance from similar lists 25 or 80 years ago." [126]

The literary canon is always changing, but it is obvious that the vast majority of classes still teach the same canonical texts, with most of the changes happening on the margins, and usually to the improvement of education. But ridiculous assertions like Clausen's have been widely quoted in the *Wall Street Journal,* the *New Criterion,* and by Dinesh D'Souza in *Illiberal Education*—who claims Clausen "reflected the emerging consensus." [127] D'Souza is right: Clausen does reflect the emerging consensus among the media and conservative intellectuals about the evils of multiculturalism. But it is a consensus based on a lie, repeated by critics whose ideological lenses have blinded them to the truth.

The MLA's "Deceptive" Survey

Despite the conservatives' laments about the multicultural revolution, surveys reveal that traditional works are still widely read in literature classes. A 1991 Modern Language Association study of nineteenth-century American literature classes found that "the great majority of respondents subscribe to traditional educational goals for their courses." [128] In response to a question asking teachers to name "up to three works among those that they consistently teach that they consider particularly important," the most frequently named authors (75 percent of all responses) were Hawthorne, Thoreau, Melville, Emerson, and Whitman, indicating a remarkable degree of consensus that traditional authors are dominant in American literature classes.

The MLA survey also found that most teachers had highly traditional goals. A large majority of respondents wanted to help students "learn the intellectual, historical, and biographical backgrounds needed to understand the literature of the period" (92.8 percent) and "derive pleasure from the wisdom and artistry displayed in literary works" (88.6 percent). While 61.7 percent of the teachers wanted students to "understand the influence of race, class, and gender on literature and interpretation," 51 percent believed it was important for students to "understand the enduring ideas and values of Western civilization," and a large group believed in both goals, indicating that there is no necessary conflict between multiculturalism and study of the classics of the West.[129]

Yet conservative critics of multiculturalism like Will Morrisey, Norman Fruman, and Thomas Short (writing in the NAS journal *Academic Questions*) claim that the MLA survey "proves that the classics have been displaced." They accuse any teacher who named a female or black writer (only 18.2 percent of teachers did) of having views "dictated, apparently, by the famous 'race, class, gender' imperative." Morrisey, Fruman, and Short also accuse the MLA survey of using a "biased design" to downplay multicultural reforms by surveying older full professors with more conservative views.[130] Actually, the MLA study overrepresented the number of younger assistant professors who had received their Ph.D.s since 1980. In view of the fact that larger numbers of these more "radical" teachers were surveyed, the real state of American literature is even more conservative than the unalarming findings of the MLA indicate.

Other conservatives have used the MLA survey to attack English professors. Celeste Colgan, formerly a top NEH staffer, complains that 62 percent of teachers include feminist approaches and 28 percent include Marxist approaches in their classes: "Students exposed to single, polemic approaches to literature are deprived of their freedom to learn."[131] Strangely, the fact that most professors make students aware of many different ways to examine literature (4.67 approaches on average) is taken as a sign of repression, while a refusal to discuss feminist or Marxist ideas presumably would be hailed by conservatives as evidence of openmindedness.

Colgan believes that universities should be subject to the same controls imposed at the NEH: "Why should parents have to pay for soapbox oratory? Fraudulent scholarship. Why should our fine research institutions harbor the bogus scholarship that sometimes goes by the name of feminist theory?"[132] Colgan and other conservatives do not want to debate feminist theory and similar approaches; they want to abolish them.

The Myth of the Decline of Western Culture

Despite fears that the Great Books are threatened, I have found no example of a traditional classic being banned from a college classroom because of its alleged racism or sexism. There is no crusade to declare the classics "politically incorrect" and then banish them. But there is a new critical way of looking at these traditional texts. One no longer assumes that they are the source of all that is noble and good; instead one closely examines the values that shaped both the author and the characters. The conservatives' crusade to banish these new analytical approaches is promoted by a deceptive campaign to save "endangered" classics.

A report in the conservative journal *Policy Review* admits: "There's a dirty little secret in the multicultural halls of American universities: dead white males are alive and well." [133] *Heterodoxy* editors David Horowitz and Peter Collier acknowledge that the classics have not been thrown out of the curriculum, but they claim that the real issue is "how they were taught." [134]

The attacks on political correctness have been successful only when traditionalists raise the issue beyond academic disputes about interpretation and falsely claim — as at Stanford — that radicals are dumping the classics. A complaint that "they're not reading Shakespeare the right way" has much less political power than the false assertion that "they're getting rid of Shakespeare and reading Alice Walker instead." Rather than address the issue of how to interpret the classics, traditionalists attack a phantom danger by claiming that traditional works are being discarded. As far as the average American could learn by reading newspapers and magazines, colleges and universities no longer teach the great works of the West. Contrary to the fears of traditionalists, it is the traditional curricular view — not the multicultural one — that prevails at nearly every college in the country. It is unquestionably true that the vast majority of students study an enormous amount of Western culture from elementary to graduate school, with much less time devoted to non-Western and minority cultures.

Multiculturalism has not politicized literature; literary study has always been a product of ideological choices about what methods to use and what books to read. Multiculturalism only expanded the range of ideas and challenged the choices made in the past. Multiculturalism has not destroyed the humanities; it has revitalized them, bringing new questions and new approaches to traditional books, as well as discovering works often overlooked in the past.

What we must seek is a balanced curriculum that includes the insights of both traditionalists and multiculturalists. Multiculturalism redefines the curriculum to reflect cultures outside America as well as the many unique and worthwhile cultures within Western culture that have been largely ignored. By rejecting the idea of culture as dead transmission of the past and proposing instead a culture that is inclusive and evolving, the multiculturalists have something valuable to offer. Race, gender, and class — even if not as all-encompassing as some might claim — are important issues that have been dismissed by traditional scholarship and teaching. If Western culture is truly pluralistic, then there should be little objection to increasing that pluralism.

It is also important to integrate the Western and non-Western, the ancient and modern, and the excluded and included. As Harvard English professor Helen Vendler notes, "It's not just Western culture that's missing, it's any culture." [135] In an age when most students in college are given an almost exclusively technical or preprofessional education, the interests of multiculturalists and traditionalists may be much more similar than they believe. We face the threat of universities devoted to empty specialization and vocational training, with no culture at all. To avoid this, we must declare, as Harvard president Charles Eliot did more than a century ago, "We would have them all, and at their best." [136] We must examine both Western culture and the cultures that have been excluded from the academy if we are to teach students the value of true diversity. We need a dialogue between Western culture and the multiculturalist critique, an ongoing argument in which the best of the past and the best of the present, the best of our traditions and the best of the attacks on them, can make students a part of the conversation debating these ideas.

W hen a Brown University junior named Douglas Hann got drunk one night and yelled abusive remarks while walking around campus, he had no idea that he would become a central figure in the national debate over speech codes. As Hann passed by a dormitory, yelling "fucking niggers" and other racial epithets at no one in particular, a student in the dorm yelled back at him. Hann turned toward the dorm and shouted, "What are you, a faggot?" and "Fucking Jew." Hann went on to tell a black woman, "My parents own your people," and had to be restrained from starting a fight.[1] A university disciplinary committee investigated the incident, and Hann was expelled for violating Brown's policy prohibiting the "subjection of another person, group or class of persons, to inappropriate, abusive, threatening, or demeaning actions, based on race, religion, gender, handicap, ethnicity, national origin or sexual orientation."

Brown's expulsion of Hann brought criticism from many conservatives and liberals who felt that free speech was being suppressed. Benno Schmidt, then president of Yale, declared: "Universities cannot censor or suppress speech, no matter how obnoxious in content, without violating their justification for existence. . . . It is to elevate fear over the capacity for a liberated and humane mind."[2] William Henry in *Time* bemoaned the fact that Brown "redefined the racist, wee-hours tirade of a drunken student as unacceptable behavior rather than as protected free speech."[3]

Yet many conservatives, like *U.S. News & World Report* columnist John Leo, admitted that Hann's drunken racist tirade was indeed unacceptable behavior: "The case could have been made that as a repeat offender on probation, the student had failed to observe minimum community standards of decency at a private university."[4] Leo seems not to object at all to the punishment, only to Brown's use of the words "harmful action" rather than "decency" to justify the decision. Ironically, in earlier years Hann probably would have been expelled without any attention at all from the media. It was the crusade against speech codes that elevated the punishment of drunken bigotry to the level of a free-speech controversy.

Speech codes have been the central villains in the great PC melodrama staged by conservatives. Judging from the attacks on speech codes, one would imagine that students live in terror of the thought police, carefully looking over their shoulders whenever they dare to tell a joke or express a conservative opinion. Charles Sykes and Brad Miner report in the *National Review College Guide* that " 'anti-harassment' codes have been established that prohibit any speech (and this includes jokes) deemed sexist, racist, or homophobic." [5] Yet fears like this had nothing to do with what was actually happening on college campuses, where no students were being expelled for telling jokes or punished for liking Rush Limbaugh.

Critics of speech codes declared that a massive wave of censorship codes had been imposed on college campuses in the past decade, threatening the free speech of anyone who dared to challenge liberal orthodoxies. Jonathan Rauch warned in *Kindly Inquisitors* that "the last few years have witnessed a rash of attempts on university campuses to restrict offensive speech, both by punishing offenders after the fact and by establishing preemptive restrictions." [6] The *Wall Street Journal* echoed many when it declared that "the proliferation of speech codes at America's institutions of higher learning stands as one of the saddest chapters in this country's intellectual history." [7]

But there was no "crisis" of censorship on American campuses. There was no proliferation of speech codes restricting student and faculty opinions. There was no conspiracy to deprive conservatives of free speech and prevent open discussion of controversial issues. Yet the attack on speech codes was so successful that a *Chronicle of Higher Education* article observed, "The phrase 'speech code' is now a dirty word on college campuses." [8]

Speech codes are nothing new. Students have been disciplined for their speech since colleges were first founded, and legitimate limits are frequently placed on words. Individuals can be sued for libel and slander. They can be prosecuted for fraud, harassing phone calls, and threats, all of which are crimes of words, not actions. Individuals are also liable for sexual harassment, even when it consists only of words. The Supreme Court has accepted limits on free speech in cases of immediate harm, captive audiences, criminal threat, obscenity, immediate riot, and time, place, and manner restrictions. [9]

How did critics manage to convince everyone that free speech was an endangered species on college campuses? First, they pretended that colleges and universities had been citadels of free expression in the past, ignoring the fact that every college has always had disciplinary procedures to punish abusive speech.

Second, critics used purely hypothetical fears to create the impression that the thought police lurked behind every Ivy-covered wall. Because Emory University bans "discriminatory harassment," which is "conduct (oral, written, graphic, or physical) directed against any person or group . . . that has the purpose or reasonably foreseeable effect of creating an offensive, demeaning, intimidating or hostile environment," the Wall Street Journal warned, "A professor at Emory better think twice about critiquing affirmative action or risk being brought up on 'anti-diversity' charges. Race, gender, and homosexuality are made taboo subjects—unless you hold the approved point of view."[10] But contrary to what the Wall Street Journal says, no student or professor has ever been charged with hate speech—let alone punished—for opposing affirmative action.

Third, critics exaggerated the pervasiveness of speech codes by claiming that they dominated college campuses. A 1991 ACLU news release declared that "a recent survey by the Carnegie Foundation for the Advancement of Teaching indicated that about 70% of colleges and universities have tried to design inhibitions on First Amendment activity."[11] In fact, the survey did not address whether disciplinary codes violated the First Amendment, and the surveyers said it was "patently untrue" that the survey showed a proliferation of speech codes, since the responses could reflect mere declarations against bigotry or policies that dealt only with unprotected conduct.[12]

No one really knows how many colleges have speech codes for the simple reason that no one has ever defined what a speech code is. If a speech code means that colleges have the authority to punish students for certain verbal expressions that are threatening or abusive or offensive, then every college has a speech code and always has had one. By some curious logic, the colleges that revised their disciplinary policies in the late 1980s were the ones accused of having speech codes, while the colleges that retained older, usually vaguer and more easily abused policies were praised for not censoring students. For example, the University of Chicago, although it claims not to have a speech code, prohibits any conduct that "threatens the security of the University community, the rights of its individual members, or its basic norms of academic integrity," and adds that "personal abuse, whether oral or written, exceeds the bounds of appropriate discourse and civil conduct." This is a standard much broader than any speech code attacked for its vagueness.[13]

A study of 384 colleges by the Freedom Forum found that colleges prohibit many kinds of behavior, including threats of violence (53.9 percent); breach of the peace (15.6 percent); disruption (79.7 percent); hazing (70.3 percent); obscenity (39.8 percent); emotional distress (14 percent); sexual harassment (78.1 percent); libel and slander (5.9 percent); fighting words (7.8 percent); lewd, indecent, and profane language (47.1 percent); verbal abuse/harassment (60.1 percent); verbal abuse/harassment based on race, gender, etc. (35.9 percent); and offensive or outrageous viewpoint (28.1 percent).[14] Certainly, most of these rules have not been enacted in recent years, although they reveal that disciplinary codes can be found at virtually every college. But the widespread older rules against disruption and lewd, indecent, and profane language are far vaguer and more subject to abuse than the more recent narrowly written provisions that have been condemned as speech codes. Free-speech advocates have not attacked hazing codes like the one in effect at Arizona State University and the University of Arizona, which prohibits even voluntary activities that "have the potential to harass, intimidate, impart pain, humiliate, invite ridicule of, cause undue mental or physical fatigue or distress, or to cause mutilation, laceration, or bodily injury."[15] Speech codes raised suspicion only when they sought to stop racial epithets and similar forms of invidious intimidation.

It is true that some speech codes are badly written and others are badly enforced. But the effects of these disciplinary rules have been greatly exaggerated. Perhaps the most famous example is from the University of Connecticut, which prohibited "causing alarm by making personal slurs," including "inappropriately directed laughter, inconsiderate jokes, . . . and conspicuous exclusions [of others] from conversations."[16] The rules sparked an outcry around the country, even though no one had ever been punished for "inappropriate laughter." George Will wrote, "The grim administrators of moral uplift at the University of Connecticut are empowered to punish students for 'inappropriate laughter.'"[17] Although the school limited the code in 1991 to words "inherently likely to provoke an immediate violent reaction," the short-lived and never-enforced "inappropriate laughter" rule is still frequently reported as if it were the paradigm of current speech codes. Since the vast majority of speech codes were unobjectionable, critics went after a few badly written codes and managed to convince the public that students were actually being expelled for laughing at the wrong moments.[18]

The speech code hysteria led critics of PC to see the speech police behind every memo. In the fall of 1990, every incoming freshman at Smith College received a pamphlet from the Office of Student Affairs which included the statement that "lookism" is "the belief that appearance is an indicator of a person's value; the construction of a standard for beauty/attractiveness; and oppression through stereotypes and generalizations of both those who do not fit that standard and those who do." [19]

While the Smith College handout is regularly ridiculed, no one has explained precisely why what it says is offensive, or how anyone reading it would be indoctrinated into leftist dogma. Silly and superficial it may be, but dangerous it is not. Yet the numerous reports about the pamphlet declared that it was the enforced policy of the college, and that anyone who dared to be a "lookist" would be disciplined. Francis Beckwith and Michael Bauman offered the Smith pamphlet as their sole example of how "many college campuses have instituted rules forbidding 'racist,' 'sexist,' or 'homophobic' speech." [20] R. Emmett Tyrrell claimed in an *American Spectator* article that "more than 130 universities have issued codes barring free discussion of dozens of topics," adding that "at Smith College the code delineates ten kinds of oppression to be avoided." [21] George Roche insisted that "Smith College had penalties for 'lookism.'" [22]

But the Smith pamphlet includes not a single word to suggest that lookism is a form of sexual harassment, or that such behavior would be punished. The Smith pamphlet offers a point of view about which activities the school feels are morally wrong; it is not a speech code regulating student behavior. But the critics of political correctness, anxious to find any anecdote to ridicule leftists, are willing to distort a statement against prejudices into a totalitarian speech code.

The crusade against speech codes was also joined by America's political leaders. Congressman Henry Hyde (R-Illinois) declared that "a regime of political correctness is now in place at many of our finest universities" and claimed that the number of colleges with speech codes "is quite large," citing the same survey misleadingly invoked by the ACLU. [23] Hyde's "Collegiate Speech Protection Act," proposed in 1991 but never passed, would have given students the right to challenge speech codes under the 1964 Civil Rights Act. When Senator Larry Craig (R-Idaho) introduced legislation in 1991 to withhold federal funding from any university with a speech code, he declared: "Students and professors who find themselves at odds with the codes are being denied tenure, asked to leave campus, and having their reputation tarnished." [24] Although Congress never passed a bill legislating free speech on campus, a similar law regulating private colleges was passed in California in 1992.

Hyde's proposal was part of the right wing's newly found devotion to the First Amendment. Like other conservatives, though, Hyde is highly selective in his defense of free speech. In 1988, he praised Edwin Meese's Commission on Pornography, saying it would "produce a lasting legacy of hope." In 1989, Hyde opposed the Supreme Court's decision defending flag burning, comparing the flag to "the Sacrament in the Catholic Church." In 1990, Hyde voted against any funding for the National Endowment for the Arts, saying he would not support "gratuitous insults."[25] Hyde's bill even exempted religious institutions (but not any other private colleges) from the "free speech" bill because he feared it might force "college administrators to accept devil worshipers on campus."[26]

But despite these high-profile defenses of "free speech," there is not and never was a censorship crisis on campus. A 1992 *Chronicle of Higher Education* investigation found that "campus codes that ban hate speech are rarely used to penalize students." Administrators reported that "few students have used the codes to lodge complaints against others," and punishments, when meted out, are rarely harsh.[27] A 1994 study of speech codes at America's twenty largest public universities found that only half have policies of any kind regulating "hostile or harassing speech or conduct," and even these are rarely enforced. The researchers concluded that "despite increasing 'hate speech' incidents, the policies go relatively unused."[28]

In the few cases where new speech codes were poorly written or enforced, the federal courts quickly struck down every code as unconstitutional. In *Doe v. University of Michigan,* a federal court rejected a speech code that was implemented at Michigan after a series of racist incidents in 1987 and 1988.[29] In response to these racial incidents and the protests against them, the university's administrators decided to enact an antidiscrimination disciplinary policy.[30] While Michigan's speech code explicitly protected "the most wide-ranging freedom of speech" in publications, it prohibited "any behavior, verbal or physical, that stigmatizes or victimizes an individual on the basis of race, ethnicity, religion, sex, sexual orientation, creed, national origin, ancestry, age, marital status, handicap or Vietnam-era veteran status" when that behavior either (1) "involves an express or implied threat to an individual's academic efforts, employment, participation in University sponsored extra-curricular activities or personal safety"; (2) "has the purpose or reasonably foreseeable effect of interfering with an individual's academic efforts, employment, participation in University sponsored extra-curricular activities or personal safety"; or (3) "creates an intimidating, hostile, or demeaning environment for educational pursuits, employment or participation in University sponsored extra-curricular activities."[31]

Under the Michigan speech code, a graduate student in the School of Social Work was investigated, but not punished, for stating his belief during a class that homosexuality was a disease and that he planned to help gay clients become straight. In a second case, a student in the School of Business Administration read a homophobic limerick in a public-speaking class; the matter was dropped when the student agreed to attend an educational "gay rap" session and write a letter of apology. In a third case, a dentistry student at an orientation session stated that "he had heard that minorities had a difficult time in the course and that he had heard that they were not treated fairly." Again, the matter was dropped after a letter of apology was written.[32]

Although none of these students were punished, the court—correctly—ruled that the speech code was unconstitutionally vague. The university also made informal settlements of various complaints, many of which probably could not be regulated by a speech code. It is important to keep the University of Michigan speech code in the proper perspective. It was adopted in response to serious racist incidents when Michigan had only an extremely vague behavior code. The speech code was never used to inflict serious punishments on students, and the worst charge against the university is that it informally settled some complaints (as any college ought to do) for acts protected by the First Amendment. If the policy had been better defined and better applied, it would have caused no free-speech objections. But instead of pointing out the flaws in Michigan's speech code, critics exaggerated its abuses and used it to attack all speech codes.

A federal court also struck down a speech code at the University of Wisconsin, even though it was much more narrowly drawn than the Michigan code. In order to violate the speech code, behavior had to: (1) be "directed at an individual"; (2) "demean the race, sex, religion, color, creed, disability, sexual orientation, national origin, ancestry or age of the individual or individuals"; and (3) "create an intimidating, hostile or demeaning environment for education, university-related work, or other university-authorized activity."[33] The Wisconsin code closely resembled the Equal Employment Opportunity Commission rules interpreting Title VII (required for all employers, including universities) hostile environment harassment.

The federal judge who rejected Wisconsin's code claimed that "since Title VII is only a statute, it cannot supersede the requirements of the First Amendment."[34] In effect, the court declared that the Title VII antidiscrimination laws of the Civil Rights Act are unconstitutional, a step that no other court has ever contemplated. The Wisconsin code did not have the flaws of the Michigan policy. It limited its coverage to the legally defined language of hostile environment harassment and included a requirement of directness. It would be strange if universities are prohibited from punishing forms of harassment that all employers are compelled by federal law to stop, although the Supreme Court has never held that institutions of higher education are exempt from antidiscrimination laws.

While speech codes can be misused to infringe on free speech, they can also protect it. When a woman at the University of Wisconsin criticized the athletic department in the student newspaper, a male student confronted her and yelled epithets at her for ten minutes, calling her a "fucking bitch" and a "fucking cunt."[35] When abusive (and threatening) speech such as this is not restricted, people hesitate to express their ideas for fear of retaliation.

The punishments at Wisconsin were not harsh. Of thirty-two complaints filed in eighteen months under the policy, thirteen cases were dismissed without a hearing and two cases were dismissed after a hearing. In only one case, an assault, was a student suspended (for seven months). The rest of the punishments placed the students on probation and sometimes required an educational project related to the offense, such as participating in alcohol abuse treatment, getting psychological counseling, completing a project on diversity, taking a course on ethics or East Asian history, or performing twenty hours of community service at a shelter for abused women.[36] All of the cases involved conduct that would have violated some other part of the student conduct code (such as disorderly conduct), and no discipline was ever imposed for anything involving an expression of opinion or a classroom discussion.[37]

In September 1992, the Wisconsin Board of Regents voted 10 to 6 to repeal a revised speech code that would have imposed penalties on those who used "epithets directed specifically toward individuals with the purpose of creating a hostile educational environment on the basis of their race, gender, or sexual preference."[38] The decision was cheered by many civil libertarians who believed that it meant the end of restrictions on speech. But it's clear that the restriction on "epithets" would have been quite narrow, especially with the additional requirements of directedness and purpose to create a hostile environment. If universities without "speech codes" punish students for epithets and similar threats (as they should), it can only be by stretching the meaning of existing university rules, which is far worse for freedom of speech than a well-defined speech code.

The presence or absence of a so-called speech code does not affect a university's ability to punish students. George Mason University in Fairfax, Virginia, punished a fraternity for an offensive skit done in blackface even though the university had never enacted a speech code.[39] Yale University, which has one of the strongest defenses of free speech in its rules, punished a student named Wayne Dick in 1988 for distributing a flyer with a parody of Yale's fifth annual Gay and Lesbian Awareness Days. Dick received two years of probation despite Yale's free-speech protections because, said Associate Dean Patricia Pierce, those protections do not apply to "worthless speech." Yale's Executive Committee found that Dick's "BAD Week" poster "constituted an act of harassment and intimidation toward the gay and lesbian community." A year later, after national publicity, Dick's punishment was finally overturned.[40]

The claim that we can solve problems on campuses and protect free speech by simply eliminating speech codes is a deception of the worst kind. Colleges must sometimes discipline students for their behavior (which may include speech as in the case of threats and harassment). By enacting a good speech code, a college does not take away free speech; it provides the groundwork for a system that can protect freedom of expression. By making better, narrower speech codes, colleges can protect student rights and defend free speech. The campaign to get rid of all speech codes is a chimera that actually threatens free speech by giving administrators untrammeled authority to punish students under much vaguer behavior codes.

The Stanford Speech Code

The crusade against speech codes reached the height of absurdity on 27 February 1995 when a superior court judge struck down Stanford University's speech code as a violation of the First Amendment, despite the fact that not a single person was punished during the four years it was in effect. Stanford's policy was a good example of a well-written and narrowly defined speech code that does not threaten free speech. The policy covers only "fighting words" in face-to-face situations addressed to a specific person and contain "words, pictures or symbols that are commonly understood to convey in a direct and visceral way, hatred or contempt" for a particular race or sex.[41]

Despite the extremely narrow focus of Stanford's policy, critics have not hesitated to attack the speech code as censorship. David Sacks says in *Heterodoxy* that the Stanford policy was "revised to prohibit speech that in any way degrades another student on the basis of race, sex, or sexual orientation."[42] Plainly, the policy does not punish anyone for merely "degrading" speech. As then Stanford president Donald Kennedy explained to first-year students in 1989, "There is room at Stanford for the expression of opinion, even if it is distasteful or misguided, about general matters of race, or ethnicity, or religion, or sexual preference. But directed insults and 'fighting words' are not protected here or, we believe, under the prevailing view of the First Amendment."[43]

Sacks is not the only one to misread the plain meaning of the Stanford policy. C. Vann Woodward claims that professors at Stanford Law School "urged censorship."[44] A headline in the conservative newspaper *Campus* reports, "Stanford Joins Speech Police."[45] John Leo says that Stanford is one place where "the new speech police have successfully imposed codes to defend the sensibilities of sexual, racial and ethnic groups."[46] Jonathan Rauch finds "no excuse for a university code like Stanford's which prohibits speech that 'is *intended* to insult or stigmatize.'"[47] But Rauch does not understand the policy. The requirement for intent limits the scope of the code, since an inadvertent insult is not covered. Rauch wrongly implies that speech that is merely intended to insult can be punished by Stanford's speech code.

Dinesh D'Souza also refers to "Stanford's censorship rule" and claims that its author, law professor Thomas Grey, "urged censorship."[48] The nine Stanford students who successfully sued the university claim that the speech code "permanently damages the quality of education" by "artificially chilling open discussion of important issues."[49] Even though no one was ever punished under Stanford's speech code and two-thirds of the students support it, the myth persists that students and faculty are being prevented from expressing their ideas.[50]

Before the new speech code was implemented at Stanford, students could be punished for not showing "respect for order, morality, personal honor, and the rights of others."[51] By any standard of free-speech protection and specificity, Stanford's new speech code is less restrictive than the code it replaced. Yet conservatives and civil libertarians who never said a word about the old, vague code attack the new code as evidence of a new totalitarianism on campus.

Harvard professor Henry Louis Gates, Jr., persuasively argues against speech codes because they give right-wingers "a gift-wrapped, bow-tied, and beribboned rallying point" which "can turn a garden-variety bigot into a First Amendment martyr." Speech codes, says Gates, "make it impossible to challenge bigotry without creating a debate over the right to speak." But Gates does not see speech codes as a massive threat to free speech. He rejects speech codes precisely because they are unimportant, since "verbal harassment is already, and pretty uncontroversially, prohibited" and "campus speech codes are rarely enforced."[52] Gates is right, although on many campuses it is not clear that harassment is prohibited. Speech codes in themselves are not important. But we must remember that it is the conservatives who have exaggerated the power and consequences of speech codes and raised the issue to a national level.

Gates calls the Stanford speech code "narrowly and responsibly tailored" and says it has "rightly been taken as a model of such careful delimitation." But, Gates adds, "chances are, the Stanford rules won't do much harm. Chances are, too, it won't do much good."[53] Gates's assessment is correct. According to a *San Francisco Chronicle* report, "nobody has ever been prosecuted under Stanford's hate-speech rules, in part because they are so carefully defined."[54] When a strictly defined, unenforced code against epithets is considered the leading threat to free speech, it shows how dishonest the fears of the "PC thought police" have been.

An improved and narrowly focused speech code can clarify the rights and responsibilities of the members of an academic community, but the current debate makes it impossible for any efforts to improve disciplinary policies to be discussed on their merits. Above all else, the myth that (in the words of *Time*) "nowhere is the First Amendment more imperiled than on college campuses" should be exposed as the lie that it is.[55]

The Attack on Speech Codes

The same critics who condemn "speech codes" openly support restrictions on free speech. Dinesh D'Souza, for example, attacks speech codes but admits that "I'm not a free speech absolutist." D'Souza suggests the following as a speech code: "Students shall not yell racial epithets at each other"—a standard vaguer and broader than the Stanford code he attacks as censorship.[56] Columnist George Will believes that an academic community "requires a particular atmosphere of civility that can be incompatible with unrestricted expression."[57] Even the ACLU admits that its support for free speech "does not prohibit colleges and universities from enacting disciplinary codes aimed at restricting acts of harassment, intimidation and invasion of privacy."[58] Nadine Strossen, the president of the ACLU, points out that "the Supreme Court never has held, and civil libertarians never have argued, that harassing, intimidating, or assaultive conduct should be immunized simply because it consists in part of words."[59] Free speech absolutist Nat Hentoff says, "Any systematic, repeated verbal harassment that substantially interferes with the target's functioning is not protected speech."[60] By depicting their opponents as "censors," critics promote an absolutist free-speech position that they have never believed in and which never existed on any college campus.

One common misconception about speech codes is that they were banned by the Supreme Court in *R.A.V. v. St. Paul* (1991), which struck down a municipal ban on hate speech. But *R.A.V.*'s main doctrine was repudiated a year later by a unanimous court in *Wisconsin v. Mitchell*, which upheld enhanced penalties for hate-motivated crimes.[61]

While all of the justices in *R.A.V.* struck down the hate speech law, Justice Scalia's majority opinion sharply attacked any law that treats race, gender, sexual orientation, or similar categories differently from other forms of hate speech. According to Scalia, bans on all fighting words are acceptable, but bans only on racially motivated fighting words are not.

Scalia's simplistic dismissal of all such regulations in *R.A.V.* was ignored by the Court in *Wisconsin v. Mitchell,* which upheld enhanced penalties for racially motivated crimes. In *Mitchell,* the Court recognized that there are good reasons for treating racially motivated attacks differently from violence based on personal animus. Crimes based on immutable characteristics of people — whether white or black, gay or straight — may create a greater social harm than random crimes because they increase social division and cause all members of a particular group to fear violence. While *R.A.V.* still outlaws vague and overbroad hate speech laws (as the concurring liberals ruled), Scalia's extreme attack on all speech codes has been effectively overruled. There is no constitutional barrier to narrowly written university speech codes, even if not all forms of fighting words are punished equally.

Another frequent false claim is that speech codes protect only minorities from racism while allowing whites to be insulted freely. Jared Taylor complains that "as whites worry about whether they are using the socially acceptable race words, blacks can call whites anything they like. No one has ever been reported to have gotten into trouble for talking about whitey, crackers, rednecks, honkies, buckra, or white trash." [62] This "fact" will come as a surprise to the black student punished at the University of Michigan for calling a white student "white trash" during an argument. Marcia Pally notes that "in the eighteen months that the University of Michigan applied its speech code, black students were accused of racist speech in over twenty cases. Students were punished twice under the code's anti-racist provisions, both times for speech by or on behalf of blacks." [63] Many opponents of speech codes, such as ACLU president Nadine Strossen, argue against them precisely because minorities, not whites, will be the ones punished: "These codes are enforced disproportionately against the very groups that think they're going to be protected by them." [64]

While there is always a danger that college administrators may punish protected speech (as they have always done), abolishing all speech codes and leaving colleges with the intellectual equivalent of a Wild West shootout where any words — no matter how abusive and threatening — can be freely spoken is not the answer. Nor is the answer to go back to the old vague and arbitrary conduct codes, which are more dangerous than the worst of the much-maligned "speech codes." Instead, colleges should adopt specific speech codes that regulate certain kinds of abusive speech and behavior — such as threats, harassment, and the mass theft of newspapers — without endangering the free expression of offensive ideas.

Trashing the Student Press

The false charge that speech codes censor politically incorrect speech is often accompanied by the claim that conservative views in student newspapers are censored by administrative punishment or theft of the newspapers. Censorship of the student press is common, but the truth is that censorship by administrators and student government officials, along with "conservative correctness," is a far greater threat to freedom of the press than political correctness.

There are cases where conservative views have been censored, and these should be condemned. The UCLA *Daily Bruin*, for example, ran a cartoon showing a rooster who was asked how he got admitted on campus. The rooster replied, "Affirmative action." The editor and the art director were suspended for using this cartoon because it violated the university's policy against derogatory stereotypes.[65] At California State University at Northridge, James Taranto, editor of the campus paper, wrote an editorial criticizing the UCLA officials for suspending the student editor and also reproduced the offensive rooster cartoon. As a result, the paper's faculty adviser gave a two-week suspension to Taranto for printing "controversial" material without permission. The ACLU intervened, and a settlement was reached.[66]

Censorship such as this must be strongly opposed, as should the theft of newspapers in order to prevent people from reading controversial material. Many of these newspaper trashings have been widely publicized. On 15 April 1993, a group of black students at the University of Pennsylvania threw away the 14,200 press run of the *Daily Pennsylvanian* because it included a column written by conservative student Gregory Pavlik, who had criticized affirmative action and Martin Luther King, Jr. Sheldon Hackney, the president of the University of Pennsylvania (and now the NEH chair), was widely condemned for failing to criticize the theft, even though Hackney said at the time: "There can be no compromise regarding the First Amendment right of an independent publication to express whatever views it chooses." Hackney also reaffirmed the ban on confiscations of newspapers. However, a disciplinary panel over which Hackney had no authority determined that the newspaper thieves had not violated any rules.[67]

A few other examples of trashings to censor conservative views have been widely publicized in the press, although the fact that the thieves were condemned and often punished (a rarity in newspaper thefts) is rarely mentioned. At the University of Maryland, bundles of the 1 November 1993 issue of the campus newspaper were taken because of charges of racism.[68] However, black leaders on campus, including two black editors of the paper, quickly denounced the theft, as did the university president.[69] The students responsible were punished by being put on probation, forced to perform sixteen hours of community service, and required to write a paper on student press censorship.

At Penn State University in April 1993, students stole four thousand copies of the right-wing student newspaper, the *Lionhearted*. That same night, protesters burned hundreds of copies of the newspaper in front of the law office of a trustee who supported the newspaper. The protesters were angered by the *Lionhearted*'s attacks on feminism, including, in the seized issue, a full-page picture of a female columnist in the main student newspaper, with her head pasted on top of a bikini-clad body. The issue also included an article calling her writings "hateful and intolerant tripe." In July 1993, university police charged two recent graduates with theft, receiving stolen property, and criminal conspiracy for taking the newspapers.[70]

At Duke University in 1993, a member of the Black Student Alliance took one hundred copies of the conservative *Duke Review*, saying, "I consider it litter, and when I see litter I throw it out." He was strongly condemned by Duke president Nan Keohane and was placed on probation after being convicted of theft by the Undergraduate Judicial Board. However, the conviction was overturned on appeal because the student was denied due process when a new definition of theft was applied retroactively.[71] Here, the university responded harshly to the removal of a small number of newspapers, and even violated the student's due process rights in its pursuit of punishment.

There is simply no evidence that a politically correct crusade of students and administrators is trying to silence conservative views. However, selective reporting about the widespread phenomenon of censorship by trashing has created a false impression that the PC thought police are roaming college campuses abducting newspapers offensive to them. In most cases, newspaper thefts have nothing to do with political correctness. The Student Press Law Center listed nineteen newspaper thefts in its spring 1994 report. Of these thefts, only one—the University of Maryland case—could be attributed to the conservative views expressed in the newspaper. Mark Goodman, director of the center, observes that student governments or campus groups mad at newspaper coverage are more often responsible than politically correct thieves.[72]

Newspapers are most often trashed when they report crimes that embarrass administrators (someone from the Stevens Institute of Technology admissions office trashed 1,250 copies of the *Stute* to keep prospective students from seeing a sexual assault story; a story on chemical dumping led to the theft of 200 copies of the University of Detroit at Mercy's *Varsity News* during an alumni event) or anger those involved in a crime (friends of a student expelled for sexual misconduct stole 1,000 copies of the *Webster University Journal;* a story about a sex crime at a fraternity house led to 2,000 copies of the *Pittsburg State University Collegio* being trashed; 1,300 copies of the *Franklin & Marshall College Student Reporter* were taken when it reported sanctions against the Black Student Union; almost every copy of the *North Adams College Beacon* was taken after it ran a front-page story about the arrest of fraternity brothers). And the most common cause of student newspapers being trashed (six out of nineteen thefts) is their endorsement or criticism of student government candidates.[73]

Contrary to the common assumption that political correctness motivates newspaper thefts, most papers are not taken for ideological reasons, and there is no sign that conservative papers are specially targeted for censorship. At Brandeis University, for example, 2,000 copies of the *Justice* were stolen because it contained a Holocaust revisionist ad (although printed with a disclaimer and with the revenues donated to the Holocaust Memorial Museum). Grace Young, publisher of the *Yale Daily News Magazine,* suspects that members of a conservative political party on campus stole one issue because it contained a story on the party's female members.[74]

In Maryland, antigay activists began repeatedly stealing copies of the *Washington Blade,* a gay and lesbian weekly, claiming that it was antifamily and should not be displayed near public libraries. Although a man was photographed taking the papers and loading them into a car, the state refused to prosecute on the grounds that "the paper gave up its possession by placing the papers in libraries." After this theft and the trashing of student newspapers at three Maryland colleges, the legislature passed a law making it a misdemeanor to take "one or more newspapers with the intent to destroy the newspapers or prevent other individuals from reading the newspapers."[75]

An alternative progressive newspaper I wrote for, the *Grey City Journal* (at the University of Chicago), was another victim of censorship by trashing. On 13 January 1993, an administrator at the University of Chicago Hospitals threw away 250 copies of the *Grey City Journal.* The administrator later claimed that she was doing "housekeeping" because the newspapers were not in vending boxes. This excuse might have been believable except for the facts that (1) this policy had not been enforced in the past, (2) this issue of the *Grey City Journal* featured a cover story on the hospital's contract negotiations with the Teamsters Union, and (3) the administrator said "I hate this paper" as she threw it away. An earlier article in the *Grey City Journal* (which won the *Nation's* I. F. Stone Prize for investigative student journalism) had exposed the hospital's discrimination against Medicaid patients. But this censorship was hardly an act that threatened the newspaper's existence. As our editorial pointed out, "the damage to the *Grey City Journal* was laughable: about $15 worth of trashed papers, in exchange for which we got more publicity than money could buy." [76]

Stealing newspapers is clearly a deplorable and indefensible act at any university that promotes free expression of ideas, and such thefts ought to be punished. But in order to punish the trashing of newspapers, it is necessary to have a clear "speech code" prohibiting behavior that infringes on the rights of others. Ironically, the crusade against speech codes has helped promote the recent increase in newspaper thefts because it convinced students that they could do or say anything they liked on campus and then invoke free speech in defense of it. When all is said and done, however, the fact is that the stealing of newspapers is not a great threat to free speech. Administrative censorship is a much more effective means of stopping investigative journalism.

Progressive newspapers are frequently the victims of official censorship. In 1989, the editors of the *Marquette University Tribune* were suspended and the business manager was fired because the newspaper had published an ad for an abortion rally, even though it ran a disclaimer noting that Marquette was not supporting the rally. Under intense media scrutiny, the university finally reinstated the student journalists. In 1992, university officials were outraged by news stories depicting the university in a negative light and by an opinion column listing student grievances titled, "Welcome to Hell, Enjoy Your Ride." Both President Albert DiUlio and Executive Vice President William Leahy chastised the editors in private meetings. In March 1993, the university refused to allow the paper to publish an unsigned editorial on abortion pill RU-486 that contradicted the university's position, claiming that it might be misinterpreted as Marquette University's views. When the student editors agreed to make the editorial a signed opinion piece, the university wanted to balance it with an opinion opposed to the abortion pill. In response to this interference, the entire student editorial board resigned, although the controversial column was eventually printed. [77]

Faculty adviser Bill Blanton has since resigned, saying that it was "not a good atmosphere to teach or practice journalism," and adding that officials at the Jesuit university "said we couldn't go against any kind of church doctrine." Journalism department chair James Scotton resigned as director of the Board of Student Publications rather than have to censor the content of the newspaper according to Catholic doctrines. Rev. John Patrick Donnelly, the new director, declares: "Freedom of the press belongs to those who own it. This being a Catholic institution, we don't expect the paper to run editorials that contradict church positions." The *Tribune* is under orders to inform administrators about any stories that contain "controversial material" before publication, and news editor Erin Grace reports, "I was told recently to keep away from things that are controversial." Student affairs official Francis Lazarus defends the university's intrusion on the grounds that "in the real world of journalism," students must "learn to work for a publisher with a particular point of view." The *Harbinger*, an alternative campus newspaper started in 1992, was not allowed to put its papers in campus buildings.[78]

At Viterbo College, a Catholic college in LaCrosse, Wisconsin, the student newspaper has frequently been harassed by the administration. In 1992, President William Medland fired the faculty adviser, the editor, and the entire thirty-three-member staff of the paper after it published a humorous article entitled "Top Ten Reasons Why You Should Use a Condom." According to Medland, the article was "tasteless and definitely not humorous," it "shocked the sensibilities of many students, faculty, staff and administrators," and it "holds up to ridicule the Catholic, Franciscan, liberal-arts nature of this institution."[79] The staff was rehired a few days later when the Society of Professional Journalists intervened. The next year, editor Darren Foster resigned, saying he faced "emotional pressure" not to run stories on controversial issues: "They have personally attacked my character for having a gay agenda, just because I wanted to run a few stories about gays."[80]

In 1991, the editor and managing editor of the student newspaper at Palm Beach Atlantic College were fired for insubordination and lost their scholarships after attempting to publish an anonymous letter and an editorial questioning the ban on homosexual activity at that Baptist college. The issue, despite being heavily censored by university officials, was criticized by several students, who, led by a student government officer, threw away about half of the 1,500 copies.[81]

At Wheaton College, a conservative Christian college in Illinois, the committee on student publications forced the editors of the literary magazine *Kodon* to remove two nude sketches of a man and a woman before it could be published.[82] At Elgin Community College in Illinois, school officials tried to censor the *Observer* and then threatened to close it down because the student magazine had run stories about gay organizations on campus and disclosed that an athlete had competed despite being academically ineligible.[83]

When *Tejas*, the Chicano student newspaper at the University of Texas at Austin, attacked Assistant Dean Joseph Horn's political and academic career (which included research on ethnic group differences in intelligence) and called for his resignation in 1991, conservatives protested the university's funding of the newspaper and successfully limited state funding to the amount needed to produce fifty copies for the journalism class, but not the previous circulation of five thousand for the student body.[84]

At the University of New Mexico, the *New Mexico Daily Lobo* included a photo essay of a gay couple and a nude man with a pierced penis. Student body president David Standridge said campus reaction was "very negative" and promised to meet with administrators to see about filing a complaint through the Student Standards and Grievance Procedures; he also promised to try to recover the $38,000 given to the paper from student fees.[85] At the University of Manitoba, the student editors of *The Manitoban* were removed for running "anti-Christian" nude cartoons and for refusing to publish Department of National Defence advertisements.[86] At Ohio State University, three editors of the student newspaper resigned and seven more were fired by the journalism school after they refused to allow prior review of the paper's stories for libel by the newspaper's faculty adviser.[87]

At Millsaps College in Jackson, Mississippi, the *Purple and White* was shut down for ten weeks by administrators after an opinions columnist jokingly suggested group sex as a way for people to transcend their differences. After alumni and trustees threatened to withdraw money from the school, the administration condemned the column as "poorly written, tasteless, offensive and unworthy of publication anywhere." The *Purple and White* was allowed to resume publication only after adopting standards for taste and decency and after a five-person editorial board unanimously approved each story before publication.[88]

Speech codes, when carefully written, can improve the campus climate for everyone by punishing egregious acts of intimidation and censorship while eliminating the old, arbitrary behavior codes still in effect at universities that do not have "speech codes." No one believes that a speech code can create racial harmony on campus. But narrowly tailored speech codes can help protect students against the worst abuses, and it is foolish to dismiss them out of hand.

The importance of free speech in higher education needs to be appreciated. The university is not a soapbox; its purpose is to educate students, not to promote absolutely free speech or ensure that every point of view has equal representation. But we must realize that freedom of expression is essential to the academic freedom of both teachers and students.

The speech code debate rarely addresses the far more important questions of indoctrination and the freedom of students to speak. No speech code has a chilling effect on public debate. What makes students hesitant to speak their minds in class, or in their term papers and final exams, has nothing to do with speech codes. Freedom of expression must never be reduced to trivial debates over formal regulations. The key issue we need to focus on, one that the uninformed obsession with speech codes ignores, is our willingness to hear different views and our commitment to the belief that we learn from understanding the views we disagree with. Openness to dissent is a virtue sorely lacking among both the Left and the Right, in our schools and in our society. Intolerance, from all sides, not political correctness, is the foe we must defeat.

➤ 5 The Myth of Sexual Correctness

On the afternoon of 19 April 1988, a nineteen-year-old student at East Stroudsburg State University in Pennsylvania walked to her boyfriend's dormitory. While waiting for him, she went to the dorm room of a friend and encountered his roommate, Robert Berkowitz. When Berkowitz asked her to "hang out for a while," she agreed, but she refused his request to give him a back rub or sit on his bed, saying she didn't trust him.

After talking for a while, Berkowitz got off the bed, sat next to her, and leaned against her until her back was on the floor. Berkowitz straddled her and started kissing her. She said, "Look, I gotta go," saying she had to meet her boyfriend. Berkowitz lifted her shirt and started fondling her. She said, "No." Berkowitz, still on top of her, continued kissing and fondling her for thirty seconds, and she continued to say "no." Berkowitz undid his pants. She kept saying "no" but reports she "really couldn't move" because he was shifting his body on top of her. She said, "No, I gotta go, let me go."

Berkowitz went to the door and locked it. He put her on the bed and straddled her again, removing her sweatpants and underwear, and she reports that she "couldn't like go anywhere." She didn't scream because "it was like a dream was happening or something." He started having sex with her and she said "no, no," repeatedly. After about thirty seconds, Berkowitz got off her and said, "Wow, I guess we just got carried away." She said, "No, we didn't get carried away, you got carried away."

Berkowitz was charged with rape, found guilty by a jury, and sentenced to one to four years in prison. But on 27 May 1994, the Pennsylvania Supreme Court overturned the jury's guilty verdict and ruled that what Berkowitz did was not rape because there was no "forcible compulsion" involved.[1]

Between 1988 and 1994, when the rape happened and when the Pennsylvania Supreme Court decided it didn't, a sexual revolution occurred. Anita Hill testified before the Senate Judiciary Committee investigating Clarence Thomas and raised public awareness about "that sexual harassment crap," as Senator Alan Simpson (R-Wyoming) put it.[2] Colleges and universities wrote new policies prohibiting sexual harassment and sexual assault, and began educating students about date rape. Antioch College, in Yellow Springs, Ohio, developed a much-ridiculed policy requiring not just consent but an active "yes" before sexual activity.

But a growing backlash against feminism condemned the increased attention to acquaintance rape and sexual harassment as "a neo-puritan preoccupation" with "a nostalgia for 1950's-style dating" that infantilized women, as Katie Roiphe wrote in a *New York Times* op-ed piece she later expanded into *The Morning After: Sex, Fear, and Feminism on Campus.* Roiphe further claimed that "these feminists are promoting the view of women as weak-willed, alabaster bodies, whose virtue must be protected from the cunning encroachments of the outside world."[3]

A sister phrase to *political correctness* was discovered in a 1993 *Newsweek* cover story: "Sexual Correctness." According to *Newsweek,* because of sexual correctness "verbal coercion can now constitute rape," and feminists are making women into "Scared Little Girls" who are "huddling in packs."[4] But like political correctness, sexual correctness is a media invention with little basis in reality. No men are being thrown in jail for verbal coercion. No women are being weakened by so-called victim feminism. No "sexually correct" dogma reigns on college campuses.

If there is a feminist conspiracy taking over universities and redefining rude behavior as date rape, it is hard to find any evidence of it. On the contrary, most colleges continue to follow the same old policies of denial and dismissal. Katie Koestner was raped in her dormitory room at the College of William and Mary in Williamsburg, Virginia, when she was a freshman. She did not receive a medical examination for twenty-four hours. Rather than filing criminal charges, she was encouraged to use an administrative hearing. At the hearing, it was determined that the rape did not deserve "severe punishment," so the rapist was allowed to remain on campus on the condition that he not enter anyone's living quarters. The college administrator who heard the case told Koestner, "I did find him guilty but I talked to him for a couple of hours this morning and I think he is a good guy. . . . You two should work through this little tiff and get back together next semester."[5] Koestner eventually transferred to another university.[6]

Many colleges are reluctant to take strong action against rape for fear that it will lead to negative publicity. Since all colleges are required to report the number of sexual assaults that occur on campus, many administrators find it more convenient to ignore rape than to encourage women to report it. Brigham Young University, after reported rapes in Provo, Utah, quadrupled, refused to allow a rape-awareness speaker on campus because the subject was "too controversial."[7] Acquaintance rape is sometimes not even recorded by campus police as a crime. One police officer reported that a theft on campus was automatically recorded, but rapes were not listed as crimes "unless the rapist was a total stranger or the victim is in the intensive-care unit."[8] Colleges sometimes respond to a rape by trying to get the victim to leave campus. When Professor Joyce Honeychurch was raped in her office at the University of Alaska, the university offered her a settlement if she would leave.[9]

The refusal to acknowledge the reality of acquaintance rape has terrible consequences for its victims. While all rape victims suffer and many have difficulty recovering from the crime, victims of acquaintance rape are taught to believe that they must have been responsible, which makes the experience even more traumatic. Although acquaintance rape victims suffer the same degree of psychological harm from the rape, they are much less likely than victims of stranger rape to report what happened to the police or tell someone else about it.[10]

Acquaintance rape on college campuses can be particularly traumatic for the victims since they know they may cross paths with their attackers. Two researchers on rape "have heard story after story of individuals transferring or dropping out of school altogether after an assault. It is also apparent from our research that a person is much more likely to transfer or to drop out if the college has failed to take her allegations seriously." They add, "We have heard of cases in which the victim is not permitted to press charges at all, either through the criminal justice system or through the campus judicial hearing process."[11] After complaints from victims that college officials had steered them away from the courts, Connecticut passed a law in 1991 making it a crime for universities to interfere with a student's right to report a crime to police.[12]

The rape myths that permeate the *Berkowitz* case are not limited to the court system; they are also reflected in the current backlash against the women's movement. According to Camille Paglia, the *Berkowitz* case "isn't even remotely about rape," because a woman is "sending a signal" when she "sits on the floor with her breasts sticking up."[13] Paglia claims that "rape has become a joke" and asserts that going to a man's room alone "is in effect consenting to sex." Like the feminists she attacks, Paglia admits that "sex is dangerous" and that "rape is one of the risk factors in getting involved with men."[14] Ironically, it is Paglia who advocates neo-Puritanical standards when she says that a woman who allows herself to be alone in a room with a man is only getting what she deserves if she is raped. No feminist urges returning to the paternalistic age of early curfew for women, open doors, and one-foot-on-the-floor rules. Instead, feminists demand that sexuality must exist in a climate free of violence.

The most influential attacks on the feminist critique of acquaintance rape have come from Neil Gilbert, a professor of social welfare at Berkeley infamous for telling one of his classes, "Comparing real rape to date rape is like comparing cancer to the common cold."[15] Gilbert has frequently attacked "radical feminists" for doing "advocacy studies" that show what he calls a "phantom epidemic" of rape. Gilbert focuses on a 1985 study by Mary Koss of 3,187 college women, the most extensive research done on the prevalence of rape. Koss found that 27.1 percent had been victims of rape (15.3 percent) or attempted rape (11.8 percent). Koss's study also showed that 84 percent of the victims knew their attacker and that 57 percent of the rapes happened on dates, suggesting that acquaintance rape is widespread.[16] This survey is the source of the common "one-in-four" statistic that Gilbert dismisses as "nonsense-type numbers."[17]

Gilbert notes that of the ten questions asked in the Koss study, most referred to the threat or use of "some degree of physical force"; Gilbert does not dispute them. But two questions, he claims, were "awkward and vaguely worded": "Have you had a man attempt sexual intercourse (get on top of you, attempt to insert his penis) when you didn't want to by giving you alcohol or drugs, but intercourse did not occur? Have you had sexual intercourse when you didn't want to because a man gave you alcohol or drugs?"[18]

However, only 8 percent of the women in the survey said that they had had sexual intercourse because a man had given them alcohol or drugs, a low level considering the frequency of alcohol use in unwanted intercourse. By contrast, 9 percent of the women had had sexual intercourse and 6 percent anal or oral intercourse because "a man threatened or used some degree of physical force (twisting your arm, holding you down, etc.)."[19] It is difficult to imagine anyone quibbling with the wording of these questions (and Gilbert is notably silent about them), since the physical force is explicit and the acts are clearly rape according to legal definitions. At most, Gilbert's challenge to the "alcohol or drugs" question reduces the number of women who had been raped from 15.3 percent to 10.6 percent, and the victims of attempted rape from 11.7 percent to 8.4 percent.[20] Even if all the women who responded to this question were not raped (and some of them certainly were by Gilbert's definition), the proportion of college women who have been victims of rape or attempted rape would decline only from one in four (27.0 percent) to one in five (19.0 percent)—a figure far above the levels Gilbert is willing to admit could be accurate.[21]

Unable to show bias in the questions, Gilbert turns to what the victims themselves said about the incidents. Of those classified as victims of rape, 27 percent said it was rape. Another 14 percent described it as a "crime, but not rape." Only 11 percent said that they didn't "feel victimized," while 49 percent called it "miscommunication."[22] Gilbert distorts this data by claiming that "seventy-three percent of those whom the researcher defined as having been raped did not perceive of themselves as victims."[23] Certainly the women who called it a crime and the respondents who called it miscommunication (without saying they were not raped) refused to describe themselves as not having been victimized.

Gilbert claims that "to deny that a woman would know whether she had been raped says essentially that women are feebleminded."[24] But many women have been taught to believe that acquaintance rape is not rape at all, but merely a bad experience. One study found that women whom Koss categorized as rape victims but who did not themselves call it rape were much more likely than women who called their experience rape to define rape as a physical attack by a stranger.[25] Clearly, one reason why women who are raped do not call it rape is because of their narrow definition of *rape*, not because they were not victims of a sexual assault.

There is no evidence that Koss categorized lesser forms of sexual victimization as rape. Since Koss had separate categories for sexual coercion—where women who "didn't want to" have sexual intercourse were "overwhelmed by a man's continual arguments and pressure" (25 percent of the women surveyed)—it seems doubtful that the cases described by Koss as rape were instead coercion, since respondents had an opportunity to describe an act of sexual victimization as something less serious than being physically forced to have sex.

Gilbert ignores another part of Koss's data, which shows that 84 percent of the women who were raped tried to reason with the attacker, 70 percent put up some form of physical resistance, and 64 percent were held down.[26] If only 27 percent of these women were "really" raped, why did so many more women react as they would in "real" rapes? This contradicts Gilbert's explanation that "later regrets" or male "sweet talk" had been redefined as rape.[27] Gilbert wrongly thinks that feminists "label every bad experience a woman has with a man as rape."[28]

Koss's conclusion that one in four college women have been raped or have faced an attempt at rape is confirmed by other studies that did not include the questions Gilbert challenges. A 1991 survey of women at Purdue found that 17 percent reported being victims of rape or attempted rape, with 69 percent of the attacks made by acquaintances.[29] A survey at the University of South Dakota found that 20.6 percent of women were "physically forced by a dating partner to have sexual intercourse." A similar study at Cornell discovered that 19 percent had experienced "intercourse against their will . . . through rough coercion, threats, force or violence," but only 2 percent said they were raped.[30]

Koss's study is also confirmed by the 1993 National Health and Social Life Survey (NHSLS) conducted by the National Opinion Research Center, the most accurate and comprehensive survey of sex in America to date. The NHSLS found that 22 percent of women have been forced to do something sexually by a man since puberty, and 30 percent of them by more than one man.[31] And even this number underestimates the true level of sexual violence in our society: "Because forced sex is undoubtedly underreported in surveys because of the socially stigmatized nature of the event, we believe that our estimates are probably conservative 'lower-bound' estimates of forced sex within the population."[32]

The NHSLS found that 25 percent of women aged eighteen to twenty-four had been forced to do something sexually. In more than three quarters of the cases, it was someone the woman knew well (22 percent), was in love with (46 percent), or married to (9 percent) — only 4 percent of the women had been attacked by a stranger.[33] The prevalence of attacks on young women found by Koss is also confirmed by the 1992 "Rape in America" study by the Justice Department, which found that girls under age eighteen were the victims in 61.6 percent of rapes.[34] A 1994 report by the Alan Guttmacher Institute found that 23 percent of fourteen-year-olds are sexually experienced, and 60 percent of their first experiences were coerced.[35]

The NHSLS researchers also explain why they did not ask respondents about forced sex by using the word *rape:* "We purposely did not use the term rape in asking about forced sex, reasoning that there is a fundamental difference between what most people mean when they use the word and what police, prosecutors, and judges will accept in court as legal rape. In addition, the word has strong emotional connotations that may make some women reluctant to apply it in situations they were in, although they may have felt that they were forced to have sex."[36] The NHSLS researchers recognize that the use of the word *rape* is a barrier to getting accurate numbers about sexual violence. In a culture where stranger rape is defined as "real rape," few women are willing to call sexual assault by its real name.

Gilbert criticizes the Koss study by pointing out that "42% of the women who were defined as having been raped had sex again with the men who had supposedly raped them," arguing that in these cases it could not have been rape.[37] Gilbert claims, "Rape is a brutal crime. If you were raped, why would you sleep with your rapist again?"[38] But the facts do not conform to how Gilbert thinks women should act. The NHSLS survey asked respondents about their first act of intercourse and found that 4.2 percent of women were forced the first time they had sex (an additional 24.5 percent did not want to have sex but were not forced). Like the Koss study, this survey determined that a large number of the women forced to have sex (35.7 percent) had intercourse with their attacker again — and half of these women had sex with him at least ten more times.[39] For a variety of reasons, many women do not leave the men who rape them, just as many battered women do not leave their attackers.

Gilbert also claims that the Koss survey must be wrong because of the "tremendous gap" between its results and those from the National Crime Survey (NCS) conducted by the Bureau of Justice Statistics. He notes that the NCS shows that rape and attempted rape fell by 30 percent between 1978 and 1988, with a current rate of 1.2 rapes per 1,000 women.[40] However, Gilbert doesn't mention that the NCS figures he cites are based on a survey that never directly asked about rape (the question supposed to elicit rape responses asked, "Did anyone TRY to attack you in some other way?").[41] These official statistics are so unreliable that the estimate of rapes went from 130,260 in 1990 to 207,610 in 1991, even though there was obviously not a 50 percent increase in rapes in one year.[42]

Those who disagree with Gilbert are never treated as sincere researchers; instead they are said to be part of a feminist, man-hating conspiracy, which uses "advocacy numbers" to "alter consciousness" and falsifies data "not through outright deceit but through a more subtle process of distortion." Gilbert claims that these "radical feminists" want "the feminist-prescribed social inoculation of every woman" because they are "disaffected" women with an "ax to grind"; thus, "Advocacy numbers on sexual assault may resonate with their feelings of being, not literally raped, but figuratively 'screwed over' by men."[43]

In an article on "scientific fraud," Gilbert even accuses Koss of "a misrepresentation of findings to the public" and a deliberate, "breathtaking disregard for the facts" in order to "make them more compatible with the author's conclusion."[44] But Koss's indisputable conclusion is that "the great majority of rape victims conceptualized their experience in highly negative terms and felt victimized whether or not they realized that legal standards for rape had been met."[45] Like any survey on a controversial topic, Koss's study deserves criticism and debate. But Gilbert's depiction of an intellectual opponent as an academic fraud is typical of the extreme efforts to construct the myth of sexual correctness.

Although Gilbert has done no original research on the subject and shows gross ignorance of basic statistical methodology (he thinks that the biased National Crime Survey is more accurate than Koss's study simply because it used "much larger samples"), he is the most widely known critic of the date rape surveys.[46] Gilbert's critiques of Koss's survey have appeared in leading magazines and national newspapers, and they are treated as gospel by the opponents of the movement against date rape. His "refutation" of the date rape crisis is cited by other attacks on feminism such as Katie Roiphe's *The Morning After* and Christina Hoff Sommers's *Who Stole Feminism?*, both of which use Gilbert's critique as their primary source when they attack the Koss survey.[47] And the distortions multiply as they trickle down: after reading Roiphe's book, Mary Matalin concluded, in a *Newsweek* article, that 73 percent of the victims "affirmed they had intercourse when they didn't want to because a man gave them drugs or alcohol. Warping the statistics trivializes the far fewer but *real* cases of acquaintance rape."[48] In this amazing warping of the statistics (less than a third of the rape victims responded to this question, not 73 percent), Koss's data are assumed to reflect the mistakes of women who got a little too drunk.

Roiphe concludes that Gilbert's arguments show that the question of rape is "a matter of opinion" and "there is a gray area in which someone's rape may be another person's bad night." But rape is a matter of opinion only if you believe that being forced to have sex is a "bad night." Like Paglia and Gilbert, Roiphe sees a conspiracy against sexual desire in the attacks on date rape: "Somebody is 'finding' this rape crisis, and finding it for a reason." The real aim of these feminists, Roiphe tells us, is not to stop rape but to "call into question all relationships between men and women."[49] In the mythical world of sexual correctness, the fight to stop violence against women is perceived as just a feminist conspiracy to destroy men.

The rape deniers also attack rape surveys on the grounds that they convey (in Gilbert's words) "a view of women as helpless victims."[50] But accurately reporting violence against women does not mean that feminists see women as helpless victims. Certainly not all women are victims of rape, and even those who are should not be depicted as helpless. Contrary to what the rape deniers believe, the cause of women is not promoted by denying the truth about sexual violence. While there is always a danger that reporting the alarming levels of victimization may cause women to be viewed as victims who need to be "protected" by limiting their freedom, this must not lead us to deny the truth. It is a far greater insult to women when the rape deniers depict them as hysterical man bashers who invent charges of rape and suffer from delusional fears.

"Inappropriate Innuendo" and Other Rape Myths

In many cases, ridiculous definitions of rape are promoted by the media to show the "extremism" of the antirape movement even though no feminist supports them. A *Chicago Tribune* headline asked, "Should Regretted Sex Be Classified as Date Rape?" as if any feminist actually believed that it ever should.[51] Katie Roiphe writes, "People have asked me if I have ever been date-raped. And thinking back on complicated nights, on too many glasses of wine, on strange and familiar beds, I would have to say yes. With such a sweeping definition of rape, I wonder how many people there are, male or female, who haven't been date-raped at one point or another. People pressure and manipulate and cajole each other into all sorts of things all the time."[52] But it is Roiphe, not a feminist, who gives rape such a sweeping definition.

In 1990, *U.S. News & World Report* columnist John Leo wrote an alarming article about the redefinition of rape: "Driven by feminist ideology, we have constantly extended the definition of what constitutes illicit male behavior. Very ambiguous incidents are now routinely flattened out into male predation and firmly listed under date rape. In Swarthmore College's rape prevention program, 'inappropriate innuendo' is actually regarded as an example of acquaintance rape."[53] Leo's anecdote about Swarthmore seems to be a powerful indictment of radical feminism. But in reality, as Jon Wiener reveals in a *Nation* article, it just isn't true.

The phrase appeared in 1985 when a two-page discussion guide written by a student was sent out with a video to teach students about acquaintance rape. One sentence in the guide declared, "Acquaintance rape as will be discussed spans a spectrum of incidents and behaviors ranging from crimes legally defined as rape to verbal harassment and inappropriate innuendo." But this guide was never given to students and was never endorsed as official Swarthmore policy or the policy of its rape prevention program. Moreover, the statement in the guide was not a feminist redefinition of rape but a poorly written effort to point out that workshops should not be limited to date rape and might encompass a wider range of behavior. Jan Boswinkel, the student who wrote the guide, told Wiener: "I didn't mean to equate innuendo with rape when I wrote that guide."[54] Although a dean and a public relations assistant had unequivocally told a *U.S. News* fact checker that the statement did not represent Swarthmore policy, Leo chose to print the false information not just once but twice, claiming that Swarthmore's policy "comes from open distaste for heterosexual sex" and would "ruin sex for the next generation."[55]

The anecdote soon took on a life of its own and began popping up in story after story. A 1991 *Time* article on date rape says that "a Swarthmore College training pamphlet once explained that acquaintance rape 'spans a spectrum of incidents and behaviors, ranging from crimes legally defined as rape to verbal harassment and inappropriate innuendo.'"[56] The "inappropriate innuendo" lie was repeated in *Playboy, Time* (again), *Reason,* the *Washington Times* (twice), the *Detroit News and Free Press, Campus,* John Taylor's infamous article in *New York* magazine (reprinted in *Reader's Digest*), and a syndicated column by *San Jose Mercury News* writer Joanne Jacobs titled "Rape by Innuendo."[57] As Wiener notes, "The story demonstrates that several of America's mainstream publications, with tens of millions of readers, have no shame about using and reusing the same discredited quote as long as it serves an antifeminist political agenda."[58]

But the "innuendo is rape" story is not simply the product of the backlash against feminism. It is also a part of the broader attack on political correctness, in which simple facts are willfully twisted beyond recognition to serve a noble lie in the culture war against radicals of all kinds. The attacks on "rape crisis feminists" fit neatly into this larger culture war, in which the backlash against feminism merges with the myth of political correctness to create the phantom called "sexual correctness."

Just Say Yes: Antioch's Sexual Conduct Policy

While sexual assaults against women are concealed or ignored, the media give tremendous attention to isolated efforts that try to address these problems. Antioch College's sexual conduct policy was reviled and ridiculed across the country as the death of sex at feminist hands. Yet a 1994 article in *Newsweek* depicts Antioch College as a sexual paradise with nude dancing and coed shower orgies in the dorms—a far cry from the "Sexual Correctness" *Newsweek* published six months earlier, which declared ominously, "The much-publicized rules governing sexual intimacy at Antioch College seem to stultify relations between men and women on the cusp of adulthood."[59]

Antioch's sexual offense policy says that "verbal consent should be obtained with each new level of physical and/or sexual contact or conduct in any given interaction, regardless of who initiates it." The Antioch policy is often ridiculed because it includes excessive provisions like, "Asking 'Do you want to have sex with me?' is not enough. The request for consent must be specific to each act." However, the Antioch policy applies only to someone who wants to initiate sexual contact; mutually and simultaneously initiated conduct is not regulated. The policy also places responsibility on both partners: "The person with whom sexual contact/conduct is initiated is responsible to express verbally and/or physically her/his willingness or lack of willingness when reasonably possible." [60]

George Will attacked Antioch's policy as "sex amidst semicolons," and the fame of Antioch's policy even reached overseas when an article in the *London Times* reported, "A new, draconian sexual code has spread like a malevolent fungus through the universities of the United States. At the most militant, Antioch College in Ohio, students sign written consent forms before engaging in sex." [61] Like so much else about Antioch and "sexual correctness," this description of "written consent forms" is pure invention.

The *New York Times* accuses Antioch of "legislating kisses" and claims, "Worrying about worst-case scenarios is appropriate since, as one disgruntled student put it: 'This is a real policy. I can get kicked out over this.'" But the "worst-case" scenarios do not exist. Antioch Dean Marian Jensen reports that students abide by the policy "to the extent that they feel comfortable," which hardly sounds like "sexual correctness" police are prowling around campus. *Newsweek* pointed out that the handful of complaints that have come up under the policy have been mediated by Dean Jensen; in nearly two years, only one student was suspended under the policy. [62] Men are not being hauled off to jail or suspended from school for failing to get explicit permission before they kiss a woman, or vice versa. Despite its excesses, the Antioch sexual offense policy states a very simple and unobjectionable rule for proper conduct: It's wrong to touch someone in a sexual way against their will. But the importance of this unenforced policy is greatly exaggerated in the "sexual correctness" backlash against feminism.

While conservatives worry vocally about "sex amidst semicolons" at one tiny liberal arts college, they have nothing to say about religious colleges that impose a far more severe form of "sexual correctness" on students. Brigham Young University strictly restricts faculty and student behavior, prohibiting alcohol, tobacco, drugs (including caffeine), gambling, sex outside marriage (including homosexuality), pornography, shorts higher than the knee, beards, and braless women. [63] Students living off campus are forced to stay in "approved student housing" where all tenants, even nonstudents, must promise to adhere to university rules. In an example of "sexual correctness" far more intrusive than anything ever urged by feminists, one nonstudent tenant was recently threatened with eviction for posting pictures of scantily clad women in his own room.[64]

At Catholic University of Puerto Rico, a female professor who remarried without having her previous marriage annulled was dismissed in 1986.[65] Christian Colletti, a senior at Messiah College in Grantham, Pennsylvania, was expelled in 1994 because he and his wife had separated, even though he had not broken the school's rule against divorce.[66] Even at secular Boston University, conservative president John Silber ordered a ban on overnight visitors of the opposite sex in dorms. The conservatives who criticize Antioch for "legislating kisses" because it prohibits nonconsensual sex never mention the numerous colleges where students can be punished for having consensual sex.

In what might be seen as the ultimate example of "sexual correctness," the U.S. Naval Academy forced out cadet Joseph Steffan a few weeks before graduation, and refused to grant him a degree, because he acknowledged being gay, even though he said he had never engaged in homosexual acts. The U.S. Court of Appeals upheld the right of the Naval Academy to deny Steffan a degree solely on the basis of his sexual orientation.[67]

Sexual Harassment in Higher Education

Despite the fear of sexual correctness and anecdotes about false charges of sexual harassment, little has really changed on college campuses. Women are still frequent targets of harassment and discrimination. While some professors have been found guilty of sexual harassment for classroom activities that are at worst questionable, it is far more common for administrators to ignore sexual harassment, knowing that women are unlikely to pursue lengthy and often futile lawsuits.

Sexual harassment is pervasive in colleges and universities. A study of women seniors at Berkeley found that 29.7 percent had experienced some kind of sexual harassment from male instructors during their college years.[68] A study at East Carolina University in Greenville, North Carolina, found that more than a third of the women students had been sexually harassed by male teachers: 20.2 percent had experienced verbal harassment; 15.4 percent, leering or ogling; 13.6 percent, remarks about clothing, body, or sexual attitudes; 8.9 percent, unwanted touching, patting, or pinching; 4.9 percent, subtle pressures for sexual activity; 2.2 percent, demands for sexual favors; and 0.9 percent had been physically assaulted.[69] A 1983 study at Harvard discovered that harassment was pervasive among female students and faculty: 34 percent of undergraduates, 41 percent of graduate students, and 49 percent of untenured faculty reported being harassed.[70] A 1987 study of 356 female graduate students found that 60 percent had experienced sexual harassment, and 9 percent reported pressure to date or have sex with a faculty member.[71] A 1994 study of 30,000 faculty members at 270 institutions found that about 15 percent of the women (and 3 percent of the men) reported being sexually harassed at their current job.[72]

Sexual harassment has severe effects on the educational opportunities and professional work of students. Forty-four percent of the victims in the Berkeley study discontinued all contact with the instructor.[73] The Harvard study discovered that 15 percent of the graduate students and 12 percent of the undergraduates who had been harassed "changed their major or educational program because of the harassment."[74] A study at the University of Illinois found that 18.7 percent of the students who were harassed suffered a decline in academic performance, 23.4 percent changed courses to avoid the harasser, and 13.9 percent changed their field of study and career plans to avoid the harasser.[75]

But too often, colleges and universities do not take sexual harassment seriously. Jean Jew, a graduate student and later a faculty member at the University of Iowa, was one victim of sexual harassment on campus. Cartoons from pornographic publications with references to her written on them were taped on hallway walls. One professor repeatedly spread rumors that she was sleeping with her adviser, the chair of the department. Another faculty member, who was denied tenure, sought to discredit the chair by threatening to produce an eyewitness who supposedly saw them having sex—even though the witness, a janitor, denied seeing anything. A third faculty member yelled at her in the hallway, "There goes that slut now!" Obscene graffiti about her sexual orientation appeared in the men's room. When she complained, the dean told her that "this is the sort of thing a single woman has to put up with."[76]

In 1983, Jew's promotion to full professor was voted down 5 to 3, with the recommendation that she stop collaborating with her former adviser. The same day she was evaluated, an obscene limerick about her was written in the men's restroom. The dean received anonymous letters calling her "Chinese pussy." A faculty panel investigating the situation concluded that Jew had been harassed and discriminated against, but the university did nothing to stop the harassment. When Jew sued the university, the university's lawyers tried to discredit her by asking about her use of birth control pills and the fact that her sister had worked as a Playboy bunny. The university declared in its closing statement, "Your Honor, this isn't sexual harassment. This is the way of the world."[77]

Annabelle Lipsett, a resident at the School of Medicine at the University of

Puerto Rico, left after three years because of the sexual harassment there: *Playboy* centerfolds covered the walls; a list of sexual nicknames for the female residents was posted; a sexually explicit drawing of Lipsett's body was put up on the bulletin board. She was repeatedly propositioned by other residents, who became hostile when she turned them down. Doctors kept her from operating and did not assign her to appropriate tasks. Her complaints to supervisors did nothing to stop the harassment. Lipsett was dismissed (ironically enough, on the ground of behavioral problems), and her appeal was denied.

The courts found that Lipsett had been harassed, and a jury awarded her $525,000 for sexual discrimination; however, a federal district court declared that she could not receive any damages under Title IX. The only punishment for the university was an injunction not to engage in future sex discrimination.[78] Although the law now allows financial penalties for harassment, legal cases are difficult to win against powerful institutions.

Administrators rarely take harsh measures to deal with sexual harassment. In 1984, the William Mitchell College of Law in St. Paul offered $4,000 each to eight women who charged the president with sexual harassment, and he was allowed to resign his post while remaining as a tenured professor there.[79] At Harvard University in the early 1980s, tenured government professor Jorge Dominguez harassed an untenured female colleague, Terry Karl, with sexual invitations, rape threats, and, finally, assault. Although Karl complained repeatedly, and Harvard found that this was "a serious abuse of authority," Dominguez was "punished" with a year's paid leave. Karl left Harvard in 1985, explaining, "I did not want to continue working in a hostile environment."[80] In 1994, the University of Houston paid a professor suspended for sexual harassment $200,000 to get him to leave. A campus judicial board had found H. Prentice Baptiste guilty of harassing a graduate student by "unwelcome intimate physical contact" — hugging her and reaching inside her pants when she was in his office.[81]

Often, only massive media attention forces a university to act. Frances Conley, a prominent neurosurgeon at Stanford University, announced in June 1991 that she would resign to protest the hostile environment for women in the medical school after Gerald Silverberg was appointed the chair of her department. Silverberg regularly referred to all women doctors and nurses as "honey." Conley notes, "In our earlier days, Silverberg would frequently ask me in front of a crowd to go to bed with him." More than twenty women came forward to testify that Silverberg had a negative impact on the environment for women. Only then did Stanford establish two special committees to deal with sexual harassment and sexism in the medical school.[82]

Sexual harassment has a strong connection to sex discrimination. Julia Bristor, a marketing professor at the University of Houston, says of her experiences in a business school at an unnamed major research university: "I found my clothes were subject to commentary no matter what I wore." And "two administrators consistently brushed against my lower back and ran their hands along my buttocks . . . ; on several occasions, a colleague petted me on the head or shoulder in front of other colleagues, as if to say I was his pet." Bristor also "constantly heard colleagues telling jokes that disparaged women." And "one colleague routinely greeted me, publicly and privately, as 'broad' or 'wench.' After I voiced my objection to these forms of address, he revised them to be more 'professional' — 'Madame chick,' for example." [83]

Perhaps the most alarming part of Bristor's story is the open sexism of faculty in their professional decision making. At a meeting held to decide whether or not to hire a woman who was finishing her Ph.D., "one colleague concluded that 'she's just going to get pregnant anyway.' Other stereotypes that influenced my colleagues' remarks included women as 'delicate'; as inveterate shoppers; as devoid of intelligence; and, at the other extreme, as subversive feminists." [84] When male professors refuse to respect female colleagues and students in their professional relations, it is not surprising to find a similar lack of respect in their professional evaluations.

Eileen Stenzel, an assistant professor of religious studies and philosophy at Saint Leo College in Florida, was not reappointed in 1986 because of "the difficulty [she had] communicating with others in an agreeable manner within the Division of Religious Studies and Philosophy." The acting chair of her department told her she was a superior teacher and scholar but lacked "a spirit of cooperation." When she asked for an explanation, Stenzel reports, "He then put his hand on my knee and said, 'The problem is that we're not buddies.'" According to Stenzel, this happened two months after a female student "had approached me concerning what she felt was inappropriate behavior" on the chair's part, including "verbal and physical behaviors that were sexual in nature, some of which had occurred in front of other students, and had caused her embarrassment and emotional stress." Stenzel also reports counseling other female students who had had similar experiences involving him. However, Stenzel did not file a sexual harassment complaint because Saint Leo did not have a grievance procedure and she was afraid of jeopardizing her job. Because she dealt with the problem of harassment directly, Stenzel was fired for not being "collegial" enough. [85]

But these legitimate sexual harassment cases rarely make the news. Instead, the media focus on dubious accusations and bungled official responses that violate the due process and free speech rights of the accused. It is true that some accusations of harassment are ridiculous, and that some penalties threaten academic freedom; but it is far more often the case that a university is simply unwilling to stop sexual harassment.

Nor is it true that charges of sexual harassment are primarily directed by feminists against professors who express conservative views. At Southern University in Baton Rouge, Louisiana, a student charged administrators with sexual harassment for telling him to "stay on top of [his project] because some students fall through the cracks." The student felt that this was a sexual innuendo because "God had given him a vision" that he was being harassed.[86] At Eastern Illinois University in Charleston, music professor Douglas DiBianco was accused of sexual and cultural harassment because he criticized Christianity and talked about phallic symbols. A student said she felt "culturally harassed" in his non-Western music class because he "slammed Christianity and other religions and said he preferred Buddhism." She also accused DiBianco of using examples of art by Robert Mapplethorpe, referring to Pinocchio's nose as a phallic symbol, and describing Snow White as "an anal-retentive, domineering woman."[87] In other cases, the response to a charge of sexual harassment is tinged with homophobia. At the University of Houston at Clear Lake, Chris Downs, an associate professor of psychology, was fired in August 1990 after a male student who had failed his course charged him with sexual harassment, even though two investigative committees had found no evidence that Downs was guilty. It took a campaign by the Texas Faculty Association and a vote of no-confidence by the faculty senate to get Downs reinstated.[88]

Some of the most famous examples of "sexual correctness" are based on exaggerated fears of censorship and repeated misreporting of the facts. Nancy Stumhofer, an English professor at the Penn State's Schuylkill campus, supposedly accused a famous painting—Goya's Naked Maja—of sexually harassing her, sparking newspaper headlines around the country like "Goosestepping on Goya." But Stumhofer never claimed that she had been "sexually harassed by the painting." She objected to the reproduction of a nude woman hanging directly behind her while she tried to teach a developmental English course because she could hear the male students laughing and making comments to each other as they stared at something directly behind me on the wall." While Stumhofer did not find the painting offensive, she wanted it moved from the classroom because she believed that the reactions of some male students distracted the class and silenced female students. As Stumhofer puts it, "It was hard for me to understand how anyone could construe moving paintings from a limited access classroom to an open access reading room in the Student Center as censorship."[89]

Ironically, a formal charge of sexual harassment was filed against Stumhofer by a faculty member and a maintenance worker after she distributed a portion of John Berger's book *Ways of Seeing*, which includes pictures of nude women. Yet none of the free-speech defenders who cried out against the "censorship" of *Naked Maja* said a word about this.[90]

Harassment codes can be abused by administrators who try to avoid negative publicity by violating the due process and free-speech rights of faculty. But conservatives say nothing when harassment charges are used to silence liberal ideas. Ohio State English professor and Vietnam veteran Phoebe Spinrad complained to the U.S. Department of Labor that the university was not in compliance with the Vietnam-Era Veterans Readjustment Act, which puts Vietnam veterans into the category of oppressed minorities. Spinrad claimed that she was being harassed because some faculty members posted "anti-military" material on their office doors. She said, "Looked at from the point of view of a vet, it was Swiftian. Imagine the outcry if there were pictured watermelon-eating blacks or bare-breasted women from auto calendars on the walls. Talk about hostile environment!"[91] By this logic, members of Vietnam Veterans against the War who put up antimilitary material could be accused of harassing themselves. The Department of Labor investigated and found the university in violation of the law because it allowed antimilitary beliefs to be expressed. The university was ordered to create affirmative action programs for Vietnam-era veterans and to keep the working environment free of harassment, intimidation, and coercion against veterans.[92] No conservatives spoke up to condemn this clear-cut violation of academic freedom; instead, Spinrad was praised in conservative journals like *Heterodoxy*.

The area of law that deals with sexual harassment is still being developed, and it is not hard to find examples of college administrators who are more concerned with public relations than with due process or freedom of speech. There is a danger that sexual harassment charges may be filed against teachers who engage students in serious academic discussions of sexuality. The answer is not to blame "sexual correctness" or claim that there is a national crisis of false charges of sexual harassment, but to ensure that clear procedures are followed by administrators and that academic freedom is protected.

The fear that women will start making false claims of sexual harassment is greatly exaggerated, much like the fear that they will invent charges of rape. The legal awards for sexual harassment are still quite small (until recently, they did not exist at all), and courts are reluctant to uphold sexual harassment except in the most extreme cases. Michael Crichton made more money from his novel *Disclosure* (about a woman who falsely accuses a man of sexual harassment) than any woman has ever been awarded in court for being sexually harassed. Few women are willing to undergo the pressure of a campus hearing or to spend years in litigation for an uncertain outcome. Women who blow the whistle on sexual harassment have little to gain and much to lose. Frances Conley realizes that what she did will ultimately be a career-ending move: "I will *not* advance further; I will *not* be an attractive candidate for positions at other academic institutions — *ever.*"[93] Jean Jew notes, "Academia is very small, very competitive, and very conservative. Universities don't want to buy trouble, and news travels fast. When someone's personal and professional reputation has been besmirched, there are very few institutions that would take a risk."[94]

The emerging law on sexual harassment does need to be refined, and free-speech concerns do need to be more fully addressed, but this doesn't change the fact that many women are the victims of sexual harassment on college campuses, and very few of their harassers are ever punished.

Conservative Correctness and the Attack on Feminism

Feminists in academia are frequently attacked as part of the campaign against sexual correctness. The field of women's studies is marginalized at most colleges and dismissed by critics like Christina Hoff Sommers as "not disciplined scholarship but feminist ideology."[95] Writing about women's studies and black studies programs, David Horowitz declares, "I think the university would be a lot healthier place if they were simply defunded."[96] Historian Page Smith believes that women's studies is "clearly out of hand." He calls it an "internal armed feminist camp" in the middle of a university and displays deep concern for its unhealthy "effect on male students."[97] A false impression has been created of women's studies as a powerful agent suppressing dissent within higher education while at the same time, the all-too-real harassment and censorship of feminists is entirely ignored in media reports of "sexual correctness."

After Professor Anita Hill testified to the U.S. Senate about Clarence Thomas's behavior, a group of Minnesota women raised $125,000 to create the Anita Faye Hill Professorship at the University of Oklahoma to study the rights of women in the workplace — enough money to qualify for matching funds from the state. Republican state representative Leonard Sullivan has led an effort to stop the professorship, declaring "All I want is to see Anita Hill in prison." Sullivan alleges that "the left-wing drafted Anita Hill, wrote the story and promised her a chair in return." Sullivan has proposed a state bill that would limit out-of-state fundraising for endowed chairs.[98]

Others who supported Anita Hill have suffered the consequences. Joel Paul, a law professor at American University whom Hill had told about the harassment, received death threats and faced a campaign of letters and phone calls attacking him, actions that delayed his tenure for six months. Harvard law professor Charles Ogletree—one of the lawyers who advised Hill—reports that there was "a great debate at Harvard as to whether or not an untenured professor had any business representing Professor Hill at this historic event."[99] Shirley Wiegand, one of Hill's best friends and also a law professor at the University of Oklahoma, faced a letter-writing campaign demanding her dismissal. David Swank, dean of the Oklahoma Law School and one of Hill's supporters, was forced out of his job because he defended Hill.[100] When Swank was proposed by the university president for a Regents' Professorship, it was turned down without explanation. University of Oklahoma president Richard Van Horn, who took early retirement in October 1993, received letters and phone calls every day from legislators and big donors still upset by the presence of Anita Hill.[101]

Sometimes the attacks on feminism take an extreme form. A feminist group at the University of Illinois in Urbana that held a twenty-four-hour "Encampment to End Sexual Violence" was repeatedly harassed. A group of teenagers and a group of students yelled at them while grabbing their own genitals, claiming that the women could be "cured." A man entered the roped-off camp area, yelled obscenities at the women, and battered one woman. Another man was arrested after calling the women "lesbo-bitches" and ripping two of their banners.[102]

At the University of Minnesota at Duluth, a female candidate for vice chancellor received numerous death and kidnapping threats, one of which warned: "Feminist bitch, don't come to Minnesota." Leaflets left in campus buildings in March 1992 threatened that the "Imperial Council of the Deer Hunter" would kill any professor who participated in workshops being held to improve the climate for women, and urged the assassination of a female history professor critical of the university's treatment of women.[103]

At Northwestern University, twenty feminists were investigated and fingerprinted after a package suspected of containing a bomb was sent to university president Arnold Weber. The package did not contain a bomb. It held some feminist material and a letter said to include "explosive rhetoric." The suspects, U.S. postal investigator Dennis Peil said, included anyone on campus who had written feminist editorials, members of women's groups, students in women's studies classes, and victims of sexual assault.[104]

On 6 December 1989, Marc Lepine armed himself and took over an engineering class at the University of Montreal. He separated the female students from the men, shouted, "You're all a bunch of feminists," and proceeded to murder fourteen women over a span of twenty minutes with his semiauto-matic rifle before killing himself. Lepine's suicide note was a long tirade against feminism, complete with a list of ninety prominent women he wanted to kill. Lepine had failed his engineering exams and believed that the women occu-pied his rightful place.

It is tempting to dismiss Lepine as a lone lunatic, since obviously no one would defend his actions. But Lepine's madness and hatred were at least in part products of the misogyny around him. A few days later, at a vigil for the victims, a young female engineering student spoke out against the sexism among the engineering faculty. Later, at the engineering school's Skit Night, when this woman appeared, some people in the crowd chanted, "Shoot the bitch." After receiving a number of death threats, she dropped out of the uni-versity and moved away. Lepine's insane act, the worst mass murder ever at a North American college, was not just the violence of a lone lunatic; it was also the extreme expression of hatred against women.[105]

Women's Studies and the Feminist Oppressor

Many attacks on feminism depict feminist professors as the oppressors of dissenting students and faculty on college campuses. In a 1993 article pub-lished in *Mother Jones,* Karen Lehrman attacks women's studies for encour-aging a feminist orthodoxy that sacrifices academic knowledge for feel-good self-expression. Lehrman complains that women's studies classes are both too academic and not academic enough: "Sometimes they are filled with unin-telligible post-structuralist jargon; sometimes they consist of consciousness-raising 'psychobabble.'" Lehrman says that women's studies classes have too much discussion and yet too little discussion. "Many professors encourage all discourse—no matter how personal or trivial," she says, but "despite the womb-like atmosphere of the classrooms, I didn't see much student question-ing of the professor or the texts."[106]

Lehrman asserts that students are reluctant to voice dissenting views because of the "political intolerance and conformity on the part of fellow students." As an example she quotes an exchange from a class at Smith College in which one student defended the ban on gays in the military and complained, "I'm sick and tired of feeling that if I have a moral problem with something, all of a sudden it's: 'You're homophobic, you're wrong, you're behind the times, go home.'" Although the professor responded, "No one is saying that support of the ban is homophobic," a couple of students said that it was. According to the dissenting student, "Women's studies creates a safe space for p.c. individuals, but doesn't maintain any space for white Christians."[107] This example of "intolerance" suggests a double standard: even though the professor took a neutral position, Lehrman worries that the few students who expressed their opinions and criticized conservatives were stifling dissent. Obviously, if women's studies are to create a "safe space" for conservatives, then professors will be required to silence their students (or at least the ones with progressive views).

Daphne Patai and Noretta Koertge, authors of *Professing Feminism,* argue that women's studies programs are places where students "learn to be on the lookout for instances of injustice" and turn out women "zombified, who start uttering stock phrases." Their conclusions are based on anonymous interviews with thirty people involved in women's studies. But it isn't difficult to find thirty people to complain about intolerance and ideological conformity in any field. Patai and Koertge rely solely on these secondhand accounts, offering no evidence to back their claim that women's studies programs are "deeply subversive of the best academic traditions" and "have no place in the university."[108]

These critics are describing not a sudden crisis of indoctrination in women's studies but a problem teachers face in every department and students face in every class they take. Rightly or wrongly, many students feel that they will get a better grade by saying what the teacher wants to hear. This does not excuse some professors in women's studies for squelching dissent, but it shows that indoctrination is not peculiar to feminism. In my own experience, I have found more discussion and open debate in women's studies classes than almost anywhere else. "More" is not perfect, and women's studies teachers and students need to encourage more open debate, but the same is true of every field. I have found women's studies classes to be intellectually challenging courses that in no way resemble the caricatures offered by critics. I was never discouraged from taking a women's studies class because I was a man. In fact, the intimidation faced by men who take women's studies classes usually comes not from feminist teachers and students but from their antifeminist peers. Male students at Mercer University in Macon, Georgia, said they had been ridiculed by their friends for taking a women's studies course.[109]

According to their critics, feminists have taken control of universities. Christina Hoff Sommers claims that "campus feminists have made the American campus a less happy place, having successfully browbeaten a once outspoken and free faculty."[110] But it is difficult to believe that a small and marginal group of women could take control of all of academia and browbeat entire faculties. Most women's studies programs are marginally funded and use "borrowed faculty." At Hunter College, for example, "We have no power

to hire, fire, or promote anybody," according to former director Rosalind Pet-
chesky.[111]

Sommers's interviews with anonymous professors reflect the widespread
bias against those who express feminist ideas. One English professor told her,
"It is very difficult to teach students who have been trained to take the 'feminist
perspective.' They have this steely look in their eyes. They distrust everything
you say. . . . You cannot argue with them."[112] Not only are such extreme fears
of criticism paranoid, but one can readily imagine the precarious position
of a feminist student whose grade depends on a professor who thinks she is
"steely-eyed" and incapable of reason.

Women report that they are careful to avoid the taint of being labeled a
feminist. Duke English professor Cathy Davidson writes, "Many female students lament, for example, how they have had to hide their feminist principles
and even subdue their personality in order not to offend this or that professor."[113] Young feminist writer Paula Kamen "always knew that coming out as
a feminist wouldn't win me any popularity contests. . . . When going out in a
group or on anything even vaguely resembling a date, I found myself hiding
the painful truth of my feminist affiliations — as if I were harboring some grisly
genetic disorder or family curse that would test even the truest and most
faithful of loves."[114]

Lisa Navin Trivedi's adviser in the history department at the University of
Chicago told her "there are no women as such" and declared, "Gender is not
a significant historiographical issue." Trivedi notes, "He truly felt that historical work which addressed women or gender issues, especially in his own field,
was pointless." The discouragement Trivedi faced was not simply because she
wanted to study women; it was also because she was a woman. Her adviser
"wondered aloud whether a woman with plans for marriage could be 'serious'
about scholarship." This adviser also referred to a female professor in the department as the "wicked witch of the West." Trivedi concludes: "I wish that
mine were an unusual story in the academy today, but it is far from it. Many of
my women friends in graduate school face the very situations I have described
here, ranging from sexual and verbal harassment to gender discrimination."[115]

Adriane Fugh-Berman, who graduated from Georgetown Medical School in
1988 (where surgeons would tell "jokes" like "Why are women's brains smaller
than men's? Because they're missing logic!"), reports what happened when
some female medical students started a women's group: "Announcements of
our meetings were defaced and women in the group began receiving threatening calls at home from someone who claimed to be watching them and who
would then accurately describe what she was wearing. One woman received

obscene notes in her school mailbox, including one that contained a rape threat. I received insulting cards in typed envelopes at my home address; my mother received similar cards at hers."[116]

Feminist professors hold a marginal position in academia. Paula Caplan notes that "some places simply will take great pains to avoid hiring you if you are known to be a feminist." A woman with a Ph.D. in business was told by her department head that "she did not fit in with the group, that they did not like her participation on the university Women's Studies committee and she was advised to resign; they did not like the feminist content in her courses."[117] A female speech communication professor was denied tenure because, in the words of the official notification, "your focus on gender and communication does not fit within the mainstream of disciplinary scholarship."[118] In a liberal arts college humanities department (where no woman had been tenured in nearly twenty years), four men were granted tenure while the only woman being considered was fired; one colleague commented that "she could hardly be described as a scholar, but only as a feminist."[119]

Candace Vogler, a philosopher at the University of Chicago, was warned at another university not to write about women until she received tenure. Political scientist Lynn Sanders says that even today feminist studies are "not regarded as having real academic worth"; those who study feminist theory must do so "in addition to something else."[120] A female professor who published two articles in scholarly women's studies journals during her first year at a major research university had her work dismissed: "She was classified as 'creative' but 'unproductive' by her evaluation committee, which regarded her women's studies articles as 'political.' The committee also expressed concern about whether her teaching was also 'politicized.'"[121]

Women's studies professors must continually justify their existence. "Anyone who has spent time in a women's studies department knows just how ridiculous is the currently fashionable notion that universities have been captured by feminist scholars and their acolytes," Deborah Cohen notes. "I remember feeling besieged—but not by sympathizers. There were people who made rude comments about women's studies at official faculty dinners, women's studies majors who had difficulty getting into classes in other departments, tussles with departments that refused to tenure scholars who just happened to belong to the Committee on Degrees in Women's Studies."[122]

Athena Theodore conducted a study of female professors in the mid-1980s that revealed numerous cases of hostility to women. Theodore discovered that women identified as feminists found it difficult to be hired. One woman reported, "On my own time, I speak and lobby for ERA. My college president told me that he had received complaints from influential persons (whom he would not identify) concerning my work for ERA. He acknowledged that he could not stop my activity on my own time, but told me to insert into the introductions of my speeches that I was not speaking for the university. . . . I have a feeling that any further promotions will not be forthcoming; I'm 'too controversial,' as our president puts it." [123]

Theodore describes a number of examples of feminists denied jobs because of their politics, including a geographer: "She has applied for 60 jobs and not given one interview because the word is out that she is a feminist. This is the 'kiss of death' in geography, which she describes as one of the most conservative academic disciplines." Theodore concludes, "Women's studies courses, even when part of the established curriculum, are highly suspect, as is also a feminist perspective in the classroom." [124]

One woman was denied tenure because her "feminist perspective affected her classroom teaching." Another female professor was denied tenure after she published her feminist views in sociology; she was told to "wear skirts and stroke a few male egos and she would not have so much trouble." A woman denied tenure was told by a member of the all-male tenure committee that everybody kept in mind that her husband could support her. A woman who initiated a petition-signing campaign for a woman's center on campus was told by an administrator that she should not count on continuing to teach "because you choose to involve yourself in activities not directly associated with your teaching." [125]

The complaints of the women Theodore interviewed were "replete with objections related to loss of academic freedom" due to "the fact of being feminists." One woman "was penalized because of the nature of the courses I taught, my research which focused on women's issues, and my participation in the Women's Studies Program." Theodore's conclusion is that feminism weighed heavily in the firing process. [126] It is true that some feminists are highly regarded and well treated in some departments at some universities. But the unpublicized fact is that in most departments at most colleges, colleagues and administrators view a feminist professor with suspicion.

At the University of Alaska at Anchorage, the dean of the School of Nursing and Health Sciences attempted to remove Rose Odum, a tenured professor of nursing, for "using her classroom as a pulpit for feminism." [127] Dean Laura MacLachlan included "unwillingness to respond to verbal greetings by dean and selected faculty" as one of the charges against Odum. [128] Odum insisted on the right to speak freely in her classes and expressed her fears for "the weakening of academic freedom and [the] job security tenure is supposed to represent. Will professors be inhibited in speaking out on controversial issues?" [129]

A faculty panel listened to eighteen hours of testimony from faculty and students, and concluded that Odum had shown "a gross insensitivity to colleagues and an inability to respond to legitimate student concerns." Although the panel recommended only a reprimand, the dean decided to dismiss her.[130] But the Alaska Supreme Court ruled that the panel (and the dean) had acted illegally and ordered her reinstatement. Students and faculty told Odum that they were afraid to testify on her behalf because they feared retribution from the dean; and also that two of the panel members were employees of the dean, who was present during the entire hearing. The Administrative Procedures Act requires an impartial hearing with an independent hearing officer and full legal representation; none of this occurred.[131]

Removal of a tenured professor is extraordinarily rare. It is almost never done for incompetence and is unusual even in cases of professional misconduct, including sexual harassment. The idea that a tenured professor could be fired for focusing too much on feminism — or any other theory — is astonishing. Academic freedom means the freedom of professors to decide what they should teach. Even today, when the politically correct are said to control universities, the situation is the same as it has always been: most of the teachers who face dismissal or official punishment are on the left, not the right.

Cecilia Farr, an English professor at Brigham Young University, is a feminist who has publicly argued for abortion rights, although she is personally opposed to abortion. Farr spoke in 1992 at a prochoice rally at the state capitol, where she carefully stated that she represented neither the Church of Latter-Day Saints nor Brigham Young University.[132] Nevertheless, a few months later, Associate Provost Todd Britsch wrote a letter to Farr's department chair noting that the governing board considered Farr's views on abortion in conflict with the Mormon church and accusing Farr of violating an agreement not to make public statements on abortion. (Farr denies making such an agreement, but the idea that faculty might be forced to make a pledge of silence is frightening in itself.) Britsch instructed Neal Lambert, the English department chair, to notify Professor Farr that she had violated "her university citizenship obligations" and told him to "place a copy of this memo in Professor Farr's file for consideration in any reviews of her performance."[133] Provost Bruce Hafen wrote to Farr that her views on abortion "can appear to convey disloyalty to the Church and its leaders, which in turn undermines the religious faith of your students."[134] Hafen also wrote, "A central question for you and for your review committee is whether your re-publication of your January, 1992, speech . . . shows a disregard of your citizenship obligation under the university's standards for continuing status reviews." Farr wrote back to Provost Hafen, asking for clarification about what she had done wrong, "so I don't make the same mistakes again."[135]

In the meantime, Farr was undergoing her third-year status review, normally a fairly routine stop on the tenure track. Department chair Neal Lambert praised her as "charismatic" and "exciting" with "considerable ability" as a scholar. He noted that Farr had a record "few third-year review candidates can field" and praised her teaching. Despite Lambert's praise, a college panel criticized Farr, and the university rejected her appeal, declaring that "her collegial behavior seem[ed] to place her own interests above the interests of the university community."[136]

People at the university have told Farr, "if you don't stop being such an outspoken feminist, you could lose your job."[137] Another professor was warned by the faculty council that her feminist views were "disturbing" and "partisan."[138] A study by the Ad-Hoc Faculty Committee on Academic Freedom compared Farr's record with those of thirteen candidates who passed their third-year review. Farr had published more articles than the average, had presented papers at seventeen conferences (six times the average), and had better teaching evaluations.[139]

In addition to the efforts of the BYU administrators to control Farr's public statements, Del Gardner, the chair of the Faculty Council on Rank and Tenure, admitted: "If the scholarship had been very strong, the citizenship may not have been a sufficient problem."[140] "Citizenship" refers to Farr's failure to follow the conservative Mormon positions on feminism and abortion. Officials at BYU openly declare that a professor's political views affect the tenure process, and that those who disagree in any way with the Mormon orthodoxy risk their jobs. More than fifteen professors have publicly announced that they are seeking other jobs in order to escape the new restrictions on freedom of thought at Brigham Young.[141]

After Lynn Kanavel Whitesides, president of the feminist Mormon Women's Forum, organized a protest against the dismissal of Farr and another BYU professor, she was "disfellowshipped" and expelled by church authorities. The church also excommunicated five scholars and writers for their liberal ideas, including Maxine Hanks, who wrote a book on Mormon feminism. Church leader Boyd Packer told a Mormon conference that feminists, homosexuals, and "so-called intellectuals and scholars" pose a serious threat to the faith.[142]

But the repression of faculty dissenters by BYU and other religious colleges has drawn little criticism from the civil libertarians who cry "political correctness." The *National Review College Guide,* which claims that "academic freedom is better respected at most religious schools than at many well-known secular colleges and universities," strongly recommends Brigham Young because "the sense of the sacred at BYU does not diminish its commitment to academic freedom." [143]

It's the antifeminists, not the feminists, who want to eliminate certain classes and departments according to their own standards of "conservative correctness." An English professor at Clemson University in South Carolina attacked his department for approving a course titled "Feminist Literary Criticism," which he said would be "mandating a regular indoctrination in feminism." [144] As editor of the conservative Princeton alumni magazine *Prospect,* Dinesh D'Souza urged the university to abolish the women's studies department "rather than let Women's Studies fester and fall away in scabs." D'Souza would allow some "worthwhile" women's studies classes into the regular curriculum but warned professors that they would have to publish extensively and that "an account of their sexual experiences would not suffice." [145]

Camille Paglia attacks the "intolerance" of feminists and urges that they be fired, but she refuses to debate her opponents. When Paglia was asked at a 1992 panel why she refuses to appear on-stage with academic feminists, she replied, "Honey, I am out of your league." [146] Camille Paglia declared on CNBC's *Equal Time,* "We must smash women's studies. Drive them out. Break the power structure. . . . Women's studies people have shown their true Stalinism."

By presenting a cartoon caricature of "Stalinist" feminism, these critics argue that it should be destroyed rather than debated. Although certainly there are feminists who deserve criticism for failing to encourage dissent in their classrooms, it is the intolerance *against* feminists, not the intolerance of feminists, that most often threatens the academic freedom of students and teachers.

Anyone standing on the quad of a typical research university in the middle of the afternoon can still see a familiar sight: a sea of white students hurrying to classes taught by overwhelmingly white male professors. The backlash against affirmative action programs has produced an increasingly popular rhetoric of "reverse discrimination" that depicts the white male as the helpless victim of affirmative action, shut out of academic jobs and denied educational opportunities while "unqualified" minorities fill the university halls. But by every indicator available—acceptance to selective schools, hiring in full-time tenure-track positions at top universities, admittance into leading graduate schools—white males are still doing dramatically better than any other group, often better than they deserve on merit alone. Whether by institutional policies benefiting well-off whites (such as preferences for children of alumni) or by the old-fashioned advantages gained from racial discrimination, white males are clearly far from oppressed. Although the view of affirmative action as reverse discrimination that destroys the careers of white students and professors is not supported by the evidence, anecdotes about white males unable to get jobs because they are all designated for minorities continue to be told. There is an ever-widening gap between the reality of continuing racism and the myth of reverse discrimination.

Conservatives have created the legend of the lonely white male Ph.D. who, like some kind of postmodern Marlboro Man, wanders the frontiers of academia, seeking any work he can find in the unfair and arbitrary world of faculty hiring, while women and minorities race up a magic path to the top. The myth that white males can't get hired persists at the same time that white males continue to be the largest group given jobs in academia.

Reverse Discrimination and the Oppressed White Male

Perhaps the best example of the rhetoric of reverse discrimination comes from Robert Weissberg, a professor of political science at the University of Illinois at Urbana-Champaign. In a 1993 *Forbes* article, Weissberg says that "a particularly painful cost of affirmative action is the 'noncareers' of bright white males who either bail out of graduate school or wind up with endless one-year temporary positions at third-rate schools. . . . They probably never will get an academic job interview, let alone a job offer. At the same time, of course, black, Hispanic and female job candidates, many of whom are not very well qualified, are on national tours going from one campus to the next receiving the most outrageous offers. All this often comes as a terrible shock to the victims." [1]

Weissberg is not alone in his alarming claims. Philosophy professor Steven Yates concludes, "Given the current climate, I would not advise a really first-rate student who happens to be white and male to pursue a teaching career in the humanities." [2] Richard Blow, a doctoral student in the history of American civilization at Harvard, writes in the *New Republic:* "If I weren't a white male, I'd have little difficulty getting a teaching job when I finish my dissertation. Female and minority Ph.D.s are so much in demand, they're courted like baseball's free agents. My female and minority peers will be snapped up as soon as they enter the job market. Merit is moot." [3]

Even liberal commentators have accepted this myth of the Great White Hopeless Male, standing with Ph.D. in hand on the unemployment line, begging for a level playing field. Philosopher Richard Rorty declares, "It is quite true that if you are a recent Ph.D. in the humanities or social sciences, your chances of finding a teaching job are very good if you are a black female and pretty bad if you are a white male." [4]

E. L. Roundtree, a doctoral candidate in history at Ohio University, objects to an advertisement for a faculty position in the American Historical Association's journal *Perspectives* that included this statement: "The University of —— is building a multicultural faculty and strongly encourages applications from female and minority candidates. Preference will be given to applicants who can serve well an increasingly diverse University community." Roundtree calls the second sentence "blatantly discriminatory" and warns: "The quality of teaching and scholarship at American universities will decline if this goal of building a multicultural faculty becomes paramount in the hiring process, replacing the accepted criteria of teaching and research ability and professional competence." [5] Roundtree's attack on "this headlong rush into a new age of discrimination" reflects a common view of affirmative action as reverse discrimination; another male doctoral candidate accuses senior historians of "simply shutting a large group of younger scholars out."[6]

The attacks persist in spite of the fact that more than three quarters of the faculty in the history profession are white males—the same proportion who received Ph.D.s between 1946 and 1988.[7] The National Research Council reports that in 1989, 57.6 percent of men with new history doctorates were hired, compared with only 53.6 percent of women Ph.D.s in history.[8] The understandable resentment of white males at the difficulty every new Ph.D. faces in a tough job market has been converted into an attack on affirmative action.

The statistical evidence strongly suggests that white males are not the victims of reverse discrimination. A 1992 survey of full-time faculty found that white males tend to hold the higher-paying jobs at research universities, while women and minorities fill the ranks of less prestigious colleges. The faculty breakdown at research universities was as follows: white males, 66.5 percent; white women, 21.0 percent; African Americans (both men and women), 3.2 percent, and Hispanics (both men and women), 1.9 percent. By contrast, at low-paying two-year colleges (the only category where white men were not the majority of the faculty), 6.1 percent of the teachers were black, 4.1 percent were Hispanic, and 37.7 percent were white women. Clearly, minorities and women hold the least desirable faculty jobs, exactly the opposite of what the reverse discrimination rhetoric says is happening.[9]

Women continue to face high hurdles in academia, and the situation is not improving. At research universities, male professors earn $7,000 more than women, male associate professors earn $3,000 more, male assistant professors earn $3,400 more, and male instructors earn $2,000 more than women. Between 1975 and 1993, salary differentials between male and female faculty increased, and the proportion of men who were tenured rose from 64 to 71 percent while the percentage of women with tenure held steady at 47 percent.[10] A recent study of higher education administrators concludes, "Being female is found to have significant direct effects on the prior placement of the individual in positions as well as on the status, salary, and responsibility achieved as a result of promotion."[11]

The best way to test whether minorities and women are being given preference over white males in faculty hiring is to look at the disparity between tenure track positions (assistant professors) and non–tenure track posts (instructors and lecturers), which are usually filled by those who cannot get tenure track jobs. In the fall of 1992, at all institutions, white men were 47.5 percent of all assistant professors but only 44.1 percent of instructors and

29.6 percent of lecturers. By contrast, blacks were only 5.8 percent of assistant professors but 6.9 percent of instructors and 6.3 percent of lecturers, and Hispanics filled all three positions in roughly equal numbers. Women of all ethnic groups were 42.5 percent of assistant professors, 47.7 percent of instructors, and 61.9 percent of lecturers.[12] Only 80.9 percent of the women held tenure track appointments, versus 92.5 percent of the men. At research universities, there were 54 percent more male assistant professors than female ones, but 62 percent more full-time female instructors than male ones.[13]

The fact that blacks, Hispanics, and women are more likely to be instructors off the tenure track than assistant professors on the tenure track reflects the lack of diversity among the assistant professors hired in the last decade. If women and minorities are gaining tremendous advantages from affirmative action, why do they hold the less desirable part-time and non–tenure track positions? And why are their numbers in academia still so small?

One reason is that discrimination remains a pervasive fact of life in academia. Law professor Julius Getman notes, "The evaluation of women for appointment and tenure in the early 1980s was often marked by barely suppressed feelings of resentment. In my experience, almost every time a woman was evaluated for promotion or tenure during that period, some hostility was manifest." Getman observes that "many of the worst cases of academic injustice" involve women "who have most directly posed a challenge to traditional elitist standards."[14] But legal action is rarely pursued because it is so difficult and costly, and women who file sex discrimination charges are unlikely to be hired by other universities.

Some of the most persuasive evidence for the importance of affirmative action comes from intelligent opponents like Kenny Williams, a black professor of English at Duke University who is also a member of the National Association of Scholars. Although she opposes Duke's affirmative action plan, Williams says that it has not brought in unqualified professors: "Although we are limited in number, most are highly qualified. Frequently they surpass their white colleagues." Many black assistant professors do not receive tenure, she says, because blacks are held to a higher, not a lower, standard: "The administration is very strict about tenure for the black faculty. When they deal with white faculty, it's often a matter of cronyism." Williams believes that academic connections are far more important than affirmative action preferences or even merit: "White professors without substantial publication records manage to get tenure, if they're cronies of whoever is in power. We have some whites here who are full professors with only one book to their credit. I don't think, under ordinary circumstances, a one-book black would make it through the system unless that person had a great deal of political support somewhere in the university." [15] The facts presented by Williams stand in sharp contrast to Abigail Thernstrom's claim that "in the hiring process, if there is a requirement for tenure slots to have one major book published with a respectable press, that requirement is waived for Blacks and Hispanics." [16] If black professors, despite affirmative action, are actually being forced to meet higher standards and are not receiving special preference, then the elimination of affirmative action would result in an even more unfair system. Affirmative action helps to counteract racial discrimination in the incestuous world of academia, where personal prejudices and connections often prevail in the backroom decisions of university departments.

Despite the paucity of women and minorities in leading faculty positions, affirmative action is blamed for destroying academic standards and oppressing innocent white males. Perhaps the most remarkable example of the "white male as victim" rhetoric is English professor Ward Parks's essay, "Anti-Male Discrimination in the Profession." [17] Parks's "evidence" of antimale discrimination is the hiring practices in his department at Louisiana State University, where five men and four women were hired over a period of five years. Parks explains that this appearance of equality really disguises inequality because more women than men were selected, but declined the job.

What Parks actually describes is the tokenism produced by affirmative action hiring programs. Because departments are under pressure to consider women and minorities as job candidates, they seek out the best-qualified women candidates along with a group of male candidates, and sometimes offer a position to a highly qualified woman. Since the same top-notch women are sought after by other colleges, the best female candidate may receive numerous offers, but she can only accept one. The other departments, having satisfied the token requirement of offering a job to a woman, then go on to the next candidate, almost invariably a white male, saying that they tried to hire a woman. The end result is that a few highly qualified women and minorities are sought after, but the overall diversity of top faculties across the country does not change.

The truth is that affirmative action has failed to breach the barriers caused by discrimination. A study of Ph.D.s in English by the Modern Language Association found that even the most recent women Ph.D.s were much worse off than their male colleagues. While women earned more than half of the English Ph.D.s in the 1980s, they were less likely than men to get tenure track positions. Only 56 percent of the women who earned English Ph.D.s from 1981 to 1986 had tenure track jobs in 1987, compared with 77.8 percent of the men, a disparity that extends to tenure and promotion. Among English Ph.D.s who graduated from 1976 to 1980, twice as many men as women were full professors by 1987.[18] It is astonishing that while men earn 12 percent fewer new doctorates than women but receive 22.3 percent more of the tenure track positions, complaints like Parks's about antimale discrimination are considered the unquestioned truth by critics of affirmative action.

The same absence of any evidence of affirmative action can be seen in the field of political science. Among Ph.D. students or graduates seeking jobs in political science from 1982 to 1992, 70.6 percent of the women and 69.5 percent of the men were successful. That is, women were given no special preference. Quite the contrary: 48 percent of the men in 1992 got the most desirable jobs at Ph.D.-granting institutions, compared to only 39 percent of the women. Nor were there any signs of greater success in the job market for minorities in 1992: 74 percent of African Americans got jobs, about the same proportion as whites, but only 62 percent of Asian Americans were successful. Although 88 percent of the Latinos were placed in political science jobs, this was a statistical aberration caused by the small number of Latino Ph.D.s, since only 50 percent of Latinos got jobs in 1990.[19]

These discrepancies also hold true in math and science. Although women make up 50 percent of undergraduate mathematics majors (and get better grades in all subjects), they are only 24 percent of the U.S. citizens receiving doctorates in math. The American Mathematical Society reports that according to the latest data, 85.5 percent of males and 88.2 percent of females with new doctorates were employed—a gap of only five jobs. A study of twenty-four top math departments found that women were hired for only 16 percent of postdoctoral positions in 1993. And a mere 16 percent of the new Ph.D.s hired by the leading mathematics departments were women. In addition, only four out of three hundred tenured professors in the top ten math departments are women, and only about 4 percent of tenure track positions at these top schools are held by women, indicating that women still face barriers to getting top jobs. Women in mathematics are also paid less than men, take longer to achieve tenure, and are less likely to be full professors.[20]

The disproportionate benefits for white males over disadvantaged groups begin in graduate school, which helps account for the small number of minorities who receive Ph.D.s. A 1993 study by the National Research Council found that only 25.4 percent of black doctoral students (versus 35 percent of Hispanics, 45.1 percent of whites, and 61.4 percent of Asians) received research assistantships. Black and Hispanic students were also more likely than whites to need loans.[21] Among 1992 Ph.D. recipients, 45.2 percent of whites finished school without debt, compared with only 36 percent of blacks and Hispanics. More than 26 percent of blacks and Hispanics were at least $15,000 in debt, compared with only 16.9 percent of the whites.[22] Nor can these discrepancies be explained by the concentration of black graduate students in fields such as education, where fellowships and assistantships are rarer. A 1985 study found that in the physical sciences, 42 percent of all students received research assistantships, but only 17 percent of the black students received them.[23] And even in education, 28 percent of the foreign Ph.D. students received financial support from their universities, versus only 12 percent of the black American Ph.D. students.[24]

The rhetoric of reverse discrimination helps explain why blacks and whites have vastly different perceptions of the effects of affirmative action and discrimination on employment opportunities in academia. A survey on tenure review found that only 6.1 percent of white males in academia believed that minorities are at a disadvantage in the tenure process, while 23.2 percent of white females and 58 percent of blacks believed this.[25] In the view of white males, affirmative action provides minorities with substantial advantages; to minorities, affirmative action is of minor consequence and does not compensate for the disadvantages they face from discrimination.

There are abuses of affirmative action, when tokenism takes the place of an honest evaluation of qualifications. There are cases of white males interviewing for jobs that have already been "reserved" for a woman or a minority. But there are also many cases of women or minorities being interviewed for jobs to satisfy the demands of affirmative action when a white male has already been chosen for the position.[26]

Women and minorities are favored over white males in some cases. It would be inaccurate to deny the existence of affirmative action in faculty hiring (or to ignore the important justifications for it). But it is a mistake to regard affirmative action as the only deviation from objective "merit" in the hiring process. Cronyism, personality conflicts, and outright bias are present throughout academia when choices for faculty and tenure decisions are made behind closed doors on the basis of highly subjective evaluations. Paul Lauter observes that "for every abuse of 'affirmative action' — and there have been some, to be sure — I can tell many a story of academic favoritism, incompetence, and silliness."[27] Affirmative action in faculty hiring is necessary to ensure equal treatment for women and minority candidates.

One of the most irrational factors in faculty hiring is the reputation of the university that granted the applicant's Ph.D. According to one study, 83 percent of the faculty at the top twelve graduate schools have degrees from these same twelve universities.[28] Much of this is because the top graduate schools attract the best applicants. But equally important are the academic prejudices and the old boy network reflected by the preference for Ph.D.s from top schools, regardless of their actual merit. It took an aggressive affirmative action program for one department to discover that a minority applicant with a Ph.D. from an obscure university and no letters of recommendation from famous scholars was actually well qualified for the job.[29]

The reverse discrimination rhetoric helps obscure the continuing discrimination against minorities. Jared Taylor, the author of the anti–affirmative action book *Paved with Good Intentions,* cites a recent study of identically qualified whites and blacks who applied for entry-level jobs in service industries. In 13 percent of the cases, both were offered jobs; 5 percent of the time, only the black got the job; and 15 percent of the time, only the white got the job. Amazingly, Taylor concludes, "It would be hard to argue that this is evidence of large-scale, antiblack bias." The fact that a white person was 55 percent more likely to be offered a job than an identically qualified black person is not a problem for Taylor, apparently, nor is it evidence of "large-scale" bias. This conclusion is all the more bizarre considering that Taylor argues that whites suffer pervasive discrimination in America as a result of the evils of affirmative action. If this is reverse discrimination, imagine what "equal opportunity" looks like in the eyes of the critics of affirmative action.[30]

Other studies have confirmed that affirmative action is essential for minorities merely to receive equal treatment. In the absence of strong efforts at diversity, discrimination is virtually inevitable. A recent study of seventy-six business students asked them to select the best candidates from a group of four applicants—two white and two black—who were equally qualified. One group of students was given a memo about the need to hire a black. A second group got a memo urging them to hire a white. A third control group received no memo. The groups that received memos tended to prefer blacks or whites, respectively. What surprised researchers was the behavior of the control group, which was virtually identical to that of the group receiving the prowhite memo. The "unbiased" control group was half as likely to select blacks as would be expected by randomly choosing between equally qualified candidates.[31]

It is clear that discrimination against minorities in the workplace is far more extensive and powerful than affirmative action programs there. And despite the belief of many professors and administrators that colleges are morally superior to other employers, the fact is that higher education is a place where affirmative action is often attacked but rarely effective in the face of pervasive discrimination.

Asian Americans, Whites, and Berkeley

Revelations of bias against Asian Americans at elite colleges during the 1980s were also misleadingly invoked to attack affirmative action. The real cause for the discrimination against Asian Americans was not affirmative action policies for blacks and Hispanics, however, but the fear that too few whites were being admitted. Preferential treatment for whites was transformed into part of the myth of reverse discrimination.

In the late 1970s and the 1980s, Asian-American enrollment skyrocketed at elite colleges and universities; the number of Asian-American students increased by 62 percent from 1976 to 1982 alone. But as the number of Asian-American students was increasing, some suspected that admissions officers were trying to limit that increase. At the University of California at Berkeley, Asian enrollment quadrupled from 1966 to 1980. But in 1984, the number of Asians admitted dropped 21 percent from the previous year. For Professor L. Ling-chi Wang, this was confirmation of some of the anecdotal evidence of discrimination he had heard, such as an English professor telling a faculty meeting that Asian students deficient in English "should not be here at all; just because they are good in math and science doesn't mean they make good undergraduate students." Patrick Hayashi, a member of the Office of Undergraduate Affairs at the time, said that "some of the people present seemed to be deliberately searching for a standard which could be used to exclude Asian immigrant applicants." A study found that the number of Asian-American applicants had increased dramatically from 1978 to 1983, even though the number of Asians admitted had barely grown.[32]

Berkeley's public relations director, Ray Colvig, explained that Berkeley had been trying to reduce its undergraduate population from 31,000 to 29,000 and said that "the Asians are far, far overrepresented in terms of percentage of the population."[33] A state auditor found that whites had a higher admission rate than Asians from 1981 to 1987, despite having no better academic credentials; and in 1986 and 1987, Asians' SAT scores were still twenty points above whites' scores, a sign that Berkeley was limiting the admission of Asian Americans and selecting only the best of the group.[34]

Conservatives blamed affirmative action for the discrimination against Asian Americans. United States Attorney General William Reynolds claimed, "The phenomenon of a 'ceiling' on Asian-Americans admissions is the inevitable result of the 'floor' that has been built for a variety of other favored racial groups."[35] James Gibney wrote in the *New Republic*, "If Asians are underrepresented based on their grades and test scores, it is largely because of affirmative action for other minority groups."[36] In 1989, Congressman Dana Rohrabacher (R-California) introduced a bill condemning universities for illegal quotas and bias against Asian Americans. But Henry Der, a member of the Berkeley Task Force that drew attention to the bias, accused him of "using our issue to try to undo affirmative action for all minority groups, and we can't go along with that."[37]

Many conservatives who raised the issue were far more concerned about white students being admitted than Asians. Berkeley professor Vincent Sarich claimed that " 'Asians' have been and are being treated 'fairly' with respect to their academic achivements" while whites "are underrepresented by some 47 percent."[38] Sarich accused Berkeley of "immoral policies" and "systematically discriminating against white students."[39] Historian C. Vann Woodward agreed: "Whites, now a minority, were underrepresented in the entering class of 1989."[40] Chester Finn complained that Berkeley's revised admissions policy would "boost the numbers of Asians admitted" and "cause a drop in white matriculations, who plainly will not make it as a minority and who may be trounced by the Asians in the merit competition."[41]

Discrimination against Asian Americans at Berkeley occurred not because preferences were given to other minorities but because preferences were given to whites. The sole proof of discrimination against Asians came from the fact that less-qualified whites were being admitted. Berkeley's assistant vice chancellor for undergraduate affairs, Thomas Travers, noted in 1986, "We could fill up half the freshman class with Asians, but that wouldn't be acceptable to the legislature." Travers added, "If we keep getting extremely well prepared Asians, and we are, we may get to the point where whites are an affirmative action group."[42]

Whites felt threatened by what happened at Berkeley in the 1980s. They were squeezed in two directions: affirmative action provided blacks and Hispanics with a representative number of places at Berkeley, while Asians outperformed whites and threatened their opportunity for purely merit-based positions. The discrimination against Asian Americans in the 1980s at elite universities was the result of this white anxiety. According to a confidential UCLA planning paper, the university planned "to curb the decline of Caucasian students. A rising concern will come from Asian students and Asians in general as the number and proportion of Asian students entering at the freshman level decline."[43] Though bias at Berkeley and other universities clearly favored whites over Asian Americans, conservatives cleverly blamed the discrimination on Berkeley's affirmative action program for underrepresented minorities. What should have been seen as an example of whites receiving preference over Asian

Americans was transformed into yet another attack on affirmative action, and, ironically, a cry that whites were the victims of discrimination. ˌ

The Mismatch Myth

The University of California at Berkeley is the most common target of the conservative opponents of affirmative action, largely because it is a unique institution. Most minority students attend less prestigious colleges with far lower admissions standards, and Ivy League colleges have affirmative action programs that admit only a very small number of minority students. Berkeley, by contrast, is a highly selective university which nevertheless maintains a strong commitment to admitting blacks and Hispanics at a rate proportional to their population in California. The conservatives' focus on Berkeley is a highly selective and deceptive way to attack affirmative action in college admissions.

Barry Gross, the president of the National Association of Scholars, uses Berkeley as his key example when he warns about "how alarmingly deficient students are who must be preferentially treated." According to Gross, "at Berkeley the five-year graduation rates are as follows: whites 66%; Asians 61%. But only 41% of the Hispanic and 27% of the black students *ever graduate at all*."[44] Gross is wrong: the five-year graduation rate for blacks is 37.5 percent, not 27 percent — and the six-year graduation rate for blacks is 51 percent, nearly twice what Gross claims, although still below the six-year graduation rate for whites of 77 percent.[45]

Critics of affirmative action charge that this racial disparity in graduation rates is caused by preferential admissions that "bump up" underqualified minorities into universities where they cannot compete. This idea is known as the mismatch theory, and its primary proponent is Thomas Sowell, who claims that "even if most minority students are able to meet the normal standards at the 'average' range of colleges and universities, the systematic mismatching of minority students begun at the top can mean that such students are generally overmatched throughout all levels of higher education. Youngsters who could have succeeded at San Jose State University may be failing at Berkeley, while youngsters who could have succeeded at a community college are failing at San Jose State."[46]

Sowell urges black students at Berkeley (where 50 percent of blacks graduate) to attend a school like San Jose State, where only 30 percent of black students graduate and the graduation rate for all students (39 percent) is much lower than it is at Berkeley (76 percent).[47] But it is hardly sound advice to tell black students that they will improve their chances for graduation by attending a college where only half as many students of any race complete their studies.

The mismatch theory cannot explain why underrepresented minorities generally have higher college dropout rates than whites, since the vast majority of minority students are admitted to college without any affirmative action preferences. The flaw in the mismatch argument is the assumption that students at different colleges will have the same dropout rates. But students at elite universities have much higher graduation rates than those at other kinds of colleges; as the colleges become less prestigious and less selective, the dropout rates increase. The six-year graduation rate for all Harvard students entering in the fall of 1987 was 97 percent, but less prestigious universities have much lower graduation rates: Boston University, 72 percent; Purdue, 69 percent; East Carolina, 49 percent; and Arizona State, 46 percent; and some universities had very low graduation rates, including Chicago State, 20 percent; Alabama State, 14 percent; and Texas Southern, 10 percent.[48] Why urge that black students, for their own good, should be placed in colleges with lower graduation rates?

Taking a student who might otherwise attend a low-status college with a high dropout rate and allowing her to attend an elite college where almost all students graduate will create the appearance of a mismatch. But there is no evidence that the individual's failure rate increases merely because she attends a more prestigious college. The only thing that changes is the lower failure rate of her classmates, which creates the mismatch illusion.

David Horowitz claims that "the dropout rate from elite campuses of minority students is about 70 percent. If half of that 70 percent had entered institutions for which they were qualified, they might have degrees and be on the path of lucrative and productive careers."[49] But there is not a single elite university where the minority dropout rate is 70 percent. The worst dropout rate, at Berkeley, is below 50 percent and that number reflects an immense affirmative action program. Myron Magnet argues that "these black students would have succeeded overwhelmingly at a good college a notch below MIT or Berkeley or Harvard or the handful of other elite schools that have snatched them up to fill their quotas."[50] But given the low graduation rate for blacks nationwide, the fact that 76 percent of blacks graduate from MIT (only slightly less than the 86 percent graduation rate for whites) should be regarded as a remarkable success.[51]

A 1994 survey by the American Council on Education found that blacks and Hispanics had significantly lower six-year graduation rates (32 percent and 41 percent, respectively) than whites (56 percent) and Asian Americans (63 percent). But the report concludes, "When differences in academic preparation and socio-economic status are controlled, the retention rates of students in these groups are equal to those of white students."[52] The factors that affected retention were student-faculty relationships, academic advising, small-group tutorials, campus climate, and financial aid. Mismatch had nothing to do with dropout rates.

Wealth is a key factor in graduation rates because students who cannot afford high tuition rates often drop out or struggle to balance a job with classes. Minority students at Berkeley are far less wealthy than white students. In 1991, the median family income of Berkeley students was $35,000 for blacks, $36,300 for Hispanics, $47,400 for Asians, and $75,000 for whites; only 18.1 percent of whites came from families with incomes less than $40,000.[53]

But Sowell's mismatch theory has gained wide acclaim among conservatives. Stephan Thernstrom, speaking on *This Week with David Brinkley,* declared that the "minority mismatch problem" had caused the "degree of frustration on the part of many minority students who have been placed through affirmative action in institutions where they're not doing very well on average."[54] Dinesh D'Souza has proposed eliminating affirmative action in order to put minority students in "an appropriate university setting" where they "would not be subject to the undue pressures of intellectual mismatch."[55] Most black and Hispanic students attend community colleges or less selective four-year colleges where affirmative action does not exist (and graduation rates are the lowest of all colleges), so it is impossible for the "minority mismatch problem" to be the cause of the high dropout rate among disadvantaged minorities.

If the mismatch theory does not explain the high dropout rate, what does? Failure to graduate usually has little to do with the admissions standards of the school. Lack of money, lack of academic preparation, and lack of interest in schoolwork are the usual reasons students drop out of college. If anything, the presence of competitive students at elite universities can be an incentive for doing better. Moreover, if minority students admitted by affirmative action cannot keep up with other students at a top-notch university, they can easily transfer to a less selective college (a factor never counted in dropout rates).

Another reason for dropping out is the discomfort many minority students feel at predominantly white institutions. A black student who left Harvard for Howard University noted, "I just couldn't continue to face the hostility I perceived."[56] Nor was this merely an excuse for poor performance. A student who made straight A's at Harvard but transferred to Tuskegee Institute said, "Although the instruction at Harvard was good, I found the atmosphere to be culturally alien and sterile."[57] Vincent Tinto, the leading researcher on dropouts, notes that "students of color, specially admitted or not, face particularly severe problems in gaining access to the mainstream of social life in largely white institutions."[58]

The mismatch myth falsely suggests that there are large differences in ability between whites and minorities. At the University of Texas Law School, which was recently sued for "reverse discrimination," the median white applicant scores on the ninety-fourth percentile of its academic index, and the median black applicant is at the eighty-ninth percentile—a difference, to be sure, but not one dramatic enough to suggest that black students are not qualified to do the work.[59] Without affirmative action, leading law schools (and future lawyers) would be nearly all white. If a black student at the eighty-ninth percentile is admitted instead of a white at the ninety-third percentile, it hardly seems to be an injustice on the order of the good old meritocratic days when Texas kept blacks out of its law school altogether, or even the current injustice done to many black students who (as Jonathan Kozol points out in *Savage Inequalities*) are systematically denied the same quality of education as white students living in wealthier areas.[60]

The problems facing minority students are clear: inadequate preparation in high school, lack of financial aid, and low expectations (or even hostility) from peers and teachers. Affirmative action did not create the economic and educational barriers to success for African Americans, and eliminating it will only further reduce opportunities. The mismatch theory is just a myth that offers a convenient way for critics to attack affirmative action without addressing the true reasons why students drop out of college.

Discrimination Today: The Legacy Preference

While tirades against affirmative action regularly fill the pages of magazines and newspapers, the most disturbing form of affirmative action—preference given to children of alumni, known as "legacies"—is usually ignored by critics. Joseph Shea of the Center for Individual Rights, for example, calls the legacy preference "statistically insignificant."[61] A group of conservative Dartmouth alumni argued that "there must be no goals or quotas for any special group or category of applicants," but added, "alumni sons and daughters should receive some special consideration."[62] Former secretary of education Lauro Cavazos declared that preferences for legacies do not violate America's "principles of justice and equity."[63] Legacies are the oldest form of affirmative action, dating from the efforts to exclude Jews from elite colleges in the 1920s, but they have been virtually immune from criticism.

Admissions consultant Richard Moll reports that legacies are given "a strong advantage in getting through the front gate." Moll says, "All admissions officers know, and a few will quietly confess, that the academic double standard for an important legacy can be more severe than for the top athlete." Moll describes a personal experience at Vassar College: "In one embarrassing situation, I succeeded in convincing the president that a very wealthy legacy would surely fail, once admitted to Vassar, only to find later that she had been invited into Yale, her father's alma mater."[64] John Larew notes in a *Washington Monthly* article that one-fifth of Harvard students receive this legacy preference and concludes, "At Harvard, a legacy is about twice as likely to be admitted as a black or Hispanic student." If they were admitted at the same rate as regular applicants, the number of legacies would drop by two hundred each year—more than the number of all underrepresented minorities who enroll at Harvard. Harvard calls the legacy preference "lineage," as in (written on one admitted student's application folder) "lineage is main thing."[65]

A 1990 Education Department Office of Civil Rights (OCR) investigation of discrimination against Asian Americans at Harvard discovered a wide discrepancy in admissions between children of alumni, recruited athletes, and regular applicants. From 1981 to 1988, 16.9 percent of all regular applicants were admitted, compared with 35.7 percent of alumni children and 48.7 percent of recruited athletes.[66] Meanwhile, only 26.6 percent of black applicants were admitted.[67] Harvard was not alone. At Yale from 1982 to 1991, 19.4 percent of all applicants were admitted, compared with 42.5 percent of legacies.[68]

On every academic scale, the legacies admitted to Harvard from 1983 to 1992 were inferior to regular admittees. Regular applicants had SAT scores 35 points higher than legacies and 130 points higher than the athletes. Other ratings for legacies were lower than the regular admittees, and the average high school class rank percentile was 96.73 for regular applicants, 92.47 for legacies, and 92.30 for athletes. The files of students admitted to the classes of 1991 and 1992 include numerous references to legacy preferences: "Well, not much to say here . . . a good student, w/average EC's, standard athletics, middle-of-the-road scores, good support and 2 legacy legs to stand on"; and "Not a great profile but just strong enough #'s and grades to get the tip from lineage."[69] Similar comments confirmed the power of legacy preferences: "Classical case that would be hard to explain to dad," "double lineage who chose the right parents," and "Without lineage, there would be little case. With it, we'll keep looking."[70]

The Office of Civil Rights concluded, "It is evident from some of these readers' comments that being the son or daughter of an alumnus of Harvard/Radcliffe was the critical or decisive factor in admitting the applicant."

The report also found that "certain alumni parents' status may be weighed more heavily than others." One comment on an applicant's file declared that the father's "connections signify lineage of more than usual weight." Another file carried the comment "We'll need confirmation that dad is a legit, S&S [a member of the alumni Schools and Scholarships Committee] because this is a 'luxury' case otherwise."[71]

Surprisingly, the OCR inquiry did not regard legacy preferences as objectionable. The report simply concluded that the apparent discrimination against Asian Americans was explained by the preferences given to legacies and athletes: "While these preferences have an adverse effect on Asian-Americans, we determined that they were long-standing and legitimate, and not a pretext for discrimination." Therefore, "Harvard's use of preferences for children of alumni and recruited athletes, while disproportionately benefitting white applicants, does not violate Title VI of the Civil Rights Act of 1964."[72]

The legacy system is particularly damaging to minorities, who were largely excluded from the Ivy League colleges until the late 1960s. Unlike affirmative action for underrepresented minorities, which seeks to compensate for past wrongs and improve racial equality, legacy preferences serve no noble purpose. This is affirmative action for rich, privileged white students, providing special treatment for students with the most advantages. Affirmative action for minorities must be seen as just one of many different kinds of preferences — and one that can balance the discriminatory effects of other preferences. Without affirmative action, "normal" employment and admissions decisions simply reestablish a racial preference — for whites.

The Stigma of Affirmative Action

There is no doubt that affirmative action often stigmatizes those who benefit from it, but mainly this is because the myth of reverse discrimination denigrates the abilities of minorities. Minorities admitted to elite colleges or hired for top faculty positions are widely presumed to be unqualified beneficiaries of an undeserved preference. The fact that the charge is untrue does not always mitigate the harmful effects it produces, from minorities doubting their own abilities to racist assumptions about them by others. But it is racism, not affirmative action, that stigmatizes minorities.

Conservatives' attacks on affirmative action often adopt a paternalistic tone. Critics say they are helping minorities escape the stigma that (they claim) is the inevitable result of affirmative action. Dinesh D'Souza's key argument in *Illiberal Education* is that affirmative action has caused the recent rise of racial hatred on college campuses. He asserts that schools with aggressive affirmative action programs "witness both widespread separatism and racial tension." D'Souza even tries to blame campus racism on black paranoia inspired by affirmative action: "The predictable result is a jealous and often bellicose group consciousness among students who do enroll."[73]

The racial incidents reported by D'Souza "represent the uncorking of a very tightly sealed bottle. A careful examination of these incidents, at Michigan and Stanford and Temple and elsewhere, reveals that most of them are connected to preferential treatment and minority double standards." D'Souza uses the example of a freshman student at Bryn Mawr who received a note that read, "Hey Spic, If you and your kind can't handle the work here, don't blame it on the racial thing. Why don't you just get out? We'd all be a lot happier."[74] But D'Souza is wrong; hardly any of the racial incidents reported in recent years had anything to do with affirmative action. It is the mere presence of a substantial number of minority students, not their SAT scores, that sparks racism. When "Nips Go Home" was written on a campus building at the University of California at Berkeley and "Stop the Asian Hordes" was spray-painted on the Engineering School, racists were not showing their anger at preferential admissions; whites were actually being given preferences over Asian Americans.[75] By blaming campus racism on university policies he dislikes, D'Souza turns bigotry into a form of protest against unfair treatment.

Critics of affirmative action rarely condemn racism itself, except in passing. Instead, they use the evil of racism as ammunition in their attack on affirmative action. D'Souza argues that unlike the old racism of ignorant prejudice, the "new racism is based on conclusions" and "direct and first-hand experience with minorities."[76] Charles Murray, author of The Bell Curve, asserts that most racial antagonism on campus is caused by white students' resentment arising from their "factually correct appraisal of the world they see around them, systematically fostered by affirmative action."[77] According to Murray and D'Souza, the new racism is a legitimate response to the unfair preferences given to minorities who are plainly unqualified to be in college.

"Because universities have exhausted the patience of the most sympathetic advocates of the victim's revolution," D'Souza explains, "the blacklash against preferential treatment and sensitivity education will continue to get worse."[78] Since D'Souza and other conservatives refuse to accept the fact that racism persists in America, they must come up with some other explanation for the clear evidence of racism on campus; conveniently, D'Souza treats racists as understandably resentful white males upset by liberal policies like affirmative action.

The truth ignored by D'Souza is that racist and sexist prejudices about the intellectual capabilities of women and minorities have been around much longer than affirmative action programs. While stigma is a very real and destructive phenomenon, the elimination of affirmative action will only harm minorities without rooting out the racist beliefs that are the true cause of stigmatization. Even if the "stigma" of affirmative action were removed by depriving women and minorities of these opportunities, they would still suffer the stigma of their race or gender.

The authors of *The Bell Curve* believe that "the same degree from the same university is perceived differently if you have a black face or a white one." They do not consider this "a misguided prejudice"; instead, they say it is an "unhappy reality."[79] D'Souza promotes this racist stigma against minorities by asking, "Who knows what the black man with the Ph.D. is really capable of doing? The Ph.D. has been placed, by affirmative action, into invisible quotation marks."[80] The irony is that blacks with Ph.D.s are being stigmatized for preferential treatment they do not receive. There is very little evidence of affirmative action in admissions to Ph.D. programs, and no one has ever presented a single case of a black man being given an undeserved Ph.D. because of his race. The dramatic failure of universities to admit and support minorities in graduate school (the "pipeline problem") is the most common excuse for their equally obvious failure to hire minority professors. Most underrepresented minorities choose to attend professional school or enter the corporate world, where their opportunities for equal treatment are better.

The problems caused by racist reactions to affirmative action are real and cannot be ignored. Law professor Stephen Carter aptly observes that "the need to prove one's professional worth over and over again has not receded."[81] "Every time I see a black person, not an Asian, but any other person of color walk by," a white student at Berkeley noted, "I think, affirmative action. It's like that's your first instinct. It's not, maybe that person was smart; it's gotta be Affirmative Action. They don't even belong here."[82] It is not surprising, then, that a black student at Berkeley feels "like I have 'Affirmative Action' stamped on my forehead."[83] But our response should be to challenge the false attacks on the qualifications of women and minorities (and to ask why students should even care about the SAT scores of fellow students), not to support the campaign to undercut affirmative action. The question for black students is not "Do you want to be stigmatized?" The question is "Do you want to be a Berkeley student with 'Affirmative Action' stamped on your forehead, or would you rather be excluded from Berkeley and still have 'Black' stamped on your forehead?"

Even when merit, not affirmative action, is the basis of a hiring or admission decision, many whites presume that racial and gender preferences are the cause. Critics simply assume that affirmative action programs lower academic standards. One recent story about Harvard Law School seemed to confirm the evils of affirmative action — that is, until it was revealed to be pure invention, and one more example of the power of the myth of reverse discrimination to replace evidence with mere suspicion when it comes to the talents of minorities.

The whispered accusations began when black law professor Charles Ogletree was hired by Harvard and an article he had written was being edited for publication by the editors of the *Harvard Law Review*. A student working on the law review claimed that "Ogletree submitted two or three pages of jottings on his career as a public defender. The entire article was manufactured by students." A law professor noted anonymously, "Of course we need more blacks. But Ogletree's a lawyer, not a scholar. He's just way beyond his depth here. I've been approached by students who tell me that law review editors wrote the whole thing." These students, the professor claimed, were intimidated by the forces of political correctness at Harvard: "The words I've heard are 'terrified' and 'petrified.' If race were not involved, they might feel able to go to the dean about it. But they're afraid they'll get pilloried. The whole thing is so unethical it's outrageous. It goes beyond affirmative action. It's . . . affirmative creation." [84]

It is a story with all the elements of political correctness and affirmative action run amok. An unqualified black, a man lacking even minimal scholarly abilities, is about to be entrenched at America's leading university, and skeptical students and professors are afraid to object for fear of being racists and persecuted by the PC thought police.

But, as Ruth Shalit reports in the *New Republic*, "the only problem with the story, for all its metaphorical elegance, was that it was untrue." Ogletree's first draft of his paper, according to six professors who saw it, was not 3 pages long but 289 pages. And "the witnesses who begged off a visit to the dean's office, citing fears of poster campaigns, were daunted not by visions of yuppie McCarthyism but by the fact that they didn't know what they were talking about." Incredibly, the tenacity of the myth of favoritism for inept minority professors is so strong that one student asked conspiratorially, "How do we know they're not just covering up their trail? They had plenty of time to prepare for reporters to descend on the law review. Are you sure the drafts were authentic?" [85]

Charles Ogletree was unanimously given tenure; presumably even the anonymous law professor who practically accused him of plagiarism voted for him. Yet the lesson Shalit draws from the story is frightening: "The excesses of victim politics have engendered a new skepticism on college campuses, a culture of suspicion in which rumors of inferiority can spiral out of control." [86] Shalit blames not racism but affirmative action itself for making such accusations seem reasonable. What should have been seen as evidence of the irrational character of the reverse discrimination rhetoric instead was presented as a blameless reaction by whites to the lowered standards allegedly spread by "victim politics."

The Myth of Equal Opportunity

Affirmative action is an imperfect solution to America's problems of bigotry and unequal opportunities for minorities. Some highly privileged minorities benefit from affirmative action while underprivileged whites are excluded from its benefits. But imperfect though it is, affirmative action is far better than nothing. Some have suggested deemphasizing race and adopting a class-based affirmative action program. On purely pragmatic grounds, this idea is good, because it would undercut the racial resistance to affirmative action. But despite the advantages given to minorities from wealthy families, the beneficiaries of affirmative action today are usually much poorer than their white counterparts.

In *Illiberal Education*, D'Souza argues that a class-based program of preferences can address injustice without raising the specter of race-based college admissions. But D'Souza's reason for having class-based affirmative action ("socioeconomic disadvantage") can be extended to justify continuing racial preferences for underrepresented minorities.[87] If overcoming disadvantage is our standard for bestowing preference, then surely we should include disadvantage caused by racial injustice as well as economic injustice. Not all minority students suffer racism directly, but then not all students from impoverished backgrounds are deprived of opportunities. On average, however, minority students are likely to have faced more barriers to getting an education (and therefore have more untapped potential) than white students.

Ideally, colleges should more carefully examine their students. Instead of giving the same preference to all underrepresented minorities, admissions officers should be more selective in providing stronger preferences to minorities who have overcome poverty as well as advantages for underprivileged whites.

However, the opposition to class-based affirmative action comes not from racial minorities but from the upper-class whites who run colleges and universities and fear the economic and social consequences of giving preference to lower-class whites. The resistance by colleges to class-based affirmative action has nothing to do with any desire to maintain the racial status quo. Rather, elite colleges fear that admitting more poor students would stretch financial aid budgets and hamper fundraising among wealthy alumni; top public universities which provide excellent education at a subsidized price to upper-middle-class students fear retaliation from state legislatures if class were given serious consideration in admissions. A more individualized system of admissions that includes a class-based preference would be relatively easy to implement, but most administrators are happy with the present system of admitting a small number of minorities, often preferring students from wealthy backgrounds who "fit in" with the other elite students.[88]

Affirmative action is not a perfect system. But we do not live in a world of perfect equality. In the fairy tale of equal opportunity, racism disappeared with the passage of the 1964 Civil Rights Act, never again to show its ugly face in American life. Affirmative action, in this view, is an unjust attempt to correct "past" wrongs—as if racism does not exist today.

Affirmative action is a just policy because it tries to counteract the de facto racial segregation in higher education that would result if so-called merit were the only basis for admission. Admission to elite colleges should not be an entitlement delivered to the wealthy and well educated who have trust funds and high SAT scores; these elite degrees are part of an intricate certification process that gives their recipients a huge advantage in the job market and a network of alums to help them. To suggest that minorities, for their own good, should be kept out of the colleges that provide the fast track to success would be comical if it didn't reflect such ignorance about our so-called meritocratic system of higher education.

Because very few underrepresented minorities—whether they are "qualified" or "unqualified"—are admitted to top-notch universities, only a trivial number of white students are actually denied admission to an elite college because of affirmative action; highly qualified white students are far more likely to be squeezed out of a space by a white son or daughter of an alumnus. But there is no crusade against legacies, especially not among the educated elite of affirmative action critics who are its beneficiaries.

Apparently preferences are objectionable only when they serve the goal of racial justice. No one cares about "unqualified" students who are musicians or athletes or children of alumni or connected to powerful politicians or who come from states like Montana. No one doubts the "meaning" of their college degrees or cries out against the injustice done to other applicants.

There are serious fundamental issues in American colleges and universities that need to be addressed. The problems of racism and sexism, discrimination, and harassment must not be ignored. But the myth of reverse discrimination misrepresents the facts and silences the debates. By falsely claiming that white male conservatives are the oppressed victims, by wrongly accusing universities of hiring unqualified women and minorities, and by ignoring the real harm and discrimination against women, minorities, gays and lesbians, and "radicals" in higher education, the political correctness debates have distracted us from addressing the real questions of equality, freedom, intellectual excellence, and justice on college campuses.

➤ Conclusion: Beyond Political Correctness

The attacks on feminism, affirmative action, and multiculturalism are linked by the fear of a changing culture. Traditional ideas are no longer merely accepted as the eternal truth but instead are challenged by new perspectives of the status quo. None of these new perspectives and controversial issues is immune from criticism. There are flaws in affirmative action, there are extreme forms of multiculturalism and feminism that invite ridicule, and there are legitimate dangers to freedom of expression to be found in speech codes.

The backlash against PC is part of the resentment against the many changes —institutional and intellectual—in American universities since the 1960s. Affirmative action programs, multicultural curricula, new research in the humanities and social sciences, and the "politicization" of the academy are all among its targets. Conservative critics say that a return to the good old days—when few people went to college, feminism and multiculturalism did not exist, and nobody caused trouble—will restore liberal education to its former glory.

Moving beyond political correctness means raising the level of debate above the misleading attacks, the exaggerated portrayals of campus life, and the angry dismissal of new ideas. Moving beyond PC also means paying attention to issues that have been obscured by the culture wars, such as the problem of unequal education in high schools and the tremendous disparities in funding between elite universities and less prestigious colleges. Above all else, moving beyond political correctness means recognizing that excellence and diversity are not at cross-purposes. There is no reason why affirmative action should lower academic standards, no reason why multiculturalism and feminism cannot expand our intellectual challenges, and no reason why freedom of speech must be sacrificed for the sake of equality.

My own experiences as a student and journalist at the University of Chicago have given me some insight into the darker side of academic life, the side that is never mentioned in those promotional pamphlets that show the university as an idyllic resort for scholarship, and also a side omitted from the scare stories about PC.

In 1991, gay students at the University of Chicago received repeated threats, including obscene phone calls and notes in the mail with white powder the writer said was a nerve poison to kill them. One of the gay students was attacked on the street late at night by two men in ski masks brandishing a syringe who told him they would kill him by injecting air into his veins. The student knocked away the syringe and ran off.

A letter slipped under the lab door of one of the students said the university should "start a cemetary" and declared that there would be further attempts to kill gay students. The death threats — which said there would be "three dead faggots" and that "no one gives a damn about faggots dying" — were signed, "Brotherhood of the Iron Fist."[1]

The Great White Brotherhood of the Iron Fist — whose "resurrection" was announced on antigay posters around campus in 1991 — was a familiar name at the University of Chicago. In 1987 this group placed phony personal ads in a free Chicago weekly, asking for responses from gay men in the Hyde Park neighborhood. After dozens of men responded, their neighbors, parents, and even employers received letters or phone calls outing them, warning that the man "may be a carrier of AIDS" and a "health threat to you and your organization," and concluding: "Avoid this homosexual at all costs."[2] The *New York Times* reported that at the University of Chicago, "a campaign involving late-night telephone threats and obscene mail has been directed at dozens of students and faculty members. Hundreds of virulent leaflets have been distributed on campus. 'Death to Faggots' bumper stickers have been plastered on the doors of teachers and students believed to be homosexuals, or their allies."[3]

Students and faculty received Christmas cards reading "Happy Death" that said they would "rot in hell." Posters appeared on campus advertising a "Kiddie Porn" show for gays and listing phone numbers of gay activists. Staff members for the *Grey City Journal,* the liberal section of the student newspaper, were harassed: newspapers were burned in their apartment lobby, antigay notices were posted in their building, and "Die!" was written on their mailbox. Swastikas were painted on two campus ministry doors, including one where a gay group met. A gay activist was sent a bull's-eye with his picture superimposed, and his parents got a threatening letter. Bumper stickers placed on buildings said, "Fight AIDS, Castrate all Gays."[4]

Two students who wrote for a conservative newspaper on campus were suspended for two years for lying about their knowledge of the 1987 harassment scheme (the responses to the ad were sent to their apartment), although one was eventually allowed to receive his degree.[5] The men who threatened and attacked the gay students in 1991 were never found.

The critics of "speech codes" rarely acknowledge that these are the kinds of incidents speech codes are designed to punish. The controversy over speech codes has also obscured the fact that many universities do little to protect students from threats and harassment. While there is always a danger that students' rights may be violated whenever a college administration is given disciplinary powers, the alternative—doing nothing—is even worse. One black student at the University of Chicago was harassed, threatened, assaulted, and called a "stupid nigger" by his fraternity brothers as a pledge in 1994. After the student newspaper described what had happened to him, the student was repeatedly harassed for nearly a year while he repeatedly asked university officials to take action. Finally, they responded by giving an informal warning to some of the fraternity brothers who had been harassing him, but no disciplinary hearings were held and no punishment was forthcoming. Harassment procedures and speech codes can be abused, but simply banishing them or ignoring them is no solution.[6]

He was not the only black student to encounter racism in Chicago. The university, stuck in the middle of the poorest black ghetto in America, is an example of how racism pervades college communities populated by even the best-intentioned liberal whites. The campus climate has not changed substantially since the 1970s, when New York Times writer Brent Staples was a graduate student and saw the fear many whites showed toward him on the street at night: "Couples locked arms or reached for each other's hand when they saw me. Some crossed to the other side of the street. People who were carrying on conversations went mute and stared straight ahead, as though avoiding my eyes would save them."[7]

The Committee for Racial Justice at the University of Chicago noted the results of a 1987 survey conducted by the Committee on University Security: "Over a five-year span 84% of individuals stopped by campus security officers were black, while only 12% of those stopped were white. Other data showed that black male students were six times as likely as white male students to be stopped by police. Of those stopped, 54% of the black students were asked to show their ID cards, while 0% of white students were asked."[8] I have never been stopped by campus security, but I am white; black and Hispanic students know that they will be viewed with suspicion by many white students, faculty, and security officers. The pundits who worry about blacks eating together and blame "black separatism" for all the racial problems on campus never mention this disturbing fact of life for minority students.

In 1992, two police officers came into the coffee shop at the main library and asked two black female graduate students to show their IDs because a library employee had reported that two black women were in the library who did not *look* like University of Chicago students. The two students wondered, "Does every Black student on this campus have to be subjected to this type of harassment to protect the white students at this University from the 'undesirables' who live in the surrounding community? . . . Does every Black student on this campus have to walk around with their ID ready to present it to anyone who asks? . . . Do we have to be constantly harassed by the university police because they can't tell the difference between Black students at the University and members of the surrounding community?"[9]

Minority faculty with unpopular opinions can be subjected to harsh public criticism. In 1995, a student at the University of Chicago wrote a letter to the student newspaper attacking a course on race relations taught by a distinguished black professor of education. The student accused the teacher of having "an agenda of black victimization" and further claimed that this professor "systematically dismissed the SAT, ACT, and even the University of Chicago as racist because blacks and other minority students do not fair [*sic*] as well as whites on the exams and in admissions." The student concluded that "basic standards of professionalism" had been "repeatedly violated" by the professor, and he asked for an investigation by administration officials.[10]

I have taken two classes from this professor, and I have never seen anything resembling a violation of professional standards by him. I have never seen him prevent free debate and critical thinking. Quite the contrary, there was always a great deal of discussion and critical thinking in his classes. When students criticized Harvard professor Stephan Thernstrom because of his opinions on racial issues, it became a highly publicized example of "political correctness." But "conservative correctness" directed against a black professor is ignored, even when (unlike Thernstrom's critics) the student urges the university to stop the class from being taught.

Sexism is also endemic in the campus environment. Its expression ranges from a "poetic" invitation to a fraternity party ("First she broke my hips, then she broke my heart: fat girls pay by the pound") to documents passed out by another fraternity to its 1992 and 1993 pledge classes that referred to "dikes," "a Jew bastard," and a song with the lines, " 'Cause the bitch she knows her duty" and "I drowned her in sperm and ruined perm / I left the dumb slut choking." [11] Women who have been raped on campus also find an unsympathetic environment and administrators primarily concerned about avoiding negative publicity. A woman who sought counseling after she was raped met with the head of student counseling services, who referred to the incident as her "undesirable sexual experience."

A similar dismissal of women's experiences appears on the academic side. One woman who graduated from my own graduate department, the Committee on Social Thought, said she "didn't feel free to do a thesis that was feminist on the Committee." [12] Another student in Social Thought told me about the "horrible maleness" of the committee. She said that some students and faculty did not treat women as equals: "I can tell they won't take me seriously because I'm a woman."

University of Chicago English professor Gerald Graff reports the resistance he encountered when he suggested gender as the new subject for part of a humanities core course. Instructors' dissatisfaction with past philosophical approaches that had focused on "Freedom and Constraint" or "The Nature of Virtue" led Graff and his colleagues to shift the topic to gender as an experiment. Graff found the change unpopular with some students and faculty: "They argued that though gender might be a legitimate enough topic for study, it was not a properly philosophical problem, and therefore was out of place in the course. Some traditionally minded instructors decided to resign from teaching the course." [13]

Graff organized a symposium for all the sections of the course to bring the conflict into the open and make students aware of these criticisms. While this is an admirable solution to the culture wars, why does the study of gender — but not of freedom or virtue — need to be debated before it can be studied? A student interested in the study of gender and sexuality told me, "I've gotten marked down on papers. If you're doing a paper on a more radical theory, you've got to be ten times better than anyone else in order to get the same grade." I have even been in a law class where a student laughed out loud (and was chastised by the professor) during another student's presentation of a feminist interpretation because he thought feminist ideas were absurd.

Obviously feminists and multiculturalists are not the only ones whose ideas are ridiculed and suppressed in classes; it happens frequently to students who believe in a wide range of ideologies. But the attacks on PC and the crusade against the leftist "thought police" have given a false impression that conservative students and faculty are the only victims of censorship.

Of course, this intolerance is not directed against all women, gays and lesbians, and minorities. Many of them have a very positive experience at the

University of Chicago, and many students find a supportive environment in which they encounter no racism, sexism, or homophobia, and feel free to express their ideas. Moreover, the University of Chicago is not unique in having problems: distrust of feminism and multiculturalism pervades nearly every campus. The list of hate incidents at the University of Chicago—although incomplete—could be matched against similar lists from almost any other college. Bigotry happens so regularly at colleges across the country that often it is not considered news, unlike the far less common but heavily publicized examples of "political correctness."

While the political correctness "debates" raged, many people never realized how deeply federal and state governments were cutting student aid and university funding, reducing educational opportunities for disadvantaged Americans. Political correctness has played a significant role in the ease with which conservatives have pushed through the defunding of higher education. It is no small irony to discover that the conservatives' attack on higher education, done in the name of the preserving the university from destruction by the barbarians within, has turned out to be the most powerful movement promoting the budget cuts that are imperiling academic standards and access to college for thousands of students.

For the vast majority of faculty and students, the threat is not PC but FC—fiscal correctness. A *New York Times* article reports about "the long-term erosion in financing for many state-supported institutions": state appropriations have declined in constant dollars since 1986, and from 1990–93 alone, appropriations for higher education fell in 36 states.[14] The current wave of cutbacks in state funding of higher education comes on the heels of an equally devastating decline in federal student aid in the 1980s, when a dramatic increase in college tuition and a sharp decline in federal student aid combined to sharply raise the cost of higher education, effectively reducing educational opportunities for thousands of students.

Perhaps even more important than access to college for all students, regardless of their wealth, are the barriers created in elementary and high school to pursuing a higher education. Students today are given such an inadequate education that they drop out of school or must struggle against the odds in college. The "savage inequalities" of our segregated and unequal school system must be dealt with to ensure that all students are truly given an opportunity to succeed, especially today when a college degree is essential to economic advancement.[15]

The conservatives' attack on American universities has succeeded beyond their wildest dreams in discrediting the academic Left. By invoking the myth of political correctness and making it into a national media phenomenon, conservatives were able to convince much of the country, and many within academia, that a conspiracy of leftist students and tenured radicals had taken control of higher education and was suppressing conservative ideas. The myth of PC, sustained by a series of exaggerated or invented anecdotes, became the mechanism by which conservatives continued their attack on the Left.

Though imperfect, universities are at the center of intellectual debate in America. For all of their problems, American universities are the freest places on earth, freer than they have ever been. Although there is sometimes abuse of power, and although many ridiculous ideas are expressed by the academic Left, there is nothing approaching totalitarian control or repression of dissent as suggested by those who claim that universities are "an island of repression in a sea of freedom." [16]

The main flaw with American higher education is not that colleges and universities are too egalitarian, but that they remain places of privilege. Despite all the complaints about affirmative action, it has actually done very little to change the dominance of white students and faculty, especially at elite universities. Despite all the complaints about multiculturalism, students today are ignorant of Western culture not because they are having to learn about other cultures but because business and preprofessional majors now predominate in college. Despite all the complaints that the Western tradition is being discarded, the curriculum at American colleges remains dominated by traditional Western works. Despite all the complaints about conservatives being censored by intolerant minorities, the average female, black, Hispanic, gay, or lesbian student is far more likely to face harassment and abuse than the average white male conservative. Despite all the complaints about "political correctness," the truth is that radical students and faculty face much more discrimination and oppression on campus. Conservative correctness, not political correctness, is the greatest threat to freedom of expression in America.

➤ Notes

Preface: PC and Me

1 Allan Bloom, *The Closing of the American Mind* (New York: Simon & Schuster, 1987), 25.

2 Cary Nelson, "Observing a Neglect for Truth," *Daily Illini*, 3 September 1991, 18.

3 *Orange and Blue Observer* (University of Illinois), August 1991, 3.

4 Nelson, 18.

5 John Taylor, "Are You Politically Correct?" *New York*, 21 January 1991, 32–40.

6 Robert Weissberg, "The Gypsy Scholars," *Forbes*, 10 May 1993, 138.

1   The Myth of Political Correctness

1 Walter Lippmann, *Public Opinion* (New York: Macmillan, 1922), 123.

2 *Chishold v. Georgia*, 2 Fed. 419, 462 (1793); see James Pfander, "Were the Framers of the Constitution PC?" *Constitutional Commentary* 11:1 (Winter 1994), 13–14.

3 Roger Geiger, *Research and Relevant Knowledge: American Research Universities since World War II* (New York: Oxford University Press, 1993), 330.

4 Herbert Kohl, "The Politically Correct Bypass: Multiculturalism and the Public Schools," *Social Policy*, Summer 1991, 33.

5 Ruth Perry, "A Short History of the Term Politically Correct," in Patricia Aufderheide, ed., *Beyond PC: Toward a Politics of Understanding* (St. Paul: Graywolf, 1992), 77.

6 Robert Kelner, "We Conservatives Wage a Phony War on Political Correctness," *Wall Street Journal*, 26 December 1991, A11.

7 Ad for *Limbaugh Letter*, 18 January 1994, Rush Limbaugh radio show.

8 *American Spectator*, March 1993, 2.

9 *American Spectator*, December 1992, 75.

10 *Chicago Tribune*, 4 November 1993, 32. A judge eventually dismissed Comedy Central's suit; see *Daily Variety*, 21 December 1993, 16.

11 Nadine Brozan, "Chronicle," *New York Times*, 11 August 1994, B8.

12 Dinesh D'Souza, *Illiberal Education: The Politics of Race and Sex on Campus* (New York: Vintage, 1992), xiv.

13 Carol Iannone, "PC with a Human Face," *Commentary*, July 1993, 44.

14 Richard Brookhiser, "The Right Should Try Journalism," *Time,* 27 September 1993, 96.

15 *Academe,* September–October 1991, 48.

16 Anthony DePalma, "Universities Grope for Lost Image," *New York Times,* 5 April 1992, education supplement, 33.

17 Catharine Stimpson, "Dirty Minds, Dirty Bodies, Clean Speech," *Michigan Quarterly Review,* Summer 1993, 326.

18 Michael Bérubé, letter, *Boston Review,* May–August 1992, 31–32.

19 Kate Griffin, "Wilmette Vehicle Sticker Looks Too 'Correct' for Some," *Chicago Tribune,* 15 November 1994, sec. 2, pp. 1, 7; Michael Lev, "On 2nd Thought, Wilmette Drops Diversity Stickers," *Chicago Tribune,* 17 November 1994, sec. 2, p. 8; editorial, "Wilmette Repels Alien Invaders," *Chicago Tribune,* 20 November 1994.

20 Arlynn Leiber Presser, "The Politically Correct Law School," *American Bar Association Journal,* September 1991, 53.

21 Rush Limbaugh, *See, I Told You So* (New York: Simon & Schuster, 1993), 344.

22 Limbaugh, 227.

23 Richard Zoglin, "The Shock of the Blue," *Time,* 25 October 1993, 71.

24 Editorial, "What about Pate?" *Chicago Tribune,* 1 December 1994, 30; Eric Zorn, "Right, Wrong, but Not Always Correct," *Chicago Tribune,* 1 November 1994, sec. 2, p. 1.

25 Bernard Weinraub, "Stereotype of Jews Is Revived," *New York Times,* 7 November 1994, B1, B4; William Cash, letter, *New York Times,* 18 November 1994.

26 President Bill Clinton, 14 December 1993; see Sam Roberts, "Clinton Warns of Harm in Accepting Violence," *New York Times,* 15 December 1993, B3.

27 Francis Clines, "First the Gay Protest, Then the Other Irish March," *New York Times,* 18 March 1993, A1, B8.

28 "Is Winning Enough? Is Margin the Key?" *New York Times,* 7 November 1994, B9.

29 Andrew Calabrese and Silvo Lenart, "Cultural Diversity and the Perversion of Tolerance," *Journal of Communication Inquiry,* Winter 1992, 34.

30 "Excerpts from President's Speech to University of Michigan Graduates," *New York Times,* 5 May 1991, 32.

31 National Council for Research on Women, *To Reclaim a Legacy of Diversity: Analyzing the "Political Correctness" Debates in Higher Education* (New York: National Council for Research on Women, 1993), 45–46.

32 Stephen Balch and Herbert London, "The Tenured Left," *Commentary,* October 1986, 43, reprinted in Les Csorba, ed., *Academic License: The War on Academic Freedom* (Evanston, Ill.: UCA Books, 1988), 13–15.

33 See "Marxism in U.S. Classrooms," *U.S. News & World Report,* 8 January 1982, 42–45, cited in Ira Shor, *Culture Wars: School and Society in the Conservative Restoration 1969–1984* (Boston: Routledge, 1986), 16.

34 Adam Begley, *Lingua Franca,* June–July 1992, 40.

35 "An Intelligent Response," *Conservative Digest,* January 1983, 12.

36 Balch and London, "The Tenured Left," 45.

37 Herbert London, "Marxism Thriving on American Campuses," *World & I,* January 1987, 189, 190.

38 Csorba, 316.

39 Csorba, 178.

40 *Grey City Journal,* 29 May 1987, 4.

41   Balch and London, in Csorba, 14.

42   Midge Decter, "More Bullying on Campus," *New York Times,* 10 December 1985, A31.

43   James Davison Hunter, *Culture Wars* (New York: Basic Books, 1991), 214.

44   Sidney Hook, *Convictions* (Buffalo: Prometheus, 1990), 113-14.

45   See Peter LaBarbera, letter to *Campus Report* distributors, January 1995 (emphasis in original).

46   Dinesh D'Souza, "The New Liberal Censorship," *Policy Review,* Fall 1986, 9.

47   Jon Wiener, "Why the Right Is Losing in Academe," *Nation,* 24 May 1986, 726.

48   See Scott Henson and Tom Philpott, "The Right Declares a Culture War," *Humanist,* March–April 1992, 46. London's extremist tactics in promoting the attacks on multiculturalism and higher education fared less well in the political arena. In 1994, when London ran unsuccessfully for New York State comptroller, he tried to smear his Democratic black opponent as anti-Semitic by running commercials that opened with the words, "Kill the Jews?" See Ian Fisher, "London and McCall Clash as Tough Race Nears End," *New York Times,* 7 November 1994, B5. London was the only Republican on the statewide ticket who lost in November, 1994.

49   Hook, 297.

50   Csorba, viii.

51   Debra Blum, "Scholars Who See Colleges in the Thrall of Politics Meet to Plan a Counterattack," *Chronicle of Higher Education,* 20 June 1990, A16.

52   Charles Sykes, *Profscam: Professors and the Demise of Higher Education* (Washington, D.C.: Regnery Gateway, 1988).

53   Roger Kimball, *Tenured Radicals: How Politics Has Corrupted Our Higher Education* (New York: Harper & Row, 1990), 146; Eve Kosofsky Sedgwick, *Tendencies* (Durham: Duke University Press, 1993), 16.

54   Richard Bernstein, "A 'Minute of Hatred' in Chapel Hill: Academia's Liberals Defend Their Carnival of Canons against Bloom's 'Killer B's,' " *New York Times,* 25 September 1988, 26, reprinted in Robert Stone, ed., *Essays on the Closing of the American Mind* (Chicago: Chicago Review Press, 1989), 15-17. The conference papers were published in *The Politics of Liberal Education,* ed. Darryl Glass and Barbara Herrnstein Smith (Durham: Duke University Press, 1992).

55   *National Review,* 19 October 1990, 18; Richard Bernstein, "The Rising Hegemony of the Politically Correct," *New York Times,* 28 October 1990, sec. 4, p. 1.

56   Jerry Adler, "Taking Offense," *Newsweek,* 24 December 1990, 48-54.

57   Dinesh D'Souza, *Falwell, Before the Millennium: A Critical Biography* (Chicago: Regnery Gateway, 1984); D'Souza, *Illiberal Education,* 19.

58   It continues: "We be culturally 'lightened too. We be takin' hard courses in many subjects, like Afro-Am Studies, Women's Studies and Policy Studies. And who be mouthin' 'bout us not bein' good read? I be practicly knowin' *Roots* cova to cova, 'til my mine be boogying to da words! An' I be watchin' the *Jeffersons* on TV 'til I be blue in da face" (Keeney Jones, "Dis Sho' Ain't No Jive, Bro," *Dartmouth Review,* 15 March 1982, quoted on *Frontline*'s "Racism 101" [1988]).

59   Michael Bérubé, *Public Access: Literary Theory and American Cultural Politics* (New York: Verso, 1994), 17-18; Dudley Clendinen, "Conservative Paper Stirs Dartmouth," *New York Times,* 13 October 1982; Louis Menand, "Illiberalisms," *New Yorker,* 20 May 1991, 101; Henson and Philpott, 15.

60   C. Vann Woodward, "Freedom and the Universities," in Patricia Aufderheide, ed., *Beyond PC: Toward a Politics of Understanding* (St. Paul: Graywolf, 1992), 49.

61   D'Souza, *Illiberal Education,* xvi.

62   Woodward, 29.

63   Robert Weissberg, "Notes from the Abyss: The Queers and Panderbears of Academe," *Chronicles,* September 1992, 16–19.

64   John Leo, *Two Steps ahead of the Thought Police* (New York: Simon & Schuster, 1994), 92.

65   *Campus,* Fall 1991, 24.

66   R. Emmett Tyrrell, "PC People," *American Spectator,* May 1991, 8–9.

67   Russell Jacoby, *Dogmatic Wisdom: How the Culture Wars Divert Education and Distract America* (New York: Doubleday, 1994), 41.

68   Robert Hughes, "The Fraying of America," *Time,* 3 February 1992, 45.

69   Taylor, 32.

70   Jon Wiener, "What Happened at Harvard," *Nation,* 30 September 1991, 386.

71   D'Souza, *Illiberal Education,* 194; Stephan Thernstrom, "McCarthyism Then and Now," *Academic Questions,* Winter 1990, 12–14.

72   Wiener, "What Happened at Harvard," 385.

73   D'Souza, *Illiberal Education,* 195–96.

74   Eugene Genovese, "Heresy, Yes—Sensitivity, No," *New Republic,* 15 April 1991, 30.

75   Thernstrom, 5; D'Souza, *Illiberal Education,* 197.

76   Thernstrom, 13.

77   Randall Kennedy, "The Political Correctness Scare," *Loyola Law Review* 37 (1991), 242.

78   D'Souza, *Illiberal Education,* 195.

79   Wiener, "What Happened at Harvard," 385.

80   Thernstrom, 10.

81   Lynne Cheney, *Telling the Truth: A Report on the State of the Humanities in Higher Education* (Washington, D.C.: National Endowment for the Humanities, 1992), 16; see Michael Bérubé, "Truth, Justice, and the American Way," in Jeffrey Williams, ed., *PC Wars* (New York: Routledge, 1995), 58.

82   Rosa Ehrenreich, "What Campus Radicals?" *Harper's,* December 1991, reprinted in Francis Beckwith and Michael Bauman, eds., *Are You Politically Correct? Debating America's Cultural Standards* (Buffalo: Prometheus, 1993), 33–39.

83   Nadine Strossen, "The Controversy over Politically Correct Speech," *USA Today,* November 1992, 59.

84   "Sensitivity Fascism," *National Review,* 27 April 1992, 19.

85   Patrick Garry, *An American Paradox: Censorship in a Nation of Free Speech* (Westport, Conn.: Praeger, 1993), 57.

86   William Bennett, *The De-Valuing of America* (New York: Summit, 1992), 175.

87   *Chronicle of Higher Education,* 17 March 1993, A16.

88   Cheney, "Beware the PC Police," *Executive Educator,* January 1992, 34.

89   Scott Heller, " 'Race, Gender, Class, and Culture': Freshman Seminar Ignites Controversy," *Chronicle of Higher Education,* 29 January 1992, A33, A35.

90   Adam Bromberg, "Lecture on Berlin Wall Becomes Racial Incident at Binghamton," *Campus,* Fall 1991, 4; Mark Tushnet, "Political Correctness, the Law, and the Legal Academy," *Yale Journal of Law & the Humanities* 4 (1992), 136; see also *Newsday,* 12 May 1991, 34.

91   David Beers, "PC? B.S." *Mother Jones,* September–October 1991, 35.

92 John Leo, "The Politically Correct Have Had a Busy Year," *St. Petersburg Times*, 1 February 1992, 22A.

93 Peter Collier and David Horowitz, eds., *Surviving the PC University* (Studio City, CA: Center for the Study of Popular Culture, 1993), 54.

94 Herbert London, "In the Bunkers of Binghamton," *Academic Questions*, Fall 1991, 16–17.

95 Originally in Alan Charles Kors, "It's Speech, Not Sex, the Dean Bans Now," *Wall Street Journal*, 12 October 1989; also described in Charles Sykes, *The Hollow Men: Politics and Corruption in Higher Education* (Washington, D.C.: Regnery Gateway, 1990), 56–57; Kimball, *Tenured Radicals*, xvi; Robert Alter, "The Folly and the Ivy," *Newsday*, 11 March 1990, 22; T. Kenneth Cribb, Jr., "Conservatism and the American Academy: Prospects for the 1990s," *Intercollegiate Review*, Spring 1990, 26; Andrew Zappia, "Free Speech Violations: A Sampling," *Campus*, Fall 1990, 6; Charles Bremner, "The Thought Police Closing Off the American Mind," *London Times*, 19 December 1990, 12; Josh Ozersky, "The Enlightenment Theology of Political Correctness," *Tikkun* 6:4 (July–August 1991), 38; Roger Kimball, " 'Tenured Radicals': A Postscript," *New Criterion*, January 1991, 8; Taylor, 34–35; D'Souza, *Illiberal Education*, 9–10; D'Souza, "Illiberal Education," *Atlantic Monthly*, March 1991; Kors, "The Politicization of the University, *in Loco Parentis*," *World & I*, May 1991, 492–93; Louis Menand, "Illiberalisms," *New Yorker*, 20 May 1991, 103; Arthur Schlesinger, *The Disuniting of America* (New York: Norton, 1992), 117; Richard Huber, *How Professors Play the Cat Guarding the Cream* (Fairfax, Va.: George Mason University Press, 1992), 62; Jack Gordon, "Rethinking Diversity, Multiculturalism," *Training* 29:1 (January 1992), 23; William Kimsey, "Fighting Restrictive Codes on Campus," *Washington Times*, 13 April 1992, E4; Stephen Chapman, "Campus Speech Codes Are on the Way to Extinction," *Chicago Tribune*, 9 July 1992, 21; Burl Osborne, "If Offensive Speech Is Silenced, Then Debate Is Censored," *St. Petersburg Times*, 20 July 1992, 7A; Nadine Strossen, "Thoughts on the Controversy over Politically Correct Speech," *SMU Law Review* 46:1 (Summer 1992), 123; Ann Leslie, "This Conspiracy to Rule All Our Minds," *Daily Mail*, 14 September 1992, 24–25; William Hoer, "Attack on Western Culture," *New American*, 21 September 1992, 18; Harlan Hoffa, "Power Politics and Arts Education," *Arts Education Policy Review*, November 1992, 29; Thomas Sowell, *Inside American Education: The Decline, the Deception, the Dogmas* (New York: Free Press, 1993), 156; Myron Magnet, *The Dream and the Nightmare: The Sixties' Legacy to the Underclass* (New York: Morrow, 1993), 193; Patrick Garry, *An American Paradox: Censorship in a Nation of Free Speech*, 58; Kors, "Bad Faith: The Politicization of the University *in Loco Parentis*," in Howard Dickman, ed., *The Imperiled Academy* (New Brunswick, N.J.: Transaction, 1993), 175; John Seigenthaler, "Politically Correct Speech: An Oxymoron," *Editor & Publisher*, 6 March 1993, 48; Bob Sipchen, "Divided We Stand?" *Los Angeles Times*, 13 April 1993, E1; Charles Sykes and Brad Miner, eds., *The National Review College Guide* (New York: Fireside, 1993), 251 (calling it "the most notorious incident" of political correctness); Dwight Lee, "Celebrating the Economic System That Makes Diversity Worth Celebrating," *Intercollegiate Review*, Spring 1994, 24; Richard Bernstein, *Dictatorship of Virtue* (New York: Simon & Schuster, 1994), 75; Steven Yates, *Civil Wrongs* (San Francisco: Institute for Contemporary Studies Press, 1994), 79; George Will, "A Kind of Compulsory Chapel," *Newsweek*, 14 November 1994, 84.

Sometimes the "red flag" anecdote got mangled in the retelling. On television with John McLaughlin, Lynne Cheney declared: "One of the classic examples of political correctness is a student who wrote an essay talking about the rights of the individual. The word individual was circled by the professor and said, 'This is a red flag word for racism.' Well, it is not"; see Federal News Service, 30 August 1991.

96   Kimball, xvi.

97   D'Souza, *Illiberal Education,* 15–16.

98   Bernstein, *Dictatorship of Virtue,* 7.

99   Stephen Balch, "Outlook," *NAS Update,* Fall 1993, 2.

100   Kimball, 29.

101   George Will, "Curdled Politics on Campus," *Newsweek,* 6 May 1991, 72.

102   Taylor, 35.

103   Bernstein, "The Rising Hegemony of the Politically Correct," 4; Terry Teachout, "Dead Center: The Myth of the Middle," *National Review,* 2 November 1992, 54.

104   Csorba, 107.

105   Walter Williams, "College Administrators Aiding Campus Leftists," *Human Events,* 20 March 1993, 9.

106   Bennett, 195. Bennett adds, "The good news is that this cultural virus has created its own antibodies" (256).

107   Balch, 3; see Csorba, 108.

108   Kimball, 204. More examples: Peter Shaw of the NAS warns of the dangers posed by "a prestigious but ideologically infected school" (Shaw, review of *National Review College Guide* in *National Review,* 20 September 1993, 75). R. Emmett Tyrrell declares that "we are all in imminent danger of long-term exposure to such campus illnesses as political correctness, multiculturalism, and—in the place of learning—jargon, cant, and sexual hygiene" (Tyrrell, "The University Left," *American Spectator,* February 1993, 14). Professor Paul Gottfried attacks "the social parasites who make up America's professoriate" (quoted in Matthew Scully, "Joining the Cultural War," *National Review,* 7 June 1993, 27). *The National Review College Guide* says that radical teachers are a "virus attacking" Western values that "has spread widely throughout higher education" (Miner and Sykes, 240).

109   Derek Bok, "Universities: Their Temptations and Tensions," *Journal of College and University Law* 18:1 (1991), 7.

110   D'Souza, *Illiberal Education,* xvii.

111   Kelner, A11.

112   D'Souza, *Illiberal Education,* xvii.

113   D'Souza, *Illiberal Education,* xvii, xviii.

114   James Carey, "Political Correctness and Cultural Studies," *Journal of Communication,* Spring 1992, 59.

115   "College Education: Paying More and Getting Less," investigation of the rising costs of a college education by the House Select Committee on Children, Youth, and Families, based on hearings of 14 September 1992. "College Education: Paying More and Getting Less Fact Sheet," 1.

116   Liz McMillen, "Olin Fund Gives Millions to Conservative Activities in Higher Education; Critics See Political Agenda," *Chronicle of Higher Education,* 22 January 1992, A32.

117   Carlin Romano, "The Periodical Table," *Lingua Franca,* November–December 1992, 23; see Ellen Messer-Davidow, "Manufacturing the Attack on Liberalized Higher Education," *Social Text,* Fall 1993, 40–80.

118   Messer-Davidow, 63.

119   Rick Haberman, "The Buying of the American Mind," *Grey City Journal* (*Chicago Maroon*), 23 September 1991, 5.

120 Bernstein, *Dictatorship of Virtue*, 349.

121 Christina Hoff Sommers, *Who Stole Feminism? How Women Have Betrayed Women* (New York: Simon & Schuster, 1994), 8.

122 Sommers, 128.

123 Messer-Davidow, 63.

124 Haberman, 5.

125 Courtney Leatherman, "A Public-Interest Law Firm Aims to Defend the Politically Incorrect," *Chronicle of Higher Education*, 23 November 1994, A18–A19.

126 McMillen, A32.

127 Henson and Philpott, 11.

128 Fox Butterfield, "The Right Breeds a College Press Network," *New York Times*, 24 October 1990, A1, B9; Henson and Philpott, 15.

129 Henson and Philpott, 16.

130 Thomas Sowell, "Unsung Heroes," *Forbes*, 6 January 1992, 70.

131 McMillen, A32.

132 Heather MacDonald, "Underdog and Pony Show," *New Criterion*, June 1992, 87; see also Gerald Graff and Gregory Jay, "The Best Ideas That Money Can Buy," *Democratic Culture*, Fall 1992, 6.

133 Lee Daniels, "Diversity, Correctness, and Campus Life," *Change*, September–October 1991, 18.

134 Philip Altbach and Lionel Lewis, "The True Crisis on Campus," *Academe*, January–February 1994, 24.

135 Susan Dodge, "Few Colleges Have Had 'Political Correctness' Controversies, Study Finds," *Chronicle of Higher Education*, 7 August 1991, A23–A24.

136 Sheila Slaughter, "Academic Freedom at the End of the Century," in Philip Altbach, Robert Berdahl, and Patricia Gumport, eds., *Higher Education in American Society*, 3d ed. (Amherst, N.Y.: Prometheus Books, 1994), 90.

2   Conservative Correctness

1 The stolen journals were the *Journal of Homosexuality, Feminist Studies, Frontiers, Gender and Society, New Directions for Women, Signs, Women, Women's Studies, Psychology of Women Quarterly,* and *Women and Politics.* See e-mail message from Stephen Rollins, associate dean of library service, University of New Mexico, 8 December 1994; Mike Maiello and William Reichard, "Zimmerman Gutted by Hate Crime," *University of New Mexico Daily Lobo,* 21 November 1994, 1; William Reichard, "Journals Found Hidden in Library," *Daily Lobo,* 30 November 1994; *Chronicle of Higher Education,* 7 December 1994, A4.

2 *Chronicle of Higher Education,* 30 November 1994, A6; 6 January 1995, A4.

3 Robert Kelner, "We Conservatives Wage a Phony War on Political Correctness," *Wall Street Journal,* 26 December 1991, A11.

4 Les Csorba, ed., *Academic License: The War on Academic Freedom* (Evanston, Ill.: UCA Books, 1988), x.

5 Thomas Sowell, *Inside American Education: The Decline, the Deception, the Dogmas* (New York: Free Press, 1993), 229.

6 Herbert London, "Marxism Thriving on American Campuses," *World & I,* January 1987, 195.

7 See Thomas Short, "'Diversity' and 'Breaking the Disciplines': Two New Assaults to the

Curriculum," *Academic Questions,* Summer 1988, 6–29; Short, "Making the Campus Safe for Bureaucracy: Reflections on the 1990 Carnegie Foundation Report," *Academic Questions,* Fall 1990, 7–22; Short, "What Shall We Defend?" *Academic Questions,* Fall 1991, 18–25.

8   Thomas Short, " 'Diversity' and 'Breaking the Disciplines,' " reprinted in Francis Beckwith and Michael Bauman, eds., *Are You Politically Correct? Debating America's Cultural Standards* (Buffalo: Prometheus, 1993), 109.

9   Jon Wiener, "God and Man at Hillsdale," *Nation,* 24 February 1992, 236; Brad Miner and Charles Sykes, eds., *The National Review College Guide* (New York: Fireside, 1993), 87.

10   Miner and Sykes, 114.

11   Thomas Sowell, "Waiting with Bated Breath in Academia," *Orange County Register,* 17 February 1992.

12   Letter, *Academic Questions,* Fall 1991, 10.

13   Wiener, 239.

14   AAUP Report, Hillsdale College, *Academe,* May–June 1988, 31.

15   Wiener, 239.

16   AAUP Report, Hillsdale College, 30, 33.

17   Miner and Sykes, 116.

18   Alice Dembner, "BU Gave Silber $300,000 Bonus during AG Probe; Pay Hike Called Unusual in Academia," *Boston Globe,* 13 May 1994, 23.

19   James Brammer, Dina Lallo, and Sarah Ney, "*Brown v. Trustees of Boston University:* The Realization of Title VII's Legislative Intent," *Journal of College and University Law* 17:4 (1991), 552–53.

20   Editorial, *Washington Post,* 26 June 1990, A20; See *Brown v. Trustees of Boston University,* 891 F.2d 337 (1st Cir. 1989), 347.

21   *Factbook on John Silber* (Boston: Concerned Faculty and Students of Boston University, 1990; reprint, 1993), 19.

22   *Factbook on John Silber,* 20.

23   Russell Jacoby, *The Last Intellectuals: American Culture in the Age of Academe* (New York: Basic Books, 1987), 137.

24   *Factbook on John Silber,* 17–18, 15, 16.

25   *Factbook on John Silber,* 16–17. Ironically, one common PC story is about Brigit Kerrigan, a student at Harvard who was criticized for putting up a Confederate flag. Although Kerrigan was permitted to keep the flag in her window, her case is presented as an example of liberal censorship by people who never mention Silber's far greater abuse of freedom of expression. See Nat Hentoff, *Free Speech for Me—But Not for Thee: How the American Left and Right Relentlessly Censor Each Other* (New York: HarperCollins, 1992), 198–201.

26   *Factbook on John Silber,* 15.

27   *Boston Globe,* 3 December 1993, correction of 1 December 1993 story by Alice Dembner, "Silber Defends Record, Calls Faculty Leader Liar," 1.

28   Alice Dembner, "Silber's Words Leave Sting; Faculty Feels Pressure of His Views, Some Say," *Boston Globe,* 24 November 1993, 27.

29   Mark Starr, "Archie Bunker with a Ph.D.," *Newsweek,* 18 June 1990, 19.

30   Courtney Leatherman, "New Eruption at Boston U.," *Chronicle of Higher Education,* 8 December 1993, A27.

31   *Factbook on John Silber,* 18, 24.

32   Richard Freeland, *Academia's Golden Age: Universities in Massachusetts, 1945–1970* (New York: Oxford University Press, 1992), 410.

33   *Factbook on John Silber,* 19.

34   Sidney Blumenthal, "Hi, Yo Silber!" *New Republic,* 22 October 1990, 12–14, 14. Among John Silber's other inane comments: "There are not very many children who come from lesbian homes because lesbians don't produce children and neither do gay people produce children"; "Why has Massachusetts suddenly become so popular for people who are accustomed to living in the tropical climate? Amazing. There has got to be a welfare magnet going on here"; "The voice of Adolf Hitler" (referring to Jesse Jackson); "There's no point in my making a speech on crime control to a bunch of drug addicts" (refusing to campaign for governor in the predominantly black Roxbury neighborhood); "The racism of Jews is quite phenomenal"; "I'm a lot closer to John Wayne than to Machiavelli"; "I've been right so much of the time"; see *Democratic Culture,* Spring 1994, 17.

35   John Silber, "Academic Freedom: A Secular Perspective," in Nicholas Cafardi, ed., *Academic Freedom in a Pluralistic Society: The Catholic University* (Pittsburgh: Duquesne University, 1990), 63, 58.

36   Peter Novick, *That Noble Dream: The "Objectivity Question" and the American Historical Profession* (Cambridge: Cambridge University Press, 1988), 564.

37   Paul Carrington, "Of Law and the River," *Journal of Legal Education* 34 (1984), 227.

38   *American Association of Law Schools Newsletter,* September 1986, 1, quoted in Jerry Frug, "McCarthyism and CLS," *Harvard Civil Rights–Civil Liberties Law Review* 22 (1987), 684.

39   Editorial, "Veritas at Harvard," *Wall Street Journal,* 3 September 1986, 26.

40   Eleanor Kerlow, *Poisoned Ivy* (New York: St. Martin's Press, 1994), 156.

41   Julius Getman, *In the Company of Scholars: The Struggle for the Soul of Higher Education* (Austin: University of Texas Press, 1992), 89.

42   Jamin Raskin, "Laying Down the Law," in John Trumpbour, ed., *How Harvard Rules* (Boston: South End Press, 1989), 344.

43   Kerlow, 51. The Massachusetts Commission against Discrimination found "probable cause" that Harvard had discriminated against her, and Laurence Tribe noted, "If a young, relatively conservative male unconnected with Critical Legal Studies had written the same, I am morally confident that person would have been given tenure"; see Kerlow, 233. Harvard University eventually settled Dalton's discrimination lawsuit by paying $260,000 to the Domestic Violence Institute she heads at Northeastern University; see *About Women on Campus,* Winter 1994, 3.

44   Kerlow, 307, 51–52.

45   David Frum, "Campus Counterrevolution," *American Spectator,* May 1991, 12–14, 13; L. Gordon Crovitz, "Harvard Law School Finds Its Counterrevolutionary," *Wall Street Journal,* 25 March 1992, A13; Raskin, 347.

46   Crovitz, A13.

47   Linda Hirshman, "Time to Lay Down the Law on Tenure," *Chicago Tribune,* 17 October 1993, sec. 6, p. 11.

48   See *Time,* 12 April 1993, 15.

49   Crovitz, A13.

50   D'Souza, *Illiberal Education,* 199. Anthony Lewis inaccurately repeats this anecdote claiming that "charges were pressed quite vigorously against the professor." See *New York Times Magazine,* 13 March 1994, reprinted in Adele Stan, ed., *Debating Sexual Correctness* (New York: Delta, 1995), 109.

51   Richard Hamilton and Lowell Hargens, "The Politics of the Professors: Self-Identifications, 1969–1984," *Social Forces* 71:3 (March 1993), 608, 614, 620.

52　Hamilton and Hargens, 624.

53　Jacoby, 202–3.

54　Peter Warren, "Delta Force," *Policy Review*, Fall 1994, 72.

55　Alice Amsden, "From P.C. to E.C.," *New York Times*, 12 January 1993, A15.

56　Paul Farhi, "Withering Away of Marxism," *International Herald Tribune*, 8 June 1989, 11, 15; cited in Trumpbour, 29.

57　Balch and London, "The Tenured Left," *Commentary*, October 1986, 28.

58　Diane Strassman, in Marianne Ferber and Julie Nelson, eds., *Beyond Economic Man* (Chicago: University of Chicago Press, 1993), 65.

59　Patricia Williams, *The Alchemy of Race and Rights* (Cambridge: Harvard University Press, 1991), 21.

60　Asoke Basu, "E Pluribus Unum," *Academe*, July–August 1986, 43.

61　Gerald Feldman, "A Collapse in Weimar Scholarship," *Central European History* 17 (June–September 1984), 159, 161; see also David Abraham, "A Reply to Gerald Feldman," *Central European History* 17 (June–September 1984), 178–244, "Response," 245–67, "Closing Remarks," 268–90.

62　Jon Wiener, *Professors, Politics, and Pop* (New York: Verso, 1991), 66, 63, 66–67, 70.

63　Tamara Lindsay, "Threats Sent to SU Professor," *Daily Orange*, 15 October 1993, 1.

64　Jeff Grabmeier, "Clashing over Political Correctness," *USA Today*, November 1992, 60.

65　See "Discouraging Hate Speech without Codes," *Academe*, January–February 1994, 18.

66　See People for the American Way, "Artistic Freedom under Attack" (Washington, D.C.: People for the American Way, 1992).

67　*Chronicle of Higher Education*, 19 January 1994, A4.

68　*Newsletter on Intellectual Freedom*, July 1993, 112.

69　While the women would have been nude, the men would have worn athletic supporters; see *Newsletter on Intellectual Freedom*, July 1993, 120.

70　*Newsletter on Intellectual Freedom*, March 1992, 46.

71　Marcia Pally, *Sex & Sensibility: Reflections on Forbidden Mirrors and the Will to Censor* (Hopewell, N.J.: Ecco Press, 1994), 6.

72　*Chronicle of Higher Education*, 23 October 1991, A5.

73　"San Francisco State Destroys Malcolm X Mural after Furor," *New York Times*, 27 May 1994, A7; *Chronicle of Higher Education*, 1 June 1994, A4.

74　Phyllis Lyon and Del Martin, *Lesbian/Woman* (Volcano, CA: Volcano Press, 1991), 332; Athena Theodore, *The Campus Troublemakers: Academic Women in Protest* (Houston: Cap and Gown Press, 1986), 79.

75　*Advocate*, no. 325, 14.

76　Lenny Giteck, "Academics: Chalking up Gay Lessons," *Advocate*, 3 September 1981, 16–19, 49.

77　John D'Emilio, *Making Trouble* (New York: Routledge, 1992), 145.

78　*Perspectives* (American Historical Association), April 1993, 13.

79　*Ratchford, President, University of Missouri et al. v. Gay Lib et al.*, cert. denied, 434 U.S. 1080, 1083–84 (1978); 558 F.2d 848 (1977).

80　*Democratic Culture*, Fall 1993, 22–23.

81　*Chronicle of Higher Education*, 11 August 1993, A5.

82　*Outlines*, June 1993, 14.

83　"Notre Dame Tells Gay Group It Can't Use Site," *Chicago Tribune*, 2 February 1995, sec. 2, p. 4.

84　*Advocate*, 23 March 1993, 23.

85 *Campus*, Spring 1994, 13.

86 *Outlines*, December 1994, 24; Katherine Mangan, "Conservative Students Challenge Support for Campus Gay Organizations," *Chronicle of Higher Education*, 27 January 1995, A38.

87 *Windy City Times*, 14 October 1993, 10.

88 Stanley Fish, *There's No Such Thing as Free Speech and It's a Good Thing, Too* (New York: Oxford University Press, 1994), 90.

89 Amy Lyn Maudlin, "Auburn Hunts Down Students in Violation of Sodomy Law," *U.*, March 1993, 7; *Windy City Times*, 12 November 1992, 10.

90 Carolyn Mooney, "Homosexuals in Academe: Fear of Backlash Clouds Reactions to Increased Tolerance," *Chronicle of Higher Education*, 23 September 1992, A17.

91 *National Gay and Lesbian Task Force Report 1990*, cited in Kevin Berrill, "Organizing against Hate on Campus: Strategies for Activists," in Gregory Herek and Kevin Berrill, eds., *Hate Crimes: Confronting Violence against Lesbians and Gay Men* (Newbury Park, CA: Sage, 1992), 260.

92 Howard, "Extremism on Campus," *Christian Century* 104 (1987), 626.

93 *National Gay and Lesbian Task Force Report 1990*, cited in Berrill, 260.

94 Grabmeier, 61.

95 Howard Ehrlich, *Campus Ethnoviolence and the Policy Options* (Baltimore: National Institute against Prejudice and Violence, 1990), 66.

96 Ehrlich, 68.

97 *National Gay and Lesbian Task Force Report 1991*, cited in Berrill, 260.

98 See Herek and Berrill, 33.

99 Catharine Stimpson, "The White Squares," *Change*, January–February 1992, 77.

100 William Norris, "Liberal Attitudes and Homophobic Acts," in Karen Harbeck, ed., *Coming out of the Classroom Closet* (New York: Harington Park Press, 1992), 92, 98–99, 104.

101 *Chronicle of Higher Education*, 27 April 1994, A6.

102 Scott Jaschik, "U.S. Charges University with Firing Instructor for Having AIDS," *Chronicle of Higher Education*, 11 May 1994, A30.

103 Mooney, A18.

104 "Outside Closes in on College," *New York Times*, 21 April 1993, B8; AAUP Report, Nyack College, *Academe*, September–October 1994, 73–78.

105 *Campus*, Winter 1993, 12–13.

106 *Democratic Culture*, Fall 1993, 7–8.

107 AAUP report, Elmira College, *Academe*, September–October 1993, 42–52.

108 Jay Crenshaw, "Gay Studies at Montana Tech," *Montana Standard*, 6 May 1994.

109 Henry Gonshak, "A Furor over Gay and Lesbian Studies," *Chronicle of Higher Education*, 21 September 1994, A56; Gonshak, "Setting the Record Less Straight," *Democratic Culture*, Spring 1995, 11.

110 Robert Rhoads, "The Campus Climate for Gay Students Who Leave 'the Closet,'" *Chronicle of Higher Education*, 27 January 1995, A56; Mary Crystal Cage, "A Course on Homosexuality," *Chronicle of Higher Education*, 14 December 1994, A19–A20; Brendan Slattery, "Kent State Debuts Gay Soc. Class," *Campus Report*, November 1994, 1, 5.

111 Christopher Phelps, "The Second Time as Farce: The Right's 'New McCarthyism,'" *Monthly Review*, October 1991, 51.

112 Mooney, A17.

113 William Tierney, *Building Communities of Difference* (Westport, Conn.: Bergin & Garvey, 1993), 55, 41.

114 Peter Monaghan, "U. of Colorado Football Coach Accused of Using His Position to Promote His Religious Views," *Chronicle of Higher Education*, 11 November 1992, A35, A37.

115 Courtney Leatherman, "Dealing with Sexual Images in Iowa Classrooms," *Chronicle of Higher Education*, 8 December 1993, A22, A24.

116 John Kenyon, "Rawlings Says Film Was Inappropriate," *Daily Iowan*, 2 October 1991, 1A, 7A.

117 Jean Fallow, "UI's Stance on Free Speech Contradictory," *Daily Iowan*, 23 September 1993.

118 Jean Fallow, Josiane Peltier, and Israel Reyes, "The Regents' Big Stick Policy," *Iowa Journal of Cultural Studies*, Spring 1994, 10 (manuscript version).

119 Tony Brecht, "UI Students Speak out against 'Sex Act' Policy," *Daily Iowan*, 20 October 1993, 1A.

120 Fallow, Peltier, and Reyes, 9–10.

121 Mary Geraghty, "TA Reprimanded after Showing Film," *Daily Iowan*, 20 September 1993, 1A.

122 Geraghty, 1A; Mary Geraghty, "TA's Reprimand Letter Rescinded in June," *Daily Iowan*, 21 September 1993, 1A.

123 John Williams, "Conservative Papers Fill Niche," *College News*, February 1993, 24.

124 *Campus Report*, January 1994, 3.

125 Tory Brecht and Mary Geraghty, "Regents Set Policy over UI Objections," *Daily Iowan*, 21 October 1993, 1A.

126 Mark Siebert, "Debate over U of I Policy Nearing End," *Des Moines Register*, 15 January 1994, 3A.

127 Jean Fallow, "Unusual and Unexpected Censorship," *Democratic Culture*, Spring 1994, 6–7.

128 Fallow, Peltier, and Reyes, 7–8.

129 Mark Draper, "Hooray for Homophobia!" *Campus Report*, May 1994, 4, 5.

130 Draper, 4, 12.

131 D'Souza, *Illiberal Education*, 12–13.

132 Michele N.-K. Collison, "Angry Protests over Diversity and Free Speech Mark Contentious Spring Semester at Harvard," *Chronicle of Higher Education*, 6 May 1992, A40; Kerlow, 35.

133 Randall Kennedy, "The Political Correctness Scare," *Loyola Law Review* 37 (1991), 235.

134 Julie Nicklin, "Arbitrator Tells U. of Delaware to Allow Grant Requests to 'Racist' Fund," *Chronicle of Higher Education*, 4 September 1991, A41, A42.

135 Jan Blits, "The Silenced Partner: Linda Gottfredson and the University of Delaware," *Academic Questions*, Summer 1991, 41.

136 "Settlement at U. of Delaware," *Science*, 15 May 1992, 962; see also *Chronicle of Higher Education*, 6 May 1992, A38.

137 Adam Begley, "Souped-up Scholar," *New York Times Magazine*, 3 May 1992, 38, 50ff.

138 "Literature Wars," *Campus*, Spring 1994, 8–9.

139 *Chronicle of Higher Education*, 1 July 1992, A5.

140 David John Ayers, "My Days and Nights in the Academic Wilderness," *Heterodoxy*, January 1993, 12.

141 Richard Siggelkow, *Dissent and Disruption: A University under Siege* (Buffalo: Prometheus, 1991), 32–33.

142 Richard Kahlenberg, *Broken Contract: A Memoir of Harvard Law School* (New York: Hill & Wang, 1992), 78–79.

143 John Leo, "Here Come the Wild Creatures," *U.S. News & World Report*, 19 October 1992, 27.

144 "Foes of Gun Control Boo Bradys off Stage," *New York Times*, 10 February 1992, A8.

145 Denise Magner, "Reagan Appointee's Speech Canceled after Students at Arizona State Ob-

ject to Her Conservative Views," *Chronicle of Higher Education*, 11 September 1991, A19–A20; see also Linda Chavez, "The Real Aim of the Promoters of Cultural Diversity Is to Exclude Certain People and to Foreclose Debate," *Chronicle of Higher Education*, 18 July 1990, B1; editorial, "The Ivory Censor," *Wall Street Journal*, 9 May 1990, A14.

146   Magner, A20.

147   Trumpbour, 111.

148   Peter Steinfels, "Conservatives Oust President of Southern Baptist Seminary," *New York Times*, 11 March 1994, A8.

149   Daniel Maguire, "Can a University Be Catholic?" *Academe*, January–February 1988, 12.

150   "Academic Freedom and the Abortion Issue," *Academe*, July–August 1986, 3A, 4A.

151   "Canceling of Abortion Forum Is Assailed," *New York Times*, date unknown.

152   *Chicago Maroon*, 17 May 1994, 5.

153   Eric Schmitt, "Powell Receives a Rousing Greeting at Harvard," *New York Times*, 11 June 1993, A8.

154   Wayne Booth, "Humanities Panel Nominee Fails the 'Distinguished Service' Test," *Chicago Tribune*, 17 July 1991, 17.

155   Viveca Novak, "The Accused," *Lingua Franca*, October 1991, 17.

156   Novak, 21; Peter Shaw, "How Non-ideological Has the Opposition Been to Nominee to National Humanities Council?" *Chronicle of Higher Education*, 1 May 1991, B2.

157   Nat Hentoff, "Heresy Hunt," *Washington Post*, 8 July 1991; editorials, "Publish and Perish," *Wall Street Journal*, 14 June 1991 and "Rally Round the Gibbet," *Wall Street Journal*, 23 May 1991; Daniel Patrick Moynihan, 19 July 1991, S 10494.

158   *Time*, "The Bonfire of the Nominee," 29 July 1991, 59.

159   Novak, 17.

160   *Lingua Franca*, June 1991, 4.

161   Stephen Burd, "Deal on Abortion Bill Said to Pave the Way for 8 Nominees to Humanities Council," *Chronicle of Higher Education*, 8 July 1992, A15.

162   Robert Royal, *1492 and All That: Political Manipulations of History* (Washington, D.C.: Ethics and Public Policy Center, 1992), 126.

163   Lynne Cheney "A Conversation with Henry Louis Gates, Jr.," *Humanities*, July–August 1991, 10.

164   Lynne Cheney, quoted in Mario Mignone, ed., *Columbus: Meeting of Cultures* (Stony Brook, N.Y.: Forum Italicum, 1993), 6.

165   "Education beyond Politics," *Partisan Review* 59 (Summer 1992), 382.

166   Royal, 129, 129, 131, 128, 132.

167   Gerry O'Sullivan, "R U P C?" *Humanist*, September–October 1991, 46–47.

168   "Education beyond Politics," *Partisan Review* 59 (Summer 1992), 381–82.

169   Stephen Burd, "Chairman of Humanities Fund Has Politicized Grants Process, Critics Charge," *Chronicle of Higher Education*, 22 April 1992, A32.

170   Burd, A32.

171   John Milne, "Ideology Fuels NEH Funding, Critics Charge," *San Francisco Examiner*, 16 August 1992, B7.

172   Milne, B7.

173   National Council for Research on Women, *To Reclaim a Legacy of Diversity: Analyzing the "Political Correctness" Debates in Higher Education* (New York: National Council for Research on Women, 1993), 50.

174   Burd, A33.

175   John Frohnmayer, *Leaving Town Alive* (New York: Houghton Mifflin, 1993), 55.

176   Karen Winkler, "Portrait," *Chronicle of Higher Education*, 16 October 1991, A5, quoted in Gerald Graff, *Beyond the Culture Wars* (New York: Norton, 1992), 167.

177   Editorial, "Mrs. Cheney's Departure," *New Criterion*, January 1993, 2.

178   George Roche, *The Fall of the Ivory Tower* (Chicago: Regnery, 1994), 61.

179   Quoted in Burd, A33.

180   Stephen Burd, "Cheney to Resign as NEH Chairman 16 Months Early," *Chronicle of Higher Education*, 9 December 1992, A25.

181   Lynne Cheney, "A Conversation with Catharine R. Stimpson," *Humanities*, September–October 1990, 6.

182   Lynne Cheney, "The End of History," *Wall Street Journal*, 20 October 1994.

183   Standard 3 of the "Revolutionary Era" requires students to learn about "the institutions and practices of government," and section B makes them "demonstrate understanding of the issues involved in the creation and ratification of the United States Constitution and the new government it established"; see *National Standards for United States History, Grades 5–12* (Los Angeles: National Center for History in the Schools, 1994), 82, 84.

184   Lynne Cheney, "Kill My Old Agency, Please," *Wall Street Journal*, 24 January 1995, A21.

185   Gertrude Himmelfarb, "What to Do about Education," *Commentary*, October 1994, 27.

186   George Will, "Literary Politics," *Newsweek*, 22 April 1991, reprinted in Patricia Aufderheide, ed., *Beyond PC: Toward a Politics of Understanding* (St. Paul: Graywolf, 1992), 25.

187   Cheney, "Conversation with Henry Louis Gates," 8.

3   The Cult of Western Culture

1   Dinesh D'Souza, " 'Bogus' Multiculturalism: How Not to Teach about the Third World," *American Educator*, Winter 1991, 30.

2   Herbert London, "Reforming Higher Education," *World & I*, May 1991, 476. The Chanting Jesse Jackson also appears in John Leo's *U.S. News & World Report* column, which refers to multiculturalism as "the same old song: 'Hey, Hey, Ho, Ho, Western Culture's Gotta Go' (lyrics by Stanford University and Jesse Jackson)." See Leo, *Two Steps ahead of the Thought Police* (New York: Simon & Schuster, 1994), 19.

3   *MacNeil-Lehrer Newshour*, 1 April 1988, quoted in William Spanos, *The End of Education: Toward Posthumanism* (Minneapolis: University of Minnesota Press, 1993), 209–10.

4   Dinesh D'Souza, *Illiberal Education* (New York: Free Press, 1991), 92.

5   "Reports and Documents on Stanford," *Minerva*, Autumn 1989, 262–63.

6   *Minerva*, 281.

7   *Minerva*, 228.

8   *Commentary*, January 1991, 7.

9   Jeffrey Seinfeld, "Culture and Curriculum Reform at Stanford University," *Centennial Review*, Spring 1992, 123.

10   Raoul Mowatt, "What Revolution at Stanford?" in Patricia Aufderheide, ed., *Beyond PC: Toward a Politics of Understanding* (St. Paul: Graywolf, 1992), 130.

11   Isaac Barchas, "Stanford after the Fall: An Insider's View," *Academic Questions*, Winter 1989, 28, 30, 32.

12   "CIV: Don't Forget the Facts," *Perspectives* (AHA), November 1992, 11.

13   D'Souza, *Illiberal Education,* 92.

14   *Minerva,* 292.

15   *Minerva,* 316.

16   *Minerva,* 394, 397.

17   *MacNeil-Lehrer Newshour,* quoted in *Minerva,* 408, 396.

18   *Minerva,* 407.

19   *Minerva,* 399, 393, 404–5; 241.

20   *Minerva,* 395, 403.

21   *Minerva,* 395.

22   Bennett's reply to Kennedy's statement on the *MacNeil-Lehrer Newshour* was: "You may want to turn this frog into a prince, but you can't. A frog is a frog"; see *Minerva,* 408.

23   *Minerva,* 395, 408.

24   *Minerva,* 405.

25   *Minerva,* 401–2.

26   *Minerva,* 405.

27   Sidney Hook, *Convictions* (Buffalo: Prometheus, 1990), 172, 179.

28   Daniel Gordon, "Inside the Stanford Mind," *Perspectives* (AHA), April 1992, 4, 8.

29   Mowatt, 131.

30   Gordon, 1, 8.

31   D'Souza, *Illiberal Education,* 61.

32   Mowatt, 131.

33   D'Souza, *Illiberal Education,* 71.

34   Dinesh D'Souza, "The Visigoths in Tweed," in Aufderheide, 15.

35   *I, Rigoberta Menchú: An Indian Woman in Guatemala,* ed. Elisabeth Burgos-Debray, trans. Ann Wright (New York: Verso, 1984), 15, 246, 1, 9, 61.

36   D'Souza, "The Visigoths in Tweed," 15.

37   *I, Rigoberta Menchú,* 225, 88.

38   D'Souza, *Illiberal Education,* 72.

39   *I, Rigoberta Menchú,* 222.

40   D'Souza, *Illiberal Education,* 71.

41   *I, Rigoberta Menchú,* 103, 113, 174, 198.

42   D'Souza, *Illiberal Education,* 67, 242.

43   C. Vann Woodward, "Freedom and the Universities," in Aufderheide, 34.

44   D'Souza, *Illiberal Education,* 71.

45   See George Will, "Curdled Politics on Campus," *Newsweek,* 6 May 1991, reprinted in Paul Berman, ed., *Debating PC: The Controversy over Political Correctness on College Campuses* (New York: Dell, 1992), 262; Richard Bernstein, *Dictatorship of Virtue* (New York: Simon & Schuster, 1994), 325.

46   Lillian Robinson, "Not Just a Matter of Course (interview with Linda Brodkey)," *Women's Review of Books,* February 1992, 23.

47   Linda Brodkey, "Writing Permitted in Designated Areas Only," in Michael Bérubé and Cary Nelson, eds., *Higher Education under Fire* (New York: Routledge, 1995), 225.

48   Julius Getman, *In the Company of Scholars: The Struggle for the Soul of Higher Education* (Austin: University of Texas Press, 1992), 138–39.

49   Bernstein, 299.

50   Lynne Cheney, "Beware the PC Police," *Executive Educator,* January 1992, 32.

51   Getman, 140.
52   Peter Collier, "Incorrect English," in Peter Collier and David Horowitz, eds., *Surviving the PC University* (Studio City, CA: Center for the Study of Popular Culture, 1993), 108.
53   Getman, 143.
54   Getman, 143, 144, 149.
55   Robinson, 23.
56   Brodkey, 114.
57   Letter to author from Margot Backus, 30 September 1994.
58   Richard Bernstein, "The Rising Hegemony of the Politically Correct," *New York Times,* 28 October 1990, sec. 4, pp. 1, 4.
59   Martin Anderson, *Impostors in the Temple* (New York: Simon & Schuster, 1992), 150.
60   Anthony DePalma, "In Battle on Political Correctness, Scholars Begin a Counteroffensive," *New York Times,* 25 September 1991, B8; Brodkey, 115; Jerry Adler, "Taking Offense," *Newsweek,* 24 December 1990, 48–54.
61   Brodkey, 116.
62   Lynne Cheney, "A Conversation with Historian C. Vann Woodward," *Humanities,* November–December 1991, 8.
63   Collier, 101.
64   Alan Gribben, "The Education of Alan Gribben," *Measure,* December 1992, 9.
65   Collier, 107; Getman, 140.
66   Brodkey, 232.
67   Bernstein, 4.
68   Anderson, 150.
69   Cheney, "Beware the PC Police," 33.
70   George Will, "Catechism of Correctness," *Washington Post,* 20 October 1991, C7.
71   "Sensitivity Fascism," *National Review,* 27 April 1992, 19.
72   Gribben, 11.
73   Bernstein, *Dictatorship of Virtue,* 333.
74   Cheney, "Beware the PC Police," 35.
75   Collier, 102.
76   Letter to author from Margot Backus, 30 September 1994.
77   Lynne Cheney, "Political Correctness and Beyond," speech delivered to the National Press Club, 25 September 1991, reprinted in Owen Peterson, ed., *Representative American Speeches, 1991–1992* (New York: H. W. Wilson, 1992), 120, 126.
78   Maureen Dowd, "Buchanan's Alternative: Not Kinder or Gentler," *New York Times,* 15 January 1992, 1.
79   See Mario Mignone, ed., *Columbus: Meeting of Cultures* (Stony Brook, N.Y.: Forum Italicum, 1993), 7.
80   Patrick Buchanan, "Yes, Mario, There Is a Cultural War," *Chicago Tribune,* 14 September 1992, 17.
81   George Roche, *The Fall of the Ivory Tower* (Chicago: Regnery, 1994), 76.
82   Midge Decter, quoted in William Bennett, *The De-Valuing of America* (New York: Summit, 1992), 258.
83   Dinesh D'Souza, "PC So Far," *Commentary,* October 1994, 44.
84   Allan Bloom, *Liberal Education and Its Enemies* (Colorado Springs: U.S. Air Force Academy Press, 1991), 9, 17.
85   *Campus Report,* January 1994, 6.

86   Eugene Genovese, "Voices Must Unite for Victory in the Cultural War," *Chicago Tribune,* 22 December 1993, 11.

87   George Will, "Curdled Politics on Campus," *Newsweek,* 6 May 1991, 72.

88   Dinesh D'Souza, "A Multicultural Reading List," *Wall Street Journal,* 24 September 1991, A18.

89   Alice Walker and Pratibha Parmar, *Warrior Marks* (New York: Harcourt Brace, 1993), 95.

90   Susan Fraiman, "Crashing the Party: Women in the Academy Now," in Mark Edmundson, ed., *Wild Orchids and Trotsky: Messages from American Universities* (New York: Penguin, 1993), 227.

91   Stephen Greenblatt, "The Best Way to Kill Our Literary Inheritance Is to Turn It into a Decorous Celebration of the New World Order," *Chronicle of Higher Education,* 12 June 1991, B2.

92   David Schoem, Linda Frankel, Ximena Zuniga, and Edith A. Lewis, eds., *Multicultural Teaching in the University* (New York: Praeger, 1993), 1.

93   Editorial, "The Derisory Tower," *New Republic,* 18 February 1991, 5–6.

94   Roger Kimball, *Tenured Radicals: How Politics Has Corrupted Our Higher Education* (New York: Harper & Row, 1990), 3.

95   Editorial, "The Ivory Censor," *Wall Street Journal,* 9 May 1990, A14.

96   John Searle, "Rationality and Realism, What Is at Stake?" *Daedalus,* Fall 1993, 72.

97   Bennett, 194.

98   Barbara Ehrenreich, "The Challenge for the Left," *Democratic Left,* July–August 1991, 3.

99   D'Souza, *Illiberal Education,* 248.

100   Roger Geiger, *Research and Relevant Knowledge: American Research Universities since World War II* (New York: Oxford University Press, 1993), 330.

101   Bernstein, *Dictatorship of Virtue,* 295.

102   *Chronicle of Higher Education,* 8 May 1991, A15.

103   Gertrude Himmelfarb, "What to Do about Education," *Commentary,* October 1994, 23. Dinesh D'Souza also inaccurately writes in *Illiberal Education* that "most American universities have diluted or displaced their 'core curriculum' in the great works of Western civilization to make room for new course requirements stressing non-Western cultures, Afro-American Studies, and Women's Studies" (5); see "Signs of a Changing Curriculum," *Change* 24:1 (1992), 25–29, cited by Betty Schmitz, "Cultural Pluralism and Core Curricula," in Maurianne Adams, ed., *Promoting Diversity in College Classrooms* (San Francisco: Jossey-Bass, 1992), 61–62.

104   Carolyn Mooney, "A Lull in the Campus Battles over 'Political Correctness,'" *Chronicle of Higher Education,* 21 April 1993, A15.

105   Keith Gawrey, "Carnegie Study Creates Stir at SUNY-Buffalo," *Campus,* Fall 1990, 3; *Chronicle of Higher Education,* 4 September 1991, A24.

106   Mooney, A15.

107   Michael Winerip, "Faculty Angst over Diversity Courses Meets the Student Zeitgeist at UMass," *New York Times,* 4 May 1994, A13.

108   *MacNeil-Lehrer Newshour,* 17 June 1991.

109   John Leo, "The Class That Deserves Cutting," *U.S. News & World Report,* 29 May 1989, 58.

110   Stephan Thernstrom, "McCarthyism Then and Now," *Academic Questions,* Winter 1990, 14.

111   David Yamane, letter, "McCarthyism or Alarmism?" *Academic Questions,* Fall 1991, 6.

112   Todd Ackerman, "Texas Schools Balk at Requiring Multiculturalism," *Houston Chronicle,* 25 December 1994, A37.

113   *Chronicle of Higher Education,* 30 June 1993, A15.

114　Ackerman, A37; *Chronicle of Higher Education,* 23 February 1994, A4.

115　Collier and Horowitz, eds., *Surviving the PC University,* 56–57.

116　William Cain, editor's introduction to *Teaching the Conflicts: Gerald Graff, Curricular Reform, and the Culture Wars* (New York: Garland, 1994), xxviii.

117　Michael Bérubé, "Public Access Limited," in Berman, 149.

118　Rosa Ehrenreich, "What Campus Radicals?" *Harper's,* December 1991, reprinted in Francis Beckwith and Michael Bauman, eds., *Are You Politically Correct? Debating America's Cultural Standards* (Buffalo: Prometheus, 1993), 35.

119　Les Csorba, ed., *Academic License: The War on Academic Freedom* (Evanston, Ill.: UCA Books, 1988), vii.

120　Herbert London, "Reforming Higher Education," *World & I,* May 1991, 476.

121　Christopher Clausen, "It Is Not Elitist to Place Major Literature at the Center of the English Curriculum," *Chronicle of Higher Education,* 13 January 1988, A52; D'Souza, *Illiberal Education,* 68.

122　Thomas Short, " 'Diversity' and 'Breaking the Disciplines': Two New Assaults on the Curriculum," *Academic Questions,* Summer 1988, 6–29, reprinted in Beckwith and Bauman, 102, 116.

123　"Department of English Course Descriptions Fall 1991," University of Illinois, 1991. Books used in some introductory courses on fiction, poetry, and drama were not listed. For a similar survey, see Gerald Graff, *Beyond the Culture Wars* (New York: Norton, 1993), 21.

124　Michael Bérubé, *Marginal Forces/Cultural Centers: Tolson, Pynchon, and the Politics of the Canon* (Ithaca: Cornell University Press, 1992), 323.

125　*Chronicle of Higher Education,* 16 November 1994, A25.

126　A 1989 survey of five hundred high schools by Arthur Applebee and the Center for the Learning and Teaching of Literature found that Shakespeare was the most popular author, just as similar surveys showed twenty-five and eighty years ago. Of the top ten authors, only one was a woman; none was a minority; see William Noble, *Bookbanning in America* (Middlebury, Vt.: S. Eriksson, 1990), 280–81; *New York Times,* 20 May 1992, B8.

127　D'Souza, *Illiberal Education,* 68.

128　Bettina Huber, "Today's Literature Classroom: Findings from the MLA's 1990 Survey of Upper-Division Courses," *ADE Bulletin,* Spring 1992, 52.

129　Huber, 46.

130　Will Morrisey, Norman Fruman, and Thomas Short, "Ideology and Literary Studies—The MLA's Deceptive Survey," *Academic Questions,* Spring 1993, 48.

131　Celeste Colgan, "Education beyond Politics," *Partisan Review* 59 (Summer 1992), 383.

132　Colgan, 383.

133　Renee Swanson, "The Living Dead," *Policy Review,* Winter 1994, 72.

134　Collier and Horowitz, 14.

135　Helen Vendler, speech delivered at the University of Chicago, 26 February 1992.

136　Charles Eliot, *A Turning Point in Higher Education: The Inaugural Address of Charles William Eliot as President of Harvard College, October 19, 1869* (Cambridge, MA: Harvard University Press, 1969), 1.

4　The Myth of Speech Codes

1　Alexander Cockburn, "Bush and P.C.—A Conspiracy So Immense," *Nation,* 27 May 1991, 690.

2   Matthew Childs, "Politically Correct Speech," *Playboy*, October 1991, 57.

3   William Henry, "Upside down in the Groves of *Academe*," *Time*, 1 April 1991, 67.

4   John Leo, "Our Misguided Speech Police," *U.S. News & World Report*, 8 April 1991, 25.

5   Charles Sykes and Brad Miner, eds., *The National Review College Guide* (New York: Fireside, 1993), iii. The authors claim that "few changes in the life of the American university are as troubling as the growth of coercive rules about speech" (268) and call colleges "the academic gulag" because of their "draconian gag rules" (239).

6   Jonathan Rauch, *Kindly Inquisitors: The New Attacks on Free Thought* (Chicago: University of Chicago Press, 1993), 131.

7   Quoted in Rush Limbaugh, *See, I Told You So* (New York: Simon & Schuster, 1993), 236.

8   Christopher Shea, "The Limits of Speech," *Chronicle of Higher Education*, 1 December 1993, A37.

9   See *Schenk v. United States*, 249 U.S. 47 (1919); *Lehman v. City of Shaker Heights*, 418 U.S. 298 (1974); *Miller v. California*, 413 U.S. 15 (1973); *Brandenberg v. Ohio*, 395 U.S. 44 (1969); *Heffron*, 452 U.S. 640 (1981).

10   Editorial, "The Ivory Censor," *Wall Street Journal*, 9 May 1990, A14.

11   "ACLU Endorses College Free Speech Bill," ACLU news release, 12 March 1991. Others reported this same "fact"; for example, Marcia Pally: "By 1991, 60 percent of American college campuses had written hate speech policies and another 11 percent were considering them"; see Pally, *Sex & Sensibility: Reflections on Forbidden Mirrors and the Will to Censor* (Hopewell, N.J.: Ecco Press, 1994), 155.

12   David Merkowitz, letter, *Washington Times*, 22 March 1991, F2; see George Fishman and Henry Hyde, "The Collegiate Speech Protection Act of 1991: A Response to the New Intolerance in the Academy," *Wayne Law Review* 37 (1991), 1470.

13   *University of Chicago Student Information Manual* (Chicago: University of Chicago, 1993–94), 30.

14   Arati Korwar, *War of Words: Speech Codes at Public Colleges and Universities* (Nashville: Freedom Forum First Amendment Center, 1994), 32.

15   Richard Page and Kay Hunnicutt, "Freedom for the Thought That We Hate," *Journal of College and University Law* 21:1 (1994), 38.

16   Benno Schmidt, "The University and Freedom," *Educational Record*, Winter 1992, 17–18.

17   George Will, *Newsweek*, 5 November 1989, reprinted in Robert Hively, ed., *The Lurking Evil: Racial and Ethnic Conflict on the College Campus* (Washington, D.C.: American Association of State Colleges and Universities, 1990), 132.

18   Among the various attacks on the old University of Connecticut code after it was changed in 1991: the 1993 *National Review College Guide* warned that students at the University of Connecticut could be suspended for "inappropriately directed laughter" and "conspicuous exclusion"—two years after these never-enforced rules had been eliminated (Miner and Sykes, 16); Richard Liby wrote in 1992, "The speech code at the University of Connecticut, for example, prohibits 'misdirected laughter' and 'conspicuous exclusion from conversation'" (Liby, "The Diverse Orthodoxy: Political Correctness in America's Universities," *Kansas Journal of Law & Public Policy*, Summer 1992, 132); Barbara Dority: "The University of Connecticut's policy bans 'inappropriately directed laughter' and 'conspicuous exclusion of students from conversations'" (Dority, "The PC Speech Police," *Humanist*, March–April 1992, 31); Gary Saul Morson: "The University of Connecticut forbids not only speech deemed offensive but also 'inappropriately directed laughter.' If one student tells an ethnic joke and another laughs at it, it would seem that both have violated the code. One

can also violate the code by silence or, in the words of the code, 'conspicuous exclusion of students from conversation'" (Morson, "Weeding In," *Academic Questions,* Winter 1992–93, 68). The problem with the old University of Connecticut code was that it failed to distinguish between bigotry that deserves condemnation and bigotry that deserves punishment. While it is certainly possible for laughter and exclusion from a conversation to be acts of bigotry, they are not sufficiently threatening to be subject to regulation.

19   Smith College pamphlet, reprinted in "Smith's New Guide for the Perplexed," *Academic Questions,* Spring 1991, 80.

20   Francis Beckwith and Michael Bauman, eds., *Are You Politically Correct? Debating America's Cultural Standards* (Buffalo: Prometheus, 1993), 10.

21   R. Emmett Tyrrell, "PC People," *American Spectator,* May 1991, 8.

22   George Roche, *The Fall of the Ivory Tower* (Chicago: Regnery, 1994), 197. John Harmon and James Bowers wrote in a political science journal: "Colleges have drafted codes warning students against speech and behavior reflecting even 'lookism'" (Harmon and Bowers, "Political Correctness and Political Science," *Perspectives on Political Science,* Fall 1994, 164). For other references to the pamphlet, see Richard Bernstein, *Dictatorship of Virtue* (New York: Simon & Schuster, 1994), 25. Lookism is not a baseless idea. Studies have found that unattractive people earn 10–20 percent less than attractive people; see Peter Passell, "An Ugly Subject," *New York Times,* 27 January 1994, C2.

23   Fishman and Hyde, 1472, 1470.

24   *Campus,* Winter 1992, 13.

25   Ted Fishman, "The Hyde Solution," *Playboy,* October 1991, 57.

26   Clarence Page, "Power and Political Correctness," *Chicago Tribune,* 15 March 1992, 3.

27   Susan Dodge, "Campus Codes That Ban Hate Speech Are Rarely Used to Penalize Students," *Chronicle of Higher Education,* 12 February 1992, A35.

28   Page and Hunnicutt, 53.

29   One of the fliers slipped under doors of black students read:
Nigger, nigger, go away,
For the white man is here to stay.
Everywhere you look,
Everywhere you'll see
The menacing branches of a tree.
And from that tree,
What do we see?
The beautiful sight of my friends and me,
Laughing at your dangling feet.
So be forewarned
And do be scared,
For I, nigger child, will see you there.
Take your black asses back to Africa,
Before it's too late.
(Trey Ellis, "Disillusioned in the Promise Land," *Playboy,* June 1989, 74)
Michigan administrators seemed to encourage the racism with insensitive comments. In 1988, Peter Steiner, dean of the College of Literature, Science, and the Arts, declared: "Our challenge is not to change this University into another kind of institution where minorities would naturally flock in much greater numbers. I need not remind you that there are

such institutions—including Wayne State and Howard University. Our challenge is not to emulate them, but to make what is the essential quality of the University of Michigan available to more minorities." After this, fliers appeared around campus saying, "Niggers, get off campus! Dean Steiner was right" (Ellis, 74–76).

30 The policy established three areas for regulation of speech: (1) in public forums such as Regents' Plaza and the *Michigan Daily*, there would be "the most wide-ranging freedom of speech"; (2) in classrooms, libraries and study centers, only conduct that "materially impedes the educational process" could be regulated; and (3) in university housing, "persons should not be required to tolerate discriminatory behavior in their homes"; see "Revised Policy on Discriminatory Acts," *University [of Michigan] Record*, 29 February 1988.

31 *Doe v. University of Michigan*, 721 F. Supp. 852 (E.D. Mich. 1989), 856.

32 *Doe v. University of Michigan*, 865–66.

33 University of Wisconsin Code, UWS 17.062, cited in *U.W.M. Post, Inc. v. Board of Regents of the University of Wisconsin*, 774 F. Supp. 1163 (E.D. Wis. 1991), 1165.

34 *U.W.M. Post*, 1177.

35 *U.W.M. Post*, 1167.

36 *U.W.M. Post*, 1167–68. For another speech code case, see *Dambrot v. Central Michigan University*, 839 F. Supp. 477 (E.D. Mich. 1993).

37 Patricia Hodulik, "Racist Speech on Campus," *Wayne Law Review* 37 (1991), 1441–44.

38 *Chronicle of Higher Education*, 23 September 1992, A5.

39 *Iota Xi Chapter of Sigma Chi Fraternity v. George Mason University*, 773 F. Supp. 792 (E.D. Va. 1991).

40 Les Csorba, ed., *Academic License: The War on Academic Freedom* (Evanston, Ill.: UCA Books, 1988), 162.

41 *Robert Corry et. al. v. Leland Stanford Junior University*, County of Santa Clara Superior Court, Case no. 740309, 27 February 1995.

42 See Peter Collier and David Horowitz, eds., *Surviving the PC University* (Studio City, CA: Center for the Study of Popular Culture, 1993), 34.

43 Collier and Horowitz.

44 C. Vann Woodward, "Freedom and the Universities," in Patricia Aufderheide, ed., *Beyond PC: Toward a Politics of Understanding* (St. Paul: Graywolf, 1992), 42.

45 *Campus*, Fall 1990, 10.

46 John Leo, *Two Steps ahead of the Thought Police* (New York: Simon & Schuster, 1994), 236.

47 Rauch, 137 (Rauch's italics).

48 D'Souza, *Illiberal Education*, 147.

49 *Chronicle of Higher Education*, 11 May 1994, A4.

50 Ben Wildavsky, "War of Words over Stanford's Speech Rule," *San Francisco Chronicle*, 4 May 1994, A14.

51 Thomas Sowell, *Inside American Education: The Decline, the Deception, the Dogmas* (New York: Free Press, 1993), 200.

52 Henry Louis Gates, Jr., "Truth or Consequences: Putting Limits on Limits," *Academe*, January–February 1994, 15.

53 Henry Louis Gates, Jr., "Let Them Talk," *New Republic*, 20 and 27 September 1993, 45.

54 Wildavsky, A14.

55 Nancy Gibbs, "Bigots in the Ivory Tower," *Time*, 23 January 1989, 56.

56 Dinesh D'Souza on the *MacNeil-Lehrer Newshour*, transcript in Paul Berman, ed., *Debating*

PC: The Controversy over Political Correctness on College Campuses (New York: Dell, 1992), 35.

57   George Will, Newsweek, 5 November 1989, in Hively, 132.

58   Nadine Strossen, "Regulating Racist Speech on Campus: A Modest Proposal," Duke Law Journal, June 1990, 571.

59   Strossen, 490.

60   Nat Hentoff, Progressive, August 1993, 5.

61   R.A.V. v. City of St. Paul, Minnesota, 112 S.Ct.2538 (1992); and Wisconsin v. Mitchell, 113 S.Ct. 2194 (1993).

62   Jared Taylor, Paved with Good Intentions: The Failure of Race Relations in Contemporary America (New York: Carroll & Graf, 1992), 221.

63   Pally, 158.

64   Strossen, 512.

65   Dana Takagi, The Retreat from Race: Asian-American Admissions and Racial Politics (New Brunswick: Rutgers University Press, 1992), 144.

66   Chester Finn, "The Campus: 'An Island of Repression in a Sea of Freedom,'" Commentary, September 1989, reprinted in Francis Beckwith and Michael Bauman, eds., Are You Politically Correct? Debating America's Cultural Standards (Buffalo: Prometheus, 1993), 66.

67   Sheldon Hackney, letter, New York Times, 16 June 1993, A16.

68   "Bundles of Paper Disappear after Accusations of Racism," New York Times, 3 November 1993, A13.

69   Newsletter on Intellectual Freedom, January 1994, 17.

70   Christopher Shea, "2 Women at Penn State Charged in Theft of Right-Wing Newspaper," Chronicle of Higher Education, 28 July 1993, A30; Tracie Tso, "Student Protesters Stop the Presses," U., October 1993, 8.

71   "Free Speech Retreat," Campus, Spring 1994, 12.

72   George Garneau, "Censorship by Theft," Editor & Publisher, 24 December 1994, 15, 31.

73   Student Press Law Center Report, Spring 1994, 32, 34.

74   Student Press Law Center Report, Spring 1994, 32, 34; Newsletter on Intellectual Freedom, September 1993, 140–41.

75   Sabra Chartrand, "In Maryland, Taking Free Papers in Protest May Soon Be a Crime," New York Times, 8 April 1994, B16.

76   Editorial, "I Hate This Paper!" Grey City Journal, 21 January 1994, 1. The article stolen was by Kim Phillips, "Dead on Arrival," Grey City Journal, 14 January 1994, 1. See also J. W. Mason, "Double Standard," Nation, 9–16 January 1995, 52.

77   Allan Wolper, "Separating Journalism from the Church," Editor & Publisher, 25 September 1993, 14, 31, 14, 16.

78   Wolper, 14, 15, 31.

79   Clarence Page, 3.

80   Newsletter on Intellectual Freedom, January 1994, 18.

81   Newsletter on Intellectual Freedom, March 1992, 48–49.

82   Newsletter on Intellectual Freedom, September 1992, 144–45.

83   Dale Eastman, "Intellectual Freedom 1993," New City (Chicago), 7 January 1993, 6.

84   Sara Diamond, "Multiculturalism Attacked," Guardian, 17 October 1990.

85   Newsletter on Intellectual Freedom, May 1993, 75.

86   Heather Robertson, "Muzzling the Student Press," Canadian Forum, October 1991, 5.

87   Newsletter on Intellectual Freedom, March 1992, 49.

88   "Column Makes Administration 'Hot and Bothered,'" *Student Press Law Center Report*, Spring 1994, 24.

5   *The Myth of Sexual Correctness*

1   *Commonwealth v. Berkowitz*, 609 A.2d 1338 (Pa.Super. 1992), 641 A.2d 1161 (Pa. 1994).

2   Karen Branan, "Out for Blood," *Ms.*, January–February 1994, 83.

3   Katie Roiphe, *The Morning After: Sex, Fear, and Feminism on Campus* (Boston: Little, Brown, 1993), 67.

4   Sarah Crichton, "Sexual Correctness: Has It Gone Too Far?" *Newsweek*, 25 October 1993, 52–56.

5   Carol Bohmer and Andrea Parrot, *Sexual Assault on Campus* (New York: Macmillan, 1993), 12.

6   Terry Steinberg, "Rape on College Campuses: Reform Through Title IX," *Journal of College and University Law* 18 (1991), 47.

7   Jon Wiener, "God and Man at Hillsdale," *Nation*, 24 February 1992, 236.

8   Carolyn Palmer, "Skepticism Is Rampant about the Statistics on Campus Crime," *Chronicle of Higher Education*, 21 April 1993, B2.

9   Bohmer and Parrot, 60.

10   Mary Koss, Thomas Dinero, Cynthia Seibel, and Susan Cox, "Stranger and Acquaintance Rape: Are There Differences in the Victim's Experience?" *Psychology of Women Quarterly* 12 (1988), 21–22.

11   Bohmer and Parrot, 41, 51.

12   Kathryn Kranhold and Katherine Farrish, "Anxiety about Sex, Dating, Rape Transforms College Life," *Hartford Courant*, 10 October 1993, A1.

13   Nancy Roman, "Scales of Justice Weigh Tiers of Sexual Assault," *Washington Times*, 16 June 1994, A8.

14   Camille Paglia, on *Later* with Bob Costas, 21 September 1992; Camille Paglia, *Sex, Art, and American Culture* (New York: Vintage, 1992), 68, 63.

15   Kathleen Hendrix, "Defining Controversy," *Los Angeles Times*, 9 July 1991, E1. In criticizing "feminist" research, Gilbert and his supporters, like many critics of political correctness, have adopted the mantle of self-anointed victimhood. Gilbert called a protest against his articles "an attempt to impose a politically correct view." See Virginia Matzek, "Rape Article Sparks Vigil," *Daily Californian*, 19 June 1991. Dean Specht said, "I'm beginning to feel that I'm being victimized" and suggested that Gilbert was "a victim of 'political correctness.'" See Jackie Stevens, "UC School of Social Welfare Still Reeling from Rape Statistics Flap," *Berkeley Express*, 8 November 1991; Harry Specht, letter, 30 July 1991. Yet it is Gilbert's defenders, not the feminists, who are intolerant of opposing views. Paul Terrell, coordinator of academic programs, invited Diane Russell to deliver the 1991 Seabury Lecture. But when Russell indicated that she planned to criticize Gilbert's writings in part of her speech, Terrell replied that the lecture had to be "a decorous, scholarly event" and that "it would be inappropriate for the Seabury lecture to become a critique of Professor Gilbert's work" (letter to Diane Russell, 13 September 1991). Dean Harry Specht admits he ordered the invitation to Russell rescinded, but he reinstated her lecture after students protested his decision.

16   Mary Koss, Christine Gidycz, and Nadine Wisniewski, "The Scope of Rape: Incidence and

Prevalence of Sexual Aggression and Victimization in a National Sample of Higher Education Students," *Journal of Consulting and Clinical Psychology* 55:2 (1987), 162–70.

17   Abby Cohn, "Rape Figures Are Inflated, Professor Says," *Woodland Hills Daily News*, 1 June 1991.

18   Neil Gilbert, "Realities and Mythologies of Rape," *Society*, May–June 1992, 4–5.

19   Koss, Gidycz, and Wisniewski, 167.

20   Christina Hoff Sommers erroneously claimed that "once you remove the positive responses to question eight, the finding that one in four college women is a victim of rape or attempted rape drops to one in nine;" see Sommers, *Who Stole Feminism? How Women Have Betrayed Women* (New York: Simon & Schuster, 1994), 213.

21   See Gilbert, 4–10.

22   Gilbert, 5.

23   Neil Gilbert, "The Phantom Epidemic of Sexual Assault," *Public Interest*, Spring 1991, 60.

24   Carol Brydolf, "Professor: Rape Figures Are Inflated," *Oakland Tribune*, 30 May 1991, A1.

25   See Arnold Kahn, Virginia Mathie, and Cyndee Torgler, "Rape Scripts and Rape Acknowledgment," *Psychology of Women Quarterly* 18 (1994), 60.

26   Mary Koss, "Hidden Rape," in Ann Wolbert Burgess, ed., *Rape and Sexual Assault II* (New York: Garland, 1988), 16; Robin Warshaw, *I Never Called It Rape* (New York: Harper & Row, 1988), 49. By contrast, only 26 percent of the women who were "sexually coerced" physically resisted, and only 9 percent said they were held down.

27   Neil Gilbert, "The Campus Rape Scare," *Wall Street Journal*, 27 June 1991.

28   Neil Gilbert, "Counterpoint: A Few Women Want to Speak for Both Sexes," *San Francisco Chronicle*, 26 June 1991.

29   Lyn Kathlene, "Beneath the Tip of the Iceberg," *Women's Review of Books*, February 1992, 30.

30   Susan Estrich, *Real Rape* (Cambridge: Harvard University Press, 1987), 112.

31   Edward Laumann, John Gagnon, Robert Michael, and Stuart Michaels, *The Social Organization of Sexuality* (Chicago: University of Chicago Press, 1994), 337; Gina Kolata, Edward Laumann, John Gagnon, and Robert Michael, *Sex in America: A Definitive Study* (Boston: Little, Brown, 1994), 225.

32   Laumann et al., 322.

33   Laumann et al., 337, 226–27.

34   "Report Cites Heavy Toll of Rapes on Young," *New York Times*, 23 June 1994, A8.

35   "Sexually Active Girls Cite Coercion," *Chicago Tribune*, 8 June 1994, 17.

36   Kolata et al., 220.

37   Gilbert, "The Phantom Epidemic of Sexual Assault," 60.

38   Michele N.-K. Collison, "A Berkeley Scholar Clashes with Feminists over Validity of Their Research on Date Rape," *Chronicle of Higher Education*, 26 February 1992, A35–A37, A37; see also Collison, "Article's Attack on 'Hype' Surrounding Date Rape Stirs Debate among Researchers, Campus Counselors," *Chronicle of Higher Education*, 7 July 1993, A41.

39   Laumann et al., 329, 333.

40   Gilbert, "Realities and Mythologies of Rape," 9.

41   See Helen Eigenberg, "The National Crime Survey and Rape: The Case of the Missing Question," *Justice Quarterly* 7:4 (December 1990).

42   David Johnston, "Survey Shows Number of Rapes Far Higher Than Official Figures," *New York Times*, 24 April 1992, A9.

43   Gilbert, "The Phantom Epidemic of Sexual Assault," 64, 63, 65, 65.

44   See Gilbert, "Realities and Mythologies of Rape," 4–10.

45   Mary Koss, "Defending Date Rape," *Journal of Interpersonal Violence* 7:1 (March 1992), 124.

46   Virginia Matzek, "Students Protest Recent Article on Date Rape," *Daily Californian,* 7 June 1991, 1.

47   Roiphe, 52; Sommers, 212–13.

48   Mary Matalin, "Stop Whining!" *Newsweek,* 25 October 1993, 62.

49   Roiphe, 54, 55, 59.

50   Neil Gilbert, "Was It Rape?" *American Enterprise,* September 1994, 75.

51   Barbara Sullivan, "The Victim Trap," *Chicago Tribune,* 14 October 1993, sec. 5, p. 1.

52   Roiphe, 79.

53   John Leo, *Two Steps ahead of the Thought Police* (New York: Simon & Schuster, 1994), 235.

54   Jon Weiner, " 'Rape by Innuendo' at Swarthmore," *Nation,* 20 January 1992, 44.

55   Wiener, " 'Rape by Innuendo,' " 45.

56   Nancy Gibbs, "When Is It Rape?" *Time,* 3 June 1991, 49.

57   Wiener, " 'Rape by Innuendo,' " 45–46. In 1992, *Campus* reported that the definition of rape "has been expanded to include, as a Swarthmore College training manual describes, the 'spectrum of incidents and behaviors ranging from crimes legally defined as rape to verbal harassment and inappropriate innuendo' "; see Roger Landry, "The Politics of Rape," *Campus,* Winter 1992, 14.

58   Wiener, " 'Rape by Innuendo,' " 47.

59   Jeff Giles, "There's a Time for Talk, and a Time for Action," *Newsweek,* 7 March 1994, 54.

60   See Antioch College, "Sexual Violence and Safety" (introduction to "Sexual Offense Policy"); Antioch College, "Sexual Offense Policy."

61   Margarette Driscoll, "Have We Gone Too Far?" *London Times,* 24 October 1993; editorial, " 'Ask First' at Antioch," *New York Times,* 11 October 1993, A10; Eric Fassin, "Playing by the Antioch Rules," *New York Times,* 26 December 1993, sec. 4, p. 11.

62   Giles, 54; James Hannah, "Applications up after College Enacts Sex Rules for 'Every Step of the Way,' " *Rocky Mountain News,* 15 January 1995, 46A.

63   Anthony DePalma, "Faith and Free Speech Wrestle for Dominance in Brigham Young Case," *New York Times,* 10 March 1993, A11.

64   *Chronicle of Higher Education,* 15 December 1993, A4.

65   *Academe,* May–June 1987, 34.

66   *Chronicle of Higher Education,* 5 January 1994, A4.

67   Scott Jaschik, "Court Upholds Naval Academy Action against Gay Student," *Chronicle of Higher Education,* 30 November 1994, A32.

68   Linda Rubin and Sherry Borgers, "Sexual Harassment in Universities during the 1980s," *Sex Roles* 23:7–8 (1990), 397–411, reprinted in Edmund Wall, ed., *Sexual Harassment: Confrontations and Decisions* (Buffalo: Prometheus, 1992), 29.

69   Rubin and Borgers, 29–30.

70   Martin Anderson, *Impostors in the Temple* (New York: Simon & Schuster, 1992), 164.

71   Rubin and Borgers, 31.

72   Melita Marie Garcia, "Study Finds High Faculty Harassment," *Chicago Tribune,* 8 April 1994, sec. 2, p. 4.

73   Rubin and Borgers, 33.

74   Anderson, 159.

75   Mary Hawkesworth, "The Politics of Knowledge: Sexual Harassment and Academic Free-

dom Reconsidered," in Malcolm Tight, ed., *Academic Freedom and Responsibility* (Philadelphia: Open University Press, 1988) 19.

76   Celia Morris, *Bearing Witness: Sexual Harassment and Beyond—Everywoman's Story* (Boston: Little, Brown, 1994), 133; *Jean Jew v. Regents of the University of Iowa,* 749 F. Supp. 946 (1990).

77   Morris, 136–37.

78   745 F.Supp. 793 (1990).

79   See *New York Times,* 23 March 1984, cited in Schilling and Fuehrer, "The Organizational Context of Sexual Harassment," in Michele Paludi, ed., *Ivory Power: Sexual Harassment on Campus* (Albany: State University of New York Press, 1990), 125.

80   Anderson, 162–64.

81   *Chronicle of Higher Education,* 19 January 1994, A21.

82   Courtney Leatherman, "Stanford Neurosurgeon Decides to Remain at University but Sees Continuing Struggle against Sex Discrimination," *Chronicle of Higher Education,* 18 September 1991, A19; Morris, 113–15.

83   Julia Bristor, "A Chilly Campus Climate: One Woman's Story," *Educational Record,* Winter 1993, 27.

84   Bristor, 27.

85   *Academe,* November–December 1989, 37, 35, 35, 35.

86   *Chronicle of Higher Education,* 21 April 1993, A22.

87   "Prof Defends Religious, Sexual Remarks," *Chicago Sun-Times,* 1 December 1993, 24.

88   Jerry Adler, "A Tale of Sex, Lies and Audiotape," *Newsweek,* 21 October 1991, 38.

89   Nancy Stumhofer, "Goya's *Naked Maja* and the Classroom Climate," *Democratic Culture,* Spring 1994, 18–22. Robert Hughes says this about the incident: "American feminism has a large repressive fringe, self-caricaturing and often abysmally trivial, like the academic thought-police who recently managed to get a reproduction of Goya's *Naked Maja* removed from a classroom at the University of Pennsylvania"; see Hughes, *Culture of Complaint: The Fraying of America* (New York: Oxford University Press, 1993), 30. Nadine Strossen says Stumhofer claimed that the painting "embarrassed her and made her female students 'uncomfortable.'" The comments by male students and the fact that the painting was placed in the student union are never mentioned; see Strossen, *Defending Pornography: Free Speech, Sex, and the Fight for Women's Rights* (New York: Scribner, 1995), 22, 128.

90   See Stumhofer, 18–22.

91   Peter Collier, "War Stories," in Peter Collier and David Horowitz, eds., *Surviving the PC University* (Studio City, Calif.: Center for the Study of Popular Culture, 1993), 224.

92   Collier, 226.

93   Morris, 115.

94   Morris, 138.

95   Sommers, 51.

96   Michelle Powers, "Ex–New Left Leader Compares '60s Radicals to '90s P.C. Activists," *Campus,* Winter 1992, 6.

97   Page Smith, *Killing the Spirit: Higher Education in America* (New York: Viking, 1990), 291.

98   Elizabeth Hudson, "In Oklahoma, the Dust Hasn't Quite Settled," *Washington Post,* national weekly edition, 13–19 September 1993, 15.

99   Branan, 84–85.

100 In Representative Sullivan's words, "There are plenty of faculty, alumni and judges who are

saying it was despicable the way the dean of the law school conducted himself by supporting her." Stephen Labaton, "For Oklahoma, Anita Hill's Story Is Open Wound," *New York Times,* 19 April 1993, A1, A9.

101 Branan, 87.

102 Jill Mackie, "Feminist Group Harassed during Anti-violence Rally," *Daily Illini,* date unknown.

103 Courtney Leatherman, "Professors and Female Administrator on Minn. Campus Receive Death Threats," *Chronicle of Higher Education,* 3 June 1992, A12, A16.

104 *Ms.,* May–June 1992, 87.

105 Linda Woodbridge, "Afterword: Poetics from the Barrel of a Gun?" in Ivo Kamps, ed., *Shakespeare Left and Right* (New York: Routledge, 1991), 288–89. Lepine also wounded thirteen women at the Ecole Polytechnique in 1989 before killing himself with the semiautomatic rifle. He left behind a rambling three-page letter blaming women for the fact that his application for admission had been turned down. See Janet Bagnall, "Dreams Not Shattered by Lepine's Fire," *Montreal Gazette,* 6 December 1994, A1.

106 Karen Lehrman, "Off Course," *Mother Jones,* September–October 1992, 46, 48, 64.

107 Lehrman, 64.

108 Daphne Patai and Noretta Koertge, *Professing Feminism: Cautionary Tales from the Strange World of Women's Studies* (New York: Basic Books, 1994), 78, 22, 184, 197.

109 *Chronicle of Higher Education,* 14 July 1993, A15.

110 Sommers, 112.

111 Andrea Simakis, "Identity Crisis," *Village Voice,* education supplement, 21 January 1992, 4.

112 Sommers, 107.

113 Cathy Davidson, " 'PH' Stands for Political Hypocrisy," *Academe,* September–October 1991, 13.

114 Paula Kamen, "My 'Bourgeois' Brand of Feminism," in Eric Liu, ed., *Next* (New York: Norton, 1994), 81, 83.

115 Lisa Navin Trivedi, "Can't Take a Joke . . . ," *Women's Review of Books,* February 1994, 14, 14, 15, 16.

116 Adriane Fugh-Berman, "Tales out of Medical School," in Amber Coverdale Sumrall and Dena Taylor, eds., *Sexual Harassment: Women Speak Out* (Freedom, Calif.: Crossing Press, 1992), 84.

117 Paula Caplan, *Lifting a Ton of Feathers* (Toronto: University of Toronto Press, 1993), 205–6.

118 Gerald Phillips, Dennis Gouran, Scott Kuehn, and Julia Wood, *Survival in the Academy* (Cresskill, N.J.: Hampton Press, 1994), 66.

119 Paul Lauter, *Canons and Contexts* (New York: Oxford University Press, 1991), 215.

120 Lucy Lisiecki, "Blood on the Walls," *Prism* (*Chicago Maroon*), 29 April 1994, 17.

121 Phillips et al., 229.

122 Deborah Cohen, "An Intellectual Home," *Women's Review of Books,* February 1994, 17.

123 Athena Theodore, *The Campus Troublemakers: Academic Women in Protest* (Houston: Cap and Gown Press, 1986), 33, 20.

124 Theodore, 34, 50.

125 Theodore, 51, 78.

126 Theodore, 78, 79, 160.

127 Rose Odum, letter, "Alaska Professor Defends Right of Free Speech," *Chronicle of Higher Education,* 21 April 1993, B4; see *Odum v. University of Alaska,* 845 F.2d 432 (1993).

128   Courtney Leatherman, "U of Alaska Former Professor Claims Firing Was Due to Her Feminist Views," *Chronicle of Higher Education,* 9 September 1992, A16.

129   Odum, B4.

130   Leatherman, A16.

131   Odum, B4.

132   Catharine Stimpson, "The Farr Case," *Change,* September–October 1993, 70.

133   Stimpson, 70.

134   Carolyn Mooney, "Conservative Brigham Young U. Contends with Small but Growing Movement for Change," *Chronicle of Higher Education,* 30 June 1993, A14.

135   Stimpson, 71.

136   Mooney, A16.

137   "Tenure Denials Raise Scholar-Freedom Issue," *New York Times,* 11 June 1993.

138   Mooney, A13.

139   Stimpson, 71.

140   Mooney, A14.

141   DePalma, A11.

142   Dirk Johnson, "Growing Mormon Church Faces Dissent by Women and Scholars," *New York Times,* 2 October 1993, 1, 7.

143   Miner and Sykes, 19, 54.

144   Mark Winchell, "When Good Men Do Nothing," *Clemson Spectator,* April 1992, 1.

145   Quoted in Scott Henson and Tom Philpott, "The Right Declares a Culture War," *Humanist,* March–April 1992, 15.

146   "Fireworks and Dazzle at Panel Talk on Beauty," *New York Times,* 9 December 1992, B13.

147   Alida Chack, "Women's Studies Frenzy: Life on the Academic Fringe," *Campus,* Spring 1994, 19.

6   *The Myth of Reverse Discrimination*

1   Robert Weissberg, "The Gypsy Scholars," *Forbes,* 10 May 1993, 138.

2   Steven Yates, letter, *American Philosophical Association Proceedings* 65:7 (June 1992), 76.

3   Richard Blow, "Mea Culpa," *New Republic,* 18 February 1991, 32; Hillsdale president George Roche also claims, " 'Males need not apply,' and 'Whites need not apply,' have become the basic messages of most faculty job advertisements today"; see Roche, *The Fall of the Ivory Tower* (Chicago: Regnery, 1994), 109.

4   Richard Rorty, "Demonizing the Academy," *Harper's,* January 1995, 16.

5   E. L. Roundtree, letter, *Perspectives* (AHA), May–June 1992, 13.

6   *Perspectives* (AHA), September 1992, 19.

7   *Perspectives* (AHA), May–June 1992, 13.

8   *Perspectives* (AHA), September 1992, 19.

9   Survey of full-time faculty teaching in fall 1992, in *Chronicle of Higher Education,* 23 November 1994, A16.

10   Paul Lauter, *Canons and Contexts* (New York: Oxford University Press, 1991), 211; *Academe,* March–April 1994, 18, 24–25.

11   Linda Johnsrud and Ronald Heck, "Administrative Promotion within a University," *Journal of Higher Education,* January–February 1994, 39.

12   Survey of full-time faculty teaching in fall 1992, *Chronicle of Higher Education,* 23 November 1994, A16.

13　See *Academe,* March–April 1994, 24–25.

14　Julius Getman, *In the Company of Scholars: The Struggle for the Soul of Higher Education* (Austin: University of Texas Press, 1992), 163, 162.

15　Kenny Williams, interviewed by Carol Iannone, "Caste and Class in a University Town," *Academic Questions,* Spring 1991, 48–49.

16　Mary-Christine Philip, "Affirmative Action Still Saddled with Negative Image," *Black Issues in Higher Education,* 24 March 1994, 25.

17　Ward Parks, "Anti-Male Discrimination in the Profession," in Peter Collier and David Horowitz, eds., *Surviving the PC University* (Studio City, CA: Center for the Study of Popular Culture, 1993), 180–92.

18　Bettina Huber, "Women in the Modern Languages, 1970–90," *Profession 90,* 62–63.

19　Michael Brintnall, "Academic Promise: Placement of New Political Scientists 1992," *PS,* June 1993, 278–80.

20　Marcia Linn, "The Tyranny of the Mean: Gender and Expectations," *Notices* (American Mathematical Society), September 1994, 767; Allyn Jackson, "Are Women Getting All the Jobs?" *Notices* (AMS), April 1994, 286–87; Judith Axler Turner, "More Women Are Earning Doctorates in Mathematics, but Few Are Being Hired by Top Universities," *Chronicle of Higher Education,* 6 December 1989, A13. At Berkeley in 1986, Jenny Harrison became the first math professor denied tenure in fifteen years. After years of litigation, an independent panel was appointed to reexamine her credentials. The panel found that she was an excellent teacher and that her research—compared with the eight men given tenure during her term at Berkeley—was better than three and equal to two others, showing that she was certainly well qualified for the position.

21　National Research Council, *Summary Report 1993* (Washington, D.C.: National Academy Press, 1993) (with appendix A, October 1994), 20–1.

22　National Research Council, *Summary Report 1992* (Washington, D.C.: National Academy Press, 1993), 26.

23　Yolanda Moses, "Black Women in Academe" (Project on the Status and Education of Women, Association of American Colleges, August 1989), 11.

24　Anthony DePalma, "As Black Ph.D.'s Taper off, Aid for Foreigners Is Assailed," *New York Times,* 21 April 1992, A1, A9.

25　Stephanie Witt, *The Pursuit of Race and Gender Equity in American Academe* (New York: Praeger, 1990), 81–83.

26　See Allyn Jackson, "Are Women Getting All the Jobs?" 286–87. For example, in the 1970s, the Berkeley mathematics department, under the pressure of affirmative action, invited women and minorities to apply for two tenure-track positions that had already been offered to two white men; see Jackson, "Fighting for Tenure," *Notices* (AMS), 191.

27　Paul Lauter, " 'Political Correctness' and the Attack on American Colleges," in Michael Bérubé and Cary Nelson, eds., *Higher Education under Fire* (New York: Routledge, 1995), 83.

28　Elizabeth Fay and Michelle Tokarczyk, eds., *Working-Class Women in the Academy* (Amherst: University of Massachusetts Press, 1993), 12.

29　G. Kindrow, "The Candidate: Inside One Affirmative Action Search," *Lingua Franca,* April 1991, 21–25; Michael Wardell, "The Candidate's Story," *Lingua Franca,* August 1991, 38–39.

30　Jared Taylor, *Paved with Good Intentions: The Failure of Race Relations in Contemporary America* (New York: Carroll & Graf, 1992), 30. Frederick Lynch cites the same study in a *Wall Street Journal* op-ed about the "oppressed class" of white men, bizarrely claiming that this indicates "only minimal levels of reverse discrimination" rather than strong evidence of antiblack discrimination; see Lynch, "Tales from an Oppressed Class," *Wall Street Journal,* 4 November 1991, A8.

31 "Discrimination Follows an Internal Script," *Wall Street Journal,* 19 October 1994, B1.

32 Dana Takagi, *The Retreat from Race: Asian-American Admissions and Racial Politics* (New Brunswick: Rutgers University Press, 1992), 21–22, 25, 26, 125.

33 Takagi, 46.

34 Dinesh D'Souza, *Illiberal Education* (New York: Free Press, 1991), 30; Vincent Sarich, "The Institutionalization of Racism at the University of California at Berkeley," *Academic Questions,* Winter 1990–91, 77.

35 Takagi, 104.

36 Takagi, 115.

37 Takagi, 133, 148.

38 Sarich, 75–76.

39 Takagi, 155.

40 C. Vann Woodward, "Freedom and the Universities," in Patricia Aufderheide, ed., *Beyond PC: Toward a Politics of Understanding* (St. Paul: Greywolf, 1992), 32.

41 Chester Finn, "The Campus: 'An Island of Repression in a Sea of Freedom,'" *Commentary,* September 1989, reprinted in Francis Beckwith and Michael Bauman, eds., *Are You Politically Correct? Debating America's Cultural Standards* (Buffalo: Prometheus, 1993), 64.

42 Takagi, 72–73.

43 People for the American Way, *Hate in the Ivory Tower: A Survey of Intolerance on College Campuses and Academia's Response* (Washington, D.C.: People for the American Way, 1991), 16.

44 Barry Gross, "The Intolerable Costs of Affirmative Action," *Reconstruction* 2:3 (1994), 59.

45 Jerome Karabel, "Berkeley and Beyond," *American Prospect* 12 (Fall 1993), 157.

46 Thomas Sowell, *Race and Culture: A World View* (New York: Basic Books, 1994), 177.

47 See "Graduation Rates for Athletes and Other Students Who Entered College in 1987–88," *Chronicle of Higher Education,* 6 July 1994, A39–A40.

48 *Chronicle of Higher Education,* 6 July 1994, A39–A40.

49 Michelle Powers, "Ex-New Left Leader Compares '60s Radicals to '90s P.C. Activists," *Campus,* Winter 1992, 7.

50 Myron Magnet, *The Dream and the Nightmare: The Sixties' Legacy to the Underclass* (New York: Morrow, 1993), 190–91.

51 Charles Murray and Richard Herrnstein, *The Bell Curve* (New York: Free Press, 1994), 473.

52 "Fewer Minorities Finish College," *Chicago Tribune,* 28 February 1994, 3.

53 Karabel, 157.

54 The program was broadcast on 5 May 1991; quoted in Alexander Cockburn, "Bush and P.C. — A Conspiracy So Immense," *Nation,* 27 May 1991, 691.

55 D'Souza, *Illiberal Education,* 253.

56 Monte Piliawsky, *Exit 13: Oppression & Racism in Academia* (Boston: South End Press, 1982), 153.

57 Piliawsky, 153.

58 Vincent Tinto, *Leaving College: Rethinking the Causes and Cures of Student Attrition,* 2d ed. (Chicago: University of Chicago Press, 1993), 74.

59 Jeffrey Rosen, "Is Affirmative Action Doomed?" *New Republic,* 17 October 1994, 35.

60 Jonathan Kozol, *Savage Inequalities: Children in America's Schools* (New York: Crown, 1994).

61 Letter, *Change*, May–June 1992, 6.

62 John Larew, "Why Are Droves of Unprepared Unqualified Kids Getting into Our Top Colleges?" *Washington Monthly*, June 1991, 14.

63 John Lamb, "The Real Affirmative Action Babies: Legacy Preferences at Harvard and Yale," *Columbia Journal of Law and Social Problems* 26 (Spring 1993), 502.

64 Richard Moll, "A Gentle War: The College Admissions Office versus the Faculty," *Change*, May–June 1992, 45–46.

65 Larew, 10–12.

66 Lamb, 503.

67 Marcia Synnott, *The Half-Opened Door: Discrimination and Admissions at Harvard, Yale, and Princeton, 1900–1970* (Westport, Conn.: Greenwood Press, 1979), 208.

68 Lamb, 505.

69 Lamb, 504–5, 501.

70 Larew, 12.

71 Lamb, 501.

72 Lamb, 502, 508.

73 D'Souza, *Illiberal Education*, 47, 51.

74 D'Souza, *Illiberal Education*, 240.

75 Walter Williams, "Campus Racism," *National Review*, 5 May 1989, 36.

76 D'Souza, *Illiberal Education*, 240–41.

77 Charles Murray, review of Andrew Hacker's *Two Nations* in *Times Literary Supplement*, 22 May 1992, quoted in William Henry, *In Defense of Elitism* (New York: Doubleday, 1994), 79.

78 D'Souza, *Illiberal Education*, 228.

79 Murray and Herrnstein, 474.

80 D'Souza, *Illiberal Education*, 240.

81 Diana Carter, "Options Limited for Minority Students as Some Institutions Seek out Wealthiest Applicants," *Black Issues in Higher Education*, 13 August 1992, 1, 8–9, 54.

82 Takagi, 110.

83 John Bunzel, *Race Relations on Campus* (Stanford: Stanford Alumni Association, 1992), 118.

84 Ruth Shalit, "Hate Story," *New Republic*, 7 June 1993, 11–14.

85 Shalit, 12, 14.

86 Shalit, 12.

87 D'Souza, *Illiberal Education*, 252.

88 See Ruben Navarrette, *A Darker Shade of Crimson: Odyssey of a Harvard Chicano* (New York: Bantam Books, 1993).

Conclusion: Beyond Political Correctness

1 Lisa Newman, "U. of C. Gays Tell of Further Threats," *Chicago Tribune*, 24 April 1991, 6; Jean Latz Griffin, "FBI Looking into Threats at U. of C.," *Chicago Tribune*, 19 April 1991, 1.

2 Jean Latz Griffin, "Responses to Phony Personal Answered with Anti-gay Letters," *Chicago Tribune*, 18 March 1987, 3.

3 Dirk Johnson, "Fear of AIDS Stirs New Attacks on Homosexuals," *New York Times*, 24 April 1987, A12.

4 Jean Latz Griffin and Lynn Emmerman, "Hate Campaign Spreads beyond U. of C. Campus,"

Chicago Tribune, 21 June 1987, 1. Steven Amsterdam, Anjail Fedson, and Laura Saltz, "The Great White Brotherhood: Why Has Nothing Been Done?" *Grey City Journal,* 29 May 1987, 4–5.

5   Blair Kamin, "U. of C. Won't Deny Diploma in Flap over Gay Harassment," *Chicago Tribune,* 28 May 1989, 5.

6   Marlin Smith, "U of C Must Reevaluate Its Harassment Policies," *Chicago Maroon,* 21 February 1995, 20.

7   Brent Staples, *Parallel Time: Growing Up in Black and White* (New York: Pantheon, 1994), 202.

8   "A Statement by the Committee for Racial Justice," University of Chicago, 1992.

9   "Black Students Harassed at Reg," *Chicago Maroon,* 14 April 1992, p. 15.

10 Dan Ralley, "Race Relations Course Poorly Taught," *Chicago Maroon,* 20 January 1995, 18.

11 "117 'facts' of Psi U life," *Prism (Chicago Maroon),* 28 October 1994, 17.

12 Committee on Social Thought Symposium, 4 April 1992.

13 Gregory Jay and Gerald Graff, "A Critique of Critical Pedagogy," in Michael Bérubé and Cary Nelson, eds., *Higher Education under Fire: Politics, Economics, and the Crisis of the Humanities* (New York: Routledge, 1995), 210.

14 William Honan, "State Universities Reshapen in the Era of Budget Cutting," *New York Times,* 22 February 1995, A1, A13; see also Ernst Benjamin, "A Faculty Response to the Fiscal Crisis: From Defense to Offense," in Bérubé and Nelson, 55.

15 See Jonathan Kozol, *Savage Inequalities: Children in America's Schools* (New York: Crown, 1991).

16 Chester Finn, "The Campus: 'An Island of Repression in a Sea of Freedom,'" *Commentary,* September 1989. The phrase is Abigail Thernstrom's.

➤ Index

About the Author
John K. Wilson is a graduate student in the Committee on Social
Thought at the University of Chicago. He is the editor of
Democratic Culture, the newsletter of Teachers for a Democratic
Culture.

Library of Congress Cataloging-in-Publication Data
Wilson, John K., 1969-
    The myth of political correctness : the conservative attack on
higher education / by John K. Wilson.
    Includes bibliographical references and index.
    ISBN 0-8223-1703-6 (cloth : alk.paper). — ISBN 0-8223-1713-3
(pbk. : alk. paper)
    1. Education, Higher — Political aspects — United States.
2. Political correctness — United States.   3. Conservatism — United
States.   4. Education, Humanistic — United States.
5. Multicultural education — United States.   6. Discrimination in
higher education — United States.   I. Title.
LC89.W55   1995
378.73 — dc20   95-22495CIP